SACREDSPACE

the prayer book 2012

Inspired by one of the most successful spirituality websites around (and for good reason), *Sacred Space* offers readers short but profound meditations on the daily scriptures. Friendly, concise, and consistently thought provoking, these books are perfect for anyone who would like to pray more and be more connected to God, but may feel too busy to do so. In other words, everyone!

James Martin, S.J.
Author of *The Jesuit Guide to (Almost) Everything*

The website Sacred Space has been helping millions to pray for some years. Now Ave Maria Press makes these very helpful and easily usable prayer-helps available in handsome and accessible form, including pocket-sized booklets for the Advent-Christmas and Lenten seasons. What a great service to God's people! I hope millions more will buy the books. God is being well served.

William A. Barry, S.J.
Author of *Paying Attention to God: Discernment in Prayer*

I don't know any other guides to prayer that are so direct, profound, and effective. It's no wonder that right around the world they have proved extraordinarily helpful in leading busy people to stay in touch with the presence of God.

Gerald O'Collins, S.J.
Author of *Jesus: A Portrait*

Sacred Space has provided countless people with a clear and concise resource to pray alone—any time and anywhere—and yet consciously united with numerous others worldwide. This timely, unassuming aid to daily prayer is a gem.

Peter van Breemen, S.J.
Author of *The God Who Won't Let Go*

SACREDSPACE

the prayer book 2012

from the website www.sacredspace.ie
The Irish Jesuits

ave maria press AMP notre dame, indiana

acknowledgment

The publisher would like to thank Piaras Jackson, S.J., and Alan McGuckian, S.J., for their kind assistance in making this book possible. Piaras Jackson, S.J., can be contacted at feedback @jesuit.ie where comments or suggestions related to the book or to www.sacredspace.ie will always be welcome.

The Scripture quotations contained herein are from the *New Revised Standard Version* Bible, © Copyright 1989 by the Division of Christian Education of the National Council of Churches of Christ in the USA and are used with permission. All rights reserved.

First published in Australia in 2011 by Michelle Anderson Publishing Pty., Ltd.

Founded in 1865, Ave Maria Press is a ministry of the United States Province of Holy Cross.

www.avemariapress.com

ISBN-10: 1-59471-277-8   ISBN-13: 978-1-59471-277-7

Cover design by Andy Wagoner.

Text design by K. Hornyak.

Printed and bound in the United States of America.

prayer for peace

Deep peace of the running waves to you,
deep peace of the flowing air to you,
deep peace of the quiet earth to you,
deep peace of the shining stars to you,
deep peace of the shades of night to you,
moon and stars always giving light to you,
deep peace of Christ, the Son of Peace, to you.

Celtic prayer

contents

How to Use This Book   viii

November 2011   1

December 2011   5

January 2012   36

February 2012   69

March 2012   98

April 2012   134

May 2012   169

June 2012   197

July 2012   228

August 2012   258

September 2012   287

October 2012   316

November 2012   344

December 2012   375

how to use this book

We invite you to make a sacred space in your day and spend ten minutes praying here and now, wherever you are, with the help of a prayer guide and scripture chosen specially for each day. Every place is a sacred space so you may wish to have this book in your desk at work or available to be picked up and read at any time of the day, whilst traveling or on your bedside table, a park bench. . . . Remember that God is everywhere, all around us, constantly reaching out to us, even in the most unlikely situations. When we know this, and with a bit of practice, we can pray anywhere.

The following pages will guide you through a session of prayer stages.

Something to think and pray about each day this week
The Presence of God
Freedom
Consciousness
The Word (leads you to the daily scripture and provides help
    with the text)
Conversation
Conclusion

It is most important to come back to these pages each day of the week as they are an integral part of each day's prayer and lead to the scripture and inspiration points.

Although written in the first person, the prayers are for "doing" rather than for reading out. Each stage is a kind of exercise or meditation aimed at helping you to get in touch with God and God's presence in your life.

We hope that you will join the many people around the world praying with us in our sacred space.

Something to think and pray about each day this week:

Seeking the Joy of Christmas
Psychiatrists say they are at their busiest in the weeks coming up to Christmas. The feast stirs up anxieties linked to memories of childhood and relationships within the family. It pushes us to difficult decisions about sending invitations, cards, or gifts. No wonder people talk about "getting over Christmas." But our real friends do not judge us by those decisions. They like us to be calm and contented in ourselves, with a clean emotional palate so that we can enter into and taste other people's joys.

The Presence of God
Lord, help me to be fully alive to your holy presence.
Enfold me in your love.
Let my heart become one with yours.

Freedom
Many countries are at this moment suffering
the agonies of war.
I bow my head in thanksgiving for my freedom.
I pray for all prisoners and captives.

Consciousness
At this moment, Lord, I turn my thoughts to You.
I will leave aside my chores and preoccupations.
I will take rest and refreshment in your presence, Lord.

The Word
The Word of God comes down to us through the scriptures.
May the Holy Spirit enlighten my mind and my heart to respond
to the Gospel teachings. (Please turn to your scripture on the following pages. Inspiration points are there should you need them.
When you are ready, return here to continue.)

Conversation
Sometimes I wonder what I might say
if I were to meet You in person, Lord.
I might say "Thank You, Lord" for always being there for me.
I know with certainty there were times when You carried me,
when through your strength I got through the dark times in my life.

Conclusion
Glory be to the Father, and to the Son, and to the Holy Spirit,
As it was in the beginning, is now, and ever shall be,
World without end. Amen.

Sunday 27th November,
First Sunday of Advent   Mark 13:33–37

Beware, keep alert; for you do not know when the time will come. It is like a man going on a journey, when he leaves home and puts his slaves in charge, each with his work, and commands the doorkeeper to be on the watch. Therefore, keep awake—for you do not know when the master of the house will come, in the evening, or at midnight, or at cockcrow, or at dawn, or else he may find you asleep when he comes suddenly. And what I say to you I say to all: Keep awake."

- Jesus' message and life was to make a difference and save the world. That's the call—to do the world a world of good. Stay awake—see how you can make someone else's life that bit better. We need to believe that each of us can make a difference to our families, to the neighbourhood, to the school. One way is to keep in touch with God.
- Advent can be a time to make sure—through prayer, through Mass, through helping the very poor—that we keep in touch with God. We allow God's grace and care to flow through us.

Monday 28th November   Matthew 8:5–11

When Jesus entered Capernaum, a centurion came to him, appealing to him and saying, "Lord, my servant is lying at home paralyzed, in terrible distress." And he said to him, "I will come and cure him." The centurion answered, "Lord, I am not worthy to have you come under my roof; but only speak the word, and my servant will be healed. For I also am a man under authority, with soldiers under me; and I say to one, 'Go,' and he goes, and to another, 'Come,' and he comes, and to my slave, 'Do this,' and the slave does it." When Jesus heard him, he was amazed and said to those who followed him, "Truly I tell you,

4

in no one in Israel have I found such faith. I tell you, many will come from east and west and will eat with Abraham and Isaac and Jacob in the kingdom of heaven."

- The centurion amazed Jesus with his forthright expression and his respect.
- Jesus saw that the kingdom of heaven was open and inclusive. I ask that I may preserve the same breadth of vision and generosity in my outlook.

Tuesday 29th November   Luke 10:21–24

At that same hour Jesus rejoiced in the Holy Spirit and said, "All things have been handed over to me by my Father; and no one knows who the Son is except the Father, or who the Father is except the Son and anyone to whom the Son chooses to reveal him." Then turning to the disciples, Jesus said to them privately, "Blessed are the eyes that see what you see! For I tell you that many prophets and kings desired to see what you see, but did not see it, and to hear what you hear, but did not hear it."

- To rejoice in the Holy Spirit is to be aware of the Father's infinite and unconditional love poured out on me. Are there moments in my life when I have felt such love? What may be preventing me from experiencing such love today?
- Jesus says, "Blessed are the eyes that see what you see." The disciples are "blessed" because, in Jesus, they are beginning to recognize the long-awaited Messiah. Do I ever count my blessings, thanking God for the gifts of life and love?

Wednesday 30th November,
St. Andrew, Apostle   Matthew 4:18–22

As he walked by the Sea of Galilee, he saw two brothers, Simon, who is called Peter, and Andrew his brother, casting a

4

net into the lake—for they were fishermen. And he said to them, "Follow me, and I will make you fish for people." Immediately they left their nets and followed him. As he went from there, he saw two other brothers, James son of Zebedee and his brother John, in the boat with their father Zebedee, mending their nets, and he called them. Immediately they left the boat and their father, and followed him.

- Andrew was always Simon Peter's brother, not the other way round; younger brothers, it seems, always remain that way.
- Do we ever outgrow that self-perception, seeing ourselves as somebody's brother or sister? Maybe with jealousy, maybe with a feeling we are not quite as good, maybe with a clinging dependence that makes it hard for us to make our own way, maybe with an unfeigned and joyful love.
- Lord, you are the brother I need never feel bad about. I know I have a good place in your mind and heart.

Thursday 1st December   Matthew 7:21, 24–27

Jesus said to the people, "Not everyone who says to me, 'Lord, Lord,' will enter the kingdom of heaven, but only one who does the will of my Father in heaven. Everyone then who hears these words of mine and acts on them will be like a wise man who built his house on rock. The rain fell, the floods came, and the winds blew and beat on that house, but it did not fall, because it had been founded on rock. And everyone who hears these words of mine and does not act on them will be like a foolish man who built his house on sand. The rain fell, and the floods came, and the winds blew and beat against that house, and it fell—and great was its fall!"

6

- Lord, you never let me forget that love is shown in deeds, not words or feelings. I could fill notebooks with resolutions and in the end be further from you.
- As William James put it: "A resolution that is a fine flame of feeling allowed to burn itself out without appropriate action, is not merely a lost opportunity, but a bar to future action."

Friday 2nd December   Matthew 9:27–31

As Jesus went on his way, two blind men followed him, crying loudly, "Have mercy on us, Son of David!" When he entered the house, the blind men came to him; and Jesus said to them, "Do you believe that I am able to do this?" They said to him, "Yes, Lord." Then he touched their eyes and said, "According to your faith let it be done to you." And their eyes were opened. Then Jesus sternly ordered them, "See that no one knows of this." But they went away and spread the news about him throughout that district.

- In matters of faith, we are all blind in some way. But if I allow Jesus to touch my heart, he will help me see more clearly the path I should follow.
- The blind men had faith in Jesus' power of healing. Do I ever experience the inner healing power of God?

Saturday 3rd December,
St. Francis Xavier   1 Corinthians 9:19, 22–23

For though I am free with respect to all, I have made myself a slave to all, so that I might win more of them. To the weak I became weak, so that I might win the weak. I have become all things to all people, so that I might by any means save some. I do it all for the sake of the gospel, so that I may share in its blessings.

- Like Francis Xavier, I bring myself to God for healing, strength, and encouragement. I listen for the words that God has for me.
- As I bring my desires to God, I ask for the focus that I need to serve God wholeheartedly.

december 4–10

Something to think and pray about each day this week:

The God Who Knows
In everything to do with prayer, we have our best model in Jesus himself. It is he who tells us both to ask for what we need and that the Father knows our needs before we ask (Matthew 6:9; 7:7). Whether we are praying for good weather for the wedding or pleading for the life of a sick friend, our prayers don't express something unknown to God. They don't bridge a gap between us and a God who is distant. God already knows. God is already with us in our desires. Our prayers are not like "making a wish" in the direction of God. All prayer involves some reaching out with childlike trust, even when the inner tone is chaotic or full of confusion. Prayer is always more than petition, even if petition is always a strand in prayer. Even if you do not use his words, all praying echoes the surrender of Jesus: not my will, but yours. We ask for what we think is best, but we try to hand everything over to the One who knows even better.

The Presence of God

God is with me; but more,
God is within me, giving me existence.
Let me dwell for a moment on God's life-giving presence
in my body, my mind, my heart,
and in the whole of my life.

Freedom

God is not foreign to my freedom.
Instead the Spirit breathes life into my most intimate desires,
gently nudging me towards all that is good.
I ask for the grace to let myself be enfolded by the Spirit.

Consciousness

Help me, Lord, to be more conscious of your presence.
Teach me to recognize your presence in others.
Fill my heart with gratitude for the times your love
has been shown to me through the care of others.

The Word

I read the Word of God slowly, a few times over, and I listen
to what God is saying to me. (Please turn to your scripture on
the following pages. Inspiration points are there should you need
them. When you are ready, return here to continue.)

Conversation

How has God's Word moved me? Has it left me cold?
Has it consoled me or moved me to act in a new way?
I imagine Jesus standing or sitting beside me;
I turn and share my feelings with him.

Conclusion

Glory be to the Father, and to the Son, and to the Holy Spirit,
As it was in the beginning, is now, and ever shall be,
World without end. Amen

Sunday 4th December, Second Sunday of Advent
Mark 1:4–6

John the baptizer appeared in the wilderness, proclaiming a baptism of repentance for the forgiveness of sins. And people from the whole Judean countryside and all the people of Jerusalem were going out to him, and were baptized by him in the river Jordan, confessing their sins. Now John was clothed with camel's hair, with a leather belt around his waist, and he ate locusts and wild honey.

- John the Baptist preached forgiveness. This is one of the special gifts of God, and one of the big celebrations of Advent. We are a forgiven people, and we welcome the forgiveness of God in our repentance.
- This means we are firstly grateful for forgiveness—that we do not have to carry forever the burden of our sin, meanness, faults, and failings. God covers them over in mercy.
- The second step of welcoming forgiveness is to try to do better in life—to move on from this sinfulness and meanness to a life of care, compassion, love, and joy, and to make steps to forgive others.

Monday 5th December
Luke 5:17–20

One day, while he was teaching, Pharisees and teachers of the law were sitting near by (they had come from every village of Galilee and Judea and from Jerusalem); and the power of the Lord was with him to heal. Just then some men came, carrying a paralyzed man on a bed. They were trying to bring him in and lay him before Jesus; but finding no way to bring him in because of the crowd, they went up on the roof and let him down with his bed through the tiles into the middle of the crowd in front of Jesus. When he saw their faith, he said, "Friend, your sins are forgiven you."

- When I come to pray, I do not come alone. I bring before Jesus all those people whose needs I know, all those for whom I have hopes. I lay them before Jesus so that they may receive the help and healing they need.
- Jesus speaks forgiveness to me. I receive the healing that he offers and ask to understand the new life Jesus seeks for me.

Tuesday 6th December   Matthew 18:12–14

Jesus said to his disciples: "What do you think? If a man has a hundred sheep, and one of them has gone astray, does he not leave the ninety-nine on the hills and go in search of the one that went astray? And if he finds it, truly I say to you, he rejoices over it more than over the ninety-nine that never went astray. So it is not the will of my father who is in heaven that one of these little ones should perish."

- Jesus is the shepherd whose heart goes after the one who is lost. When I feel forlorn or lost, I have a special place in Jesus' heart. I allow myself to feel vulnerable, to be cherished, sought, and found.
- I may sometimes want to have everything squared away and in order. It may be that I want to rely more on myself than on Jesus. Being in need is not demeaning when I am closer to the heart of Jesus.

Wednesday 7th December   Matthew 11:28–30

Jesus said, "Come to me, all you that are weary and are carrying heavy burdens, and I will give you rest. Take my yoke upon you, and learn from me; for I am gentle and humble in heart, and you will find rest for your souls. For my yoke is easy, and my burden is light."

- The scribes and Pharisees laid heavy burdens on people by imposing on them the so-called "traditions of the elders," rules and regulations not found in the Jewish scriptures. Jesus scorned these "traditions."

- Instead he urged his followers to take his "yoke," to accept his direction. Jesus' yoke is easy because what he teaches, no matter how challenging, gives meaning, direction, and peace of soul to a person's life.

Thursday 8th December, The Immaculate
Conception of the Blessed Virgin Mary   Luke 1:30–33

The angel said to her, "Do not be afraid, Mary, for you have found favor with God. And now, you will conceive in your womb and bear a son, and you will name him Jesus. He will be great, and will be called the Son of the Most High, and the Lord God will give to him the throne of his ancestor David. He will reign over the house of Jacob forever, and of his kingdom there will be no end."

- Mary might well have felt afraid as she became aware of the presence of God. I spend this time in the presence of the same God and give thanks for the welcome and reassurance that God gives me. I ask Mary to be with me, to help me open my heart to God as she did.

- Mary said "Yes" to the plan that was outlined in the great sweep of the angel's words. I sometimes quail at the day-to-day challenges that I face. I ask God's help to remember that I can make God's ways evident even in small and ordinary ways.

Friday 9th December   Matthew 11:16–19

Jesus spoke to the crowds, "But to what will I compare this generation? It is like children sitting in the marketplaces and calling to one another, 'We played the flute for you, and you did not dance; we wailed, and you did not mourn.' For John came neither eating nor drinking, and they say, 'He has a demon'; the Son of Man came eating and drinking, and they say, 'Look, a glutton and a drunkard, a friend of tax collectors and sinners!' Yet wisdom is vindicated by her deeds."

- The children playing in the marketplace might have seemed a trivial distraction to many, but to Jesus they offered an image of life. Perhaps I can take time to notice the small things in my life—the incidental happenings—and listen to what God may be saying to me in them.
- Jesus knew that he could not please all of the people around him. He remained true to his vision and truth. I pray that I may not become distracted from following Jesus by trying to win the approval of others.

Saturday 10th December   Matthew 17:10–13

And the disciples asked him, "Why, then, do the scribes say that Elijah must come first?" He replied, "Elijah is indeed coming and will restore all things; but I tell you that Elijah has already come, and they did not recognize him, but they did to him whatever they pleased. So also the Son of Man is about to suffer at their hands." Then the disciples understood that he was speaking to them about John the Baptist.

- The disciples brought their questions to Jesus, to hear what he might have to say. I bring the things that make me wonder, that raise questions for me, and lay them before Jesus in prayer. I listen carefully for his word.
- Neither John the Baptist nor Jesus were always recognized. I pray for the humility I need to act as Jesus did.

december 11–17

Something to think and pray about each day this week:

The Deepest Thirst

Follow the story in John's gospel of Jesus' encounter at the well of Jacob. Imagine yourself the Samaritan woman. I come to the well on a simple errand, to fetch water for the house. To my surprise, a stranger accosts me and asks for a favor. He is a foreigner, the sort of man I would expect to be hostile. I try to work out what he is up to. Soon my need for water is forgotten. He explores my history. He knows me better than my closest friends. He speaks of a thirst that is deeper than my everyday appetite. He opens a vision of a world beyond our present divisions. I cannot keep this to myself. It is too important, too life enhancing not to talk about. I go home and spread the news: "Come, see a man who told me all that I ever did. Can this be the Christ?"

The Presence of God
What is present to me is what has a hold on my becoming.
I reflect on the presence of God always there in love,
amidst the many things that have a hold on me.
I pause and pray that I may let God
affect my becoming in this precise moment.

Freedom
There are very few people
who realize what God would make of them
if they abandoned themselves into his hands,
and let themselves be formed by his grace (St. Ignatius).
I ask for the grace to trust myself totally to God's love.

Consciousness
In the presence of my loving Creator,
I look honestly at my feelings over the last day,
the highs, the lows, and the level ground.
Can I see where the Lord has been present?

The Word
God speaks to each one of us individually. I need to listen to hear
what he is saying to me. Read the text a few times, then listen.
(Please turn to your scripture on the following pages. Inspiration
points are there should you need them. When you are ready, return here to continue.)

Conversation
What is stirring in me as I pray?
Am I consoled, troubled, left cold?
I imagine Jesus himself standing or sitting at my side,
and share my feelings with him.

Conclusion
Glory be to the Father, and to the Son, and to the Holy Spirit,
As it was in the beginning, is now, and ever shall be,
World without end. Amen.

16

Sunday 11th December,
Third Sunday of Advent
John 1:6–8, 19–28

There was a man sent from God, whose name was John. He came as a witness to testify to the light, so that all might believe through him. He himself was not the light, but he came to testify to the light. This is the testimony given by John when the Jews sent priests and Levites from Jerusalem to ask him, "Who are you?" He confessed and did not deny it, but confessed, "I am not the Messiah." And they asked him, "What then? Are you Elijah?" He said, "I am not." "Are you the prophet?" He answered, "No." Then they said to him, "Who are you? Let us have an answer for those who sent us. What do you say about yourself?" He said, "I am the voice of one crying out in the wilderness, 'Make straight the way of the Lord,'" as the prophet Isaiah said. Now they had been sent from the Pharisees. They asked him, "Why then are you baptizing if you are neither the Messiah, nor Elijah, nor the prophet?" John answered them, "I baptize with water. Among you stands one whom you do not know, the one who is coming after me; I am not worthy to untie the thong of his sandal." This took place in Bethany across the Jordan where John was baptizing.

- We are in the atmosphere of something about to happen. John the Baptist is still on the scene, pointing where to look, where to wait, how to expect the one who is to come. We get so used to Christmas and the coming of Christ that we hardly have any sense of expectation.
- Christmas is not meant to be quiet. It's meant to draw out many responses in us. This could be a week of active expectancy—to do something to prepare well for the Lord.
- How will you prepare for Christmas? Can you do something for the poor each day? Thank somebody genuinely each day for their

place in your life? Say you are sorry to someone you hurt, or forgive someone who hurt you?

Monday 12th December   Matthew 21:23–27

When Jesus entered the temple, the chief priests and the elders of the people came to him as he was teaching, and said, "By what authority are you doing these things, and who gave you this authority?" Jesus said to them, "I will also ask you one question; if you tell me the answer, then I will also tell you by what authority I do these things. Did the baptism of John come from heaven, or was it of human origin?" And they argued with one another, "If we say, 'From heaven,' he will say to us, 'Why then did you not believe him?' But if we say, 'Of human origin,' we are afraid of the crowd; for all regard John as a prophet." So they answered Jesus, "We do not know." And he said to them, "Neither will I tell you by what authority I am doing these things."

- Jesus does not engage in futile discussion. There are times when words may get in the way, when no amount of speech will help.
- Am I sometimes like the priests and elders? Quizzing, figuring out, arguing, debating? Jesus values a faith that is lively, engaged, generous, and uncomplicated. I spend time with Jesus, careful not to be always talking and quizzing.

Tuesday 13th December   Matthew 21:28–32

Jesus said, "What do you think? A man had two sons; he went to the first and said, 'Son, go and work in the vineyard today.' He answered, 'I will not'; but later he changed his mind and went. The father went to the second and said the same; and he answered, 'I go, sir'; but he did not go. Which of the two did the will of his father?" They said, "The first." Jesus said to them, "Truly I tell you, the tax collectors and the prostitutes are going into the kingdom of God ahead of you. For John came to you in the way of righteousness and you did not believe him, but the tax collectors and the prostitutes believed him; and even after you saw it, you did not change your minds and believe him."

- Jesus speaks this parable to me. I avoid applying it to others right now and simply accept Jesus' warmth as he sees how I have served. I listen for his invitation as he shows me where I hold back.
- To live in the kingdom is to be ready to rub shoulders with all kinds. God's love is given freely and is accepted by many. I pray for a heart that is open to those who are not like me.

Wednesday 14th December · Luke 7:18–23

The disciples of John reported all these things to him. So John summoned two of his disciples and sent them to the Lord to ask, "Are you the one who is to come, or are we to wait for another?" When the men had come to him, they said, "John the Baptist has sent us to you to ask, 'Are you the one who is to come, or are we to wait for another?'" Jesus had just then cured many people of diseases, plagues, and evil spirits, and had given sight to many who were blind. And he answered them, "Go and tell John what you have seen and heard: the blind receive their sight, the lame walk, the lepers are cleansed, the deaf hear, the dead are raised, the poor have good news brought to them. And blessed is anyone who takes no offense at me."

- Jesus sends John an answer, but it is not a declaration. It is a picture of a world in which God's Spirit is powerfully at work. This image is to encourage John, to give him heart in prison.
- Jesus wants to give me heart by pointing my attention to where the Spirit is at work. I review my current concerns with God, asking for light and hope.

Thursday 15th December   **Luke 7:24–30**

When John's messengers had gone, Jesus began to speak to the crowds about John: "What did you go out into the wilderness to look at? A reed shaken by the wind? What then did you go out to see? Someone dressed in soft robes? Look, those who put on fine clothing and live in luxury are in royal palaces. What then did you go out to see? A prophet? Yes, I tell you, and more than a prophet. This is the one about whom it is written, 'See, I am sending my messenger ahead of you, who will prepare your way before you.' I tell you, among those born of women no one is greater than John; yet the least in the kingdom of God is greater than he."

- Jesus reminds the people of what they sought and found in John the Baptist: they did not search for some trivial reed or elegant courtesan, but encountered a sign of God's presence. I take some time to recall and savour again the people who have helped me to discover God's ways.
- As I am one of the least in the kingdom of God, I consider that Jesus thinks me great.

Friday 16th December   **John 5:33–36**

Jesus said to the Jews: "You sent messengers to John, and he testified to the truth. Not that I accept such human testimony, but I say these things so that you may be saved. He was a burning and shining lamp, and you were willing to rejoice for a while in his light. But I have a testimony greater than John's. The works that the Father has given me to complete, the very works that I am doing, testify on my behalf that the Father has sent me."

- Always Jesus draws us back from words to works. He tells the Jews that while he respects the testimony of John the Baptist, for crucial evidence they should look at the works that Jesus has done in obedience to his Father.

- So, Lord, do I dare to ask people to look at my life, my actions, rather than rely on spoken evidence? Are my works on a par with my profession?

Saturday 17th December   Matthew 1:1–7

An account of the genealogy of Jesus the Messiah, the son of David, the son of Abraham. Abraham was the father of Isaac, and Isaac the father of Jacob, and Jacob the father of Judah and his brothers, and Judah the father of Perez and Zerah by Tamar, and Perez the father of Hezron, and Hezron the father of Aram, and Aram the father of Aminadab, and Aminadab the father of Nahshon, and Nahshon the father of Salmon, and Salmon the father of Boaz by Rahab, and Boaz the father of Obed by Ruth, and Obed the father of Jesse, and Jesse the father of King David. And David was the father of Solomon by the wife of Uriah, and Solomon the father of Rehoboam. . . .

- This litany of names deserves to be read reverently, as all names do. I think of the lists that can easily dehumanize and pray that the dignity and experience of each person be respected. I consider that a life's story lies behind each name that I see today.
- I think of how my life and faith depend on so many others about whom I know so little. I pray for them with thanks.

Something to think and pray about each day this week:

Meditating on Advent

Now more than at any other time we need to insulate ourselves from the constant pressure from advertisers and media, telling us what to buy and how to spend at Christmas. Come back to some simple reminder of the meaning of the feast, like Alice Meynell's *Advent Meditation*:

> No sudden thing of glory and fear
> Was the Lord's coming; but the dear
> Slow Nature's days followed each other
> To form the Saviour from His Mother
> —One of the children of the year.

The Presence of God
God is with me; but more, God is within me.
Let me dwell for a moment on God's life-giving presence
in my body, in my mind, in my heart,
as I sit here, right now.

Freedom
A thick and shapeless tree-trunk would never believe
that it could become a statue, admired as a miracle of sculpture,
and would never submit itself to the chisel of the sculptor,
who sees by her genius what she can make of it (St. Ignatius).
I ask for the grace to let myself be shaped by my loving Creator.

Consciousness
Knowing that God loves me unconditionally,
I can afford to be honest about how I am.
How has the last day been, and how do I feel now?
I share my feelings openly with the Lord.

The Word
I read the Word of God slowly, a few times over, and I listen
to what God is saying to me. (Please turn to your scripture on
the following pages. Inspiration points are there should you need
them. When you are ready, return here to continue.)

Conversation
Do I notice myself reacting as I pray with the Word of God?
Do I feel challenged, comforted, angry?
Imagining Jesus sitting or standing by me,
I speak out my feelings, as one trusted friend to another.

Conclusion
Glory be to the Father, and to the Son, and to the Holy Spirit,
As it was in the beginning, is now, and ever shall be,
World without end. Amen.

Sunday 18th December,
Fourth Sunday of Advent   Luke 1:26–38

In the sixth month the angel Gabriel was sent by God to a town in Galilee called Nazareth, to a virgin whose name was Mary. And he came to her and said, "Greetings, favored one! The Lord is with you." But she was much perplexed by his words and pondered what sort of greeting this might be. The angel said to her, "Do not be afraid, Mary, for you have found favor with God. And now, you will conceive in your womb and bear a son, and you will name him Jesus. He will be great, and will be called the Son of the Most High, and the Lord God will give to him the throne of his ancestor David. He will reign over the house of Jacob forever, and of his kingdom there will be no end." Mary said to the angel, "How can this be, since I am a virgin?" The angel said to her, "The Holy Spirit will come upon you, and the power of the Most High will overshadow you; therefore the child to be born will be holy; he will be called Son of God. And now, your relative Elizabeth in her old age has also conceived a son; and this is the sixth month for her who was said to be barren. For nothing will be impossible with God." Then Mary said, "Here am I, the servant of the Lord; let it be with me according to your word." Then the angel departed from her.

- Christmas highlights the belief that God is in all of us. We can ignore that, or we can help God be found in all of us. God is active through each of us for each other.
- In the visit of Mary, God came close to Elizabeth in the ordinary and homely moments of every day. These Advent and Christmas days give us the space to allow the huge, eternal mystery become part of the everyday.

Monday 19th December   Luke 1:5–25

In the days of King Herod of Judea, there was a priest named Zechariah, who belonged to the priestly order of Abijah. His wife was a descendant of Aaron, and her name was Elizabeth. Both of them were righteous before God, living blamelessly according to all the commandments and regulations of the Lord. But they had no children, because Elizabeth was barren, and both were getting on in years. Once when he was serving as priest before God and his section was on duty, he was chosen by lot, according to the custom of the priesthood, to enter the sanctuary of the Lord and offer incense. Now at the time of the incense-offering, the whole assembly of the people was praying outside. Then there appeared to him an angel of the Lord, standing at the right side of the altar of incense. When Zechariah saw him, he was terrified; and fear overwhelmed him. But the angel said to him, "Do not be afraid, Zechariah, for your prayer has been heard. Your wife Elizabeth will bear you a son, and you will name him John. You will have joy and gladness, and many will rejoice at his birth, for he will be great in the sight of the Lord. He must never drink wine or strong drink; even before his birth he will be filled with the Holy Spirit. He will turn many of the people of Israel to the Lord their God. With the spirit and power of Elijah he will go before him, to turn the hearts of parents to their children, and the disobedient to the wisdom of the righteous, to make ready a people prepared for the Lord." Zechariah said to the angel, "How will I know that this is so? For I am an old man, and my wife is getting on in years." The angel replied, "I am Gabriel. I stand in the presence of God, and I have been sent to speak to you and to bring you this good news. But now, because you did not believe my words, which will be fulfilled in their time, you will become mute, unable to speak, until the day these things occur." Meanwhile, the people were waiting for Zechariah, and wondered at his delay in the sanctuary. When he did come out, he could not speak to them, and they realized that he had seen a vision in the sanctuary. He kept motioning to them and remained unable to speak. When his time of service was ended, he went to his home. After those days his wife Elizabeth conceived, and for five months she remained in seclusion. She said, "This is what the Lord has done for me when he looked favorably on me and took away the disgrace I have endured among my people."

- Zechariah served as a priest in the Jerusalem Temple. One of the duties of the priests was to keep the brazier burning that stood on the altar of incense in front of the Holy of Holies. They would fill the brazier with fresh incense before the morning sacrifice, and again at the evening sacrifice.

- It was during such an occasion that God's messenger, Gabriel, appears and foretells the birth of John the Baptist. Later, when his wife, Elizabeth, against all odds, finds herself pregnant, she proclaims, "This is what the Lord has done for me when he looked favorably on me and took away the disgrace I have endured among my people." Barrenness was considered a humiliation, and even a punishment from God.

- As I contemplate this scene, am I ever awed by the great things God has done for me during my life?

Tuesday 20th December **Luke 1:38**

Then Mary said, "Here am I, the servant of the Lord; let it be with me according to your word." Then the angel departed from her.

- Mary's "Here am I" has such direct simplicity that it reminds me that I am often distracted. I consider how too much looking ahead or back distracts me from being present to myself—where God wants to meet me.

- "The angel departed." Mary did not live in the glow of the angel's presence but took the message of God's presence into her daily life. I value this time of quiet and ask that it nourish me in the busy moments of my life.

Wednesday 21st December   Luke 1:39–45

In those days Mary set out and went with haste to a Judean town in the hill country, where she entered the house of Zechariah and greeted Elizabeth. When Elizabeth heard Mary's greeting, the child leapt in her womb. And Elizabeth was filled with the Holy Spirit and exclaimed with a loud cry, "Blessed are you among women, and blessed is the fruit of your womb. And why has this happened to me, that the mother of my Lord comes to me? For as soon as I heard the sound of your greeting, the child in my womb leapt for joy. And blessed is she who believed that there would be a fulfillment of what was spoken to her by the Lord."

- The Spirit of God in Elizabeth rejoiced in the presence of Mary. I pray for those who have been friends to me, for all whose companionship or example lifts my heart.
- An expectant mother, Mary set out on her journey. She carried the Word within her. I draw inspiration from this scene and see in it a reminder of who I am this day: I carry the Word of God in me as nourishment for me and for those around me.

Thursday 22nd December   Luke 1:46–56

And Mary said, "My soul magnifies the Lord, and my spirit rejoices in God my Savior, for he has looked with favor on the lowliness of his servant. Surely, from now on all generations will call me blessed; for the Mighty One has done great things for me, and holy is his name. His mercy is for those who fear him from generation to generation. He has shown strength with his arm; he has scattered the proud in the thoughts of their hearts. He has brought down the powerful from their thrones, and lifted up the lowly; he has filled the hungry with good things, and sent the rich away empty. He has helped his servant Israel, in remembrance of his mercy, according to the promise he made to our ancestors, to Abraham and to his descendants forever." And Mary remained with Elizabeth about three months and then returned to her home.

- With Mary, I count my blessings, not as a matter of pride or achievement, but to recognize where God is at work in my life.
- Pride and humility are in the picture as Mary prays her *Magnificat.* Mary rejoices in being a blessed, lowly servant. I think of how this description relates to how I am now.

Friday 23rd December   Luke 1:57–66

Now the time came for Elizabeth to give birth, and she bore a son. Her neighbors and relatives heard that the Lord had shown his great mercy to her, and they rejoiced with her. On the eighth day they came to circumcise the child, and they were going to name him Zechariah after his father. But his mother said, "No; he is to be called John." They said to her, "None of your relatives has this name." Then they began motioning to his father to find out what name he wanted to give him. He asked for a writing tablet and wrote, "His name is John." And all of them were amazed. Immediately his mouth was opened and his tongue freed, and he began to speak, praising God. Fear came over all their neighbors, and all these things were talked about throughout the entire hill country of Judea. All who heard them pondered them and said, "What then will this child become?" For, indeed, the hand of the Lord was with him.

- Even in his old age, Zechariah was ready to break from the old patterns. I ask for the help that I need to step away from usual patterns and to follow God's call.
- I pray for all children: may the joy and hope that they experience live and grow into a deep appreciation of God's goodness.

Saturday 24th December   Luke 1:67–79

Then his father Zechariah was filled with the Holy Spirit and spoke this prophecy: "Blessed be the Lord God of Israel, for he has looked favorably on his people and redeemed them. He has raised up a mighty savior for us in the house of his servant David, as he spoke through the mouth of his holy prophets from of old, that we would be saved from our enemies and from the hand of all who hate us. Thus he has shown the mercy promised to our ancestors, and has remembered his holy covenant, the oath that he swore to our ancestor Abraham, to grant us that we, being rescued from the hands of our enemies, might serve him without fear, in holiness and righteousness before him all our days. And you, child, will be called the prophet of the Most High; for you will go before the Lord to prepare his ways, to give knowledge of salvation to his people by the forgiveness of their sins. By the tender mercy of our God, the dawn from on high will break upon us, to give light to those who sit in darkness and in the shadow of death, to guide our feet into the way of peace."

- Every day, this prayer of Zechariah becomes the morning prayer of thousands of people across the world. I read it slowly, letting the words reveal their meaning for me today.
- Zechariah is profoundly aware of his heritage, seeing God's action in the past as having promise for the future. I draw encouragement from my own story, allowing God to bless me with hope and confidence in continued blessing.

december 25–31

Something to think and pray about each day this week:

God Incarnate

A married woman once told a group of her friends: When my husband looks at me, I am so much greater and richer than when I look at myself. I sense so much more potential in me. Her husband added: When I experience my wife's loving gaze, I feel a sense of inner growth which seems to be lacking if I just look at myself in the mirror.

We experience this in Jesus' birth. God looks at us through human eyes for the first time, and in that gaze we begin to know our value and preciousness. The Incarnation reveals to us our worth in the sight of God. He loves us enough to share this mortal flesh with us. In prayer I think how God is waiting for me, looking at me.

The Presence of God

As I sit here, the beating of my heart,
the ebb and flow of my breathing, the movements of my mind
are all signs of God's ongoing creation of me.
I pause for a moment, and become aware
of this presence of God within me.

Freedom

I ask for the grace
to let go of my own concerns
and be open to what God is asking of me,
to let myself be guided and formed by my loving Creator.

Consciousness

In the presence of my loving Creator,
I look honestly at my feelings over the last day,
the highs, the lows, and the level ground.
Can I see where the Lord has been present?

The Word

I take my time to read the Word of God, slowly, a few times, allowing myself to dwell on anything that strikes me. (Please turn to your scripture on the following pages. Inspiration points are there should you need them. When you are ready, return here to continue.)

Conversation

Remembering that I am still in God's presence,
I imagine Jesus himself standing or sitting beside me
and say whatever is on my mind, whatever is in my heart,
speaking as one friend to another.

Conclusion

Glory be to the Father, and to the Son, and to the Holy Spirit,
As it was in the beginning, is now, and ever shall be,
World without end. Amen.

32

Sunday 25th December,
Feast of the Nativity of the Lord   John 1:1–5

In the beginning was the Word, and the Word was with God, and the Word was God. He was in the beginning with God. All things came into being through him, and without him not one thing came into being. What has come into being in him was life, and the life was the light of all people. The light shines in the darkness, and the darkness did not overcome it.

- No love that in a family dwells,
  No carolling in frosty air,
  Nor all the steeple-shaking bells
  Can with this single Truth compare —
  That God was Man in Palestine
  And lives today in Bread and Wine. (G.K. Chesterton)

Monday 26th December,
St. Stephen, the first martyr   Matthew 10:17–22

Jesus said to his apostles, "Beware of them, for they will hand you over to councils and flog you in their synagogues; and you will be dragged before governors and kings because of me, as a testimony to them and the Gentiles. When they hand you over, do not worry about how you are to speak or what you are to say; for what you are to say will be given to you at that time; for it is not you who speak, but the Spirit of your Father speaking through you. Brother will betray brother to death, and a father his child, and children will rise against parents and have them put to death; and you will be hated by all because of my name. But the one who endures to the end will be saved."

- Immediately after remembering the birth of Jesus, the Church remembers the first martyr. Birth and death are intimately connected with Jesus. The word for the place he was born is the same as the word for the upper room where he had the Last Supper. We know that the destiny of this child is for a cruel death.

- The upper room was also the place for the coming of the Spirit. In all of life, birth, and death and all that is in-between is the blessing of the Spirit.

Tuesday 27th December,
St. John, Evangelist   John 20:1a, 2–8

Early on the first day of the week, while it was still dark, Mary Magdalene came to the tomb and saw that the stone had been removed from the tomb. So she ran and went to Simon Peter and the other disciple, the one whom Jesus loved, and said to them, "They have taken the Lord out of the tomb, and we do not know where they have laid him." Then Peter and the other disciple set out and went toward the tomb. The two were running together, but the other disciple outran Peter and reached the tomb first. He bent down to look in and saw the linen wrappings lying there, but he did not go in. Then Simon Peter came, following him, and went into the tomb. He saw the linen wrappings lying there, and the cloth that had been on Jesus' head, not lying with the linen wrappings but rolled up in a place by itself. Then the other disciple, who reached the tomb first, also went in, and he saw and believed.

- It is sometimes tempting to cling to the glow of Christmas. While I value the gift of this season, this Easter scene reminds me that faith calls me to move on, to seek the risen Lord.
- When Mary Magdalene did not find Jesus where she expected, she went first to her community. As questions arise for me, I bring them to God and to others whom I trust.

34

Wednesday 28th December,
The Holy Innocents   Matthew 2:16–18

When Herod saw that he had been tricked by the wise men, he was infuriated, and he sent and killed all the children in and around Bethlehem who were two years old or under, according to the time that he had learned from the wise men. Then was fulfilled what had been spoken through the prophet Jeremiah: "A voice was heard in Ramah, wailing and loud lamentation, Rachel weeping for her children; she refused to be consoled, because they are no more."

- This terrible scene evokes the genocides and atrocities that still happen today.
- Herod's action was motivated by his pride and self-seeking. As I pray for all leaders, I ask God to heal me of any false image I have of myself. I pray with compassion for all who are affected by violence and cruelty.

Thursday 29th December   Luke 2:27–32

Guided by the Spirit, Simeon came into the temple; and when the parents brought in the child Jesus, to do for him what was customary under the law, Simeon took him in his arms and praised God, saying, "Master, now you are dismissing your servant in peace, according to your word; for my eyes have seen your salvation, which you have prepared in the presence of all peoples, light for revelation to the Gentiles and for glory to your people Israel."

- Simeon's example is of patient hope, as he waited around the Temple for a sign of God's salvation. I ask for a strengthening of my hope and faith as I wait on the Lord.
- Each day, thousands across the world make this their night prayer. Perhaps I might read it this evening, with acceptance and quiet joy, in gratitude for God's work through each one of us.

Friday 30th December, The Holy Family
Matthew 2:13–15

Now after they had left, an angel of the Lord appeared to Joseph in a dream and said, "Get up, take the child and his mother, and flee to Egypt, and remain there until I tell you; for Herod is about to search for the child, to destroy him." Then Joseph got up, took the child and his mother by night, and went to Egypt, and remained there until the death of Herod. This was to fulfill what had been spoken by the Lord through the prophet, "Out of Egypt I have called my son."

- Just after the wonders and signs of the visit of the Magi, Joseph is ready to move on. I pray that I may be able to relish inspiration wherever I find it, yet always remain poised to act.
- Joseph, Mary, and Jesus lived the lives of exiles. I pray for all who are away from home at this time because of political conditions, and I think of the exiles I encounter.

Saturday 31st December
John 1:16–18

From his fullness we have all received, grace upon grace. The law indeed was given through Moses; grace and truth came through Jesus Christ. No one has ever seen God. It is God the only Son, who is close to the Father's heart, who has made him known.

- This time of prayer is one way in which I receive the truth and grace that God wants to offer me. I prepare myself to receive blessings from the very heart of God.
- "Grace upon grace"; I picture an abundance of blessing, a cascade of goodness. This is what God desires for me. I ask that I not be content with less.

january 1–7

Something to think and pray about each day this week:

The Work of Healing Love

Jesus, faced with a man who had been crippled for thirty-eight years, asked a peculiar question, "Do you want to be healed?" (John 5:1). The man had been coming daily to the pool of Bethzatha; it was part of his routine. Being delicate can become a way of life. Some grow accustomed to being a victim, to being helped, to being dependent, to being unable to walk, or to having to fend for themselves. Jesus restores people not just to the absence of complaints but to energy and service. When he cured Simon's mother-in-law, she got out of bed and prepared a meal.

What bit of ourselves do we want to be healed? Everyone has a weakness where stress shows: nose, tummy, nerves, addiction, sleep, anxiety, fears, pains, rashes. We can be too limited and unambitious in our prayer for healing. A lovely description of mental health (from Freud) is "the capacity to love and to work." Shalom means wholeness.

Jesus' ministry focussed on the sick, that they should have life and have it more abundantly. God is pure act. Heaven is more than eternal rest. The music of heaven is full of energy, not just Massanet's *Meditation* or monastic chant, but folk or rock and roll—any music to dance to.

The Presence of God
I pause for a moment
and reflect on God's life-giving presence
in every part of my body, in everything around me,
in the whole of my life.

Freedom
Many countries are at this moment suffering
the agonies of war.
I bow my head in thanksgiving for my freedom.
I pray for all prisoners and captives.

Consciousness
Knowing that God loves me unconditionally,
I look honestly over the last day, its events, and my feelings.
Do I have something to be grateful for? Then I give thanks.
Is there something I am sorry for? Then I ask forgiveness.

The Word
God speaks to each one of us individually. I need to listen to hear
what he is saying to me. Read the text a few times, then listen.
(Please turn to your scripture on the following pages. Inspiration
points are there should you need them. When you are ready, return here to continue.)

Conversation
How has God's Word moved me? Has it left me cold?
Has it consoled me or moved me to act in a new way?
I imagine Jesus standing or sitting beside me;
I turn and share my feelings with him.

Conclusion
Glory be to the Father, and to the Son, and to the Holy Spirit,
As it was in the beginning, is now, and ever shall be,
World without end. Amen.

Sunday 1st January,
Solemnity of Mary, Mother of God — Luke 2:16–21

So they went with haste and found Mary and Joseph, and the child lying in the manger. When they saw this, they made known what had been told them about this child; and all who heard it were amazed at what the shepherds told them. But Mary treasured all these words and pondered them in her heart. The shepherds returned, glorifying and praising God for all they had heard and seen, as it had been told them. After eight days had passed, it was time to circumcise the child; and he was called Jesus, the name given by the angel before he was conceived in the womb.

- God's messengers tell the shepherds something astonishing, that a baby boy lying in a manger is both Messiah and Lord, God and Saviour! They, in their turn, repeat the angels' extraordinary message to Mary and Joseph.
- As Jesus grew and developed, Mary must have pondered all these things as she laced his sandals, prepared his meals, soothed him when he cried, and watched over him as he learned how to use carpenter's tools. Like any mother, she must have pondered what the future had in store for her son.
- I too am called to ponder Jesus' life so that his ways of thinking and his value system may become mine.

Monday 2nd January — John 1:19–28

This is the testimony given by John when the Jews sent priests and Levites from Jerusalem to ask him, "Who are you?" He confessed and did not deny it, but confessed, "I am not the Messiah." And they asked him, "What then? Are you Elijah?" He said, "I am not." "Are you the prophet?" He answered, "No." Then they said to him, "Who are you? Let us have an answer for those who sent us. What do you say about yourself?" He said, "I am the voice of one crying out in the wilderness, 'Make straight the way of the Lord,'" as the prophet Isaiah said. Now they had been sent from the Pharisees. They asked him, "Why then are you baptizing if you are neither the Messiah, nor Elijah, nor the prophet?" John answered them, "I baptize with water. Among you stands one whom you do not know, the one who is coming after me; I am not worthy to untie the thong of his sandal." This took place in Bethany across the Jordan where John was baptizing.

- When asked who he is, John the Baptist replies that he is "the voice of one crying in the wilderness, 'Make straight the way of the Lord.'" John compares himself to an engineer shouting out orders as the royal road is being prepared for the arrival of the king, or, in this case, for Jesus.
- What preparations am I making so that I am ready to welcome Jesus into my heart today?

Tuesday 3rd January — John 1:29–34

The next day John saw Jesus coming toward him and declared, "Here is the Lamb of God who takes away the sin of the world! This is he of whom I said, 'After me comes a man who ranks ahead of me because he was before me.' I myself did not know him; but I came baptizing with water for this reason, that he might be revealed to Israel." And John testified, "I saw the Spirit descending from heaven like a dove, and it remained on him. I myself did not know him, but the one who sent me to baptize with water said to me, 'He on whom you see the Spirit descend and remain is the one who baptizes with the Holy Spirit.' And I myself have seen and have testified that this is the Son of God."

- Our prayer brings us in touch with the Son of God who walked our earth. We pray in the presence of the One who lives in the heaven of God's presence, and is also close to each of us. His essential quality is firstly that he takes away the sin of the world.
- Prayer purifies us each day, forgives us, and calls us into fuller friendship with the One who is Son of God and son of Mary, child of heaven and born of earth.

Wednesday 4th January   John 1:35–39

The next day John again was standing with two of his disciples, and as he watched Jesus walk by, he exclaimed, "Look, here is the Lamb of God!" The two disciples heard him say this, and they followed Jesus. When Jesus turned and saw them following, he said to them, "What are you looking for?" They said to him, "Rabbi" (which translated means Teacher), "where are you staying?" He said to them, "Come and see." They came and saw where he was staying, and they remained with him that day.

- Jesus asks all would-be followers to spend time with him. He asks them to "come and see." By contemplating and meditating on the gospels, I come to know Jesus more intimately and more personally.
- The various disciples invited one another to "come and see" Jesus. Do I ever share my experience of knowing, loving, and serving Jesus with others?

Thursday 5th January   John 1:43–51

The next day Jesus decided to go to Galilee. He found Philip and said to him, "Follow me." Now Philip was from Bethsaida, the city of Andrew and Peter. Philip found Nathanael and said to him, "We have found him about whom Moses in the law and also the prophets wrote, Jesus son of Joseph from Nazareth." Nathanael said to him, "Can anything good come out of

Nazareth?" Philip said to him, "Come and see." When Jesus saw Nathanael coming toward him, he said of him, "Here is truly an Israelite in whom there is no deceit!" Nathanael asked him, "Where did you get to know me?" Jesus answered, "I saw you under the fig tree before Philip called you." Nathanael replied, "Rabbi, you are the Son of God! You are the King of Israel!" Jesus answered, "Do you believe because I told you that I saw you under the fig tree? You will see greater things than these." And he said to him, "Very truly, I tell you, you will see heaven opened and the angels of God ascending and descending upon the Son of Man."

- "Can anything good come out of Nazareth?" Nathanael asks rather cynically. People are often judged by where they come from, by the way they speak, by their status in society. Do I do that?

Friday 6th January   Mark 1:7

John proclaimed, "The one who is more powerful than I is coming after me; I am not worthy to stoop down and untie the thong of his sandals. I have baptized you with water; but he will baptize you with the Holy Spirit."

- Mark's gospel reveals John the Baptist as the beacon, showing us the way to the "more powerful" one who is to come, Jesus. As Isaiah has foretold, John shows us the coming of the Lord.
- How do I reveal Jesus to those in my life—my family, friends, work colleagues?

Saturday 7th January   Matthew 4:12–17, 23–25

Now when Jesus heard that John had been arrested, he withdrew to Galilee. He left Nazareth and made his home in Capernaum by the lake, in the territory of Zebulun and Naphtali, so that what had been spoken through the prophet Isaiah might be fulfilled: "Land of Zebulun, land of Naphtali, on the road by the sea, across the Jordan, Galilee of the Gentiles—the people who sat in darkness have seen a great light, and for those who sat in the region and shadow of death light has dawned." From that time Jesus began to proclaim, "Repent, for the kingdom of heaven has come near." Jesus went throughout Galilee, teaching in their synagogues and proclaiming the good news of the kingdom and curing every disease and every sickness among the people. So his fame spread throughout all Syria, and they brought to him all the sick, those who were afflicted with various diseases and pains, demoniacs, epileptics, and paralytics, and he cured them. And great crowds followed him from Galilee, the Decapolis, Jerusalem, Judea, and from beyond the Jordan.

- Jesus sought security in a Galilee that was at least half Gentile in population, half pagan in cult, and bilingual—the people spoke Greek as well as Aramaic. According to Matthew, Jesus becomes a "light" for these people through his teaching and healing.
- Is Jesus the light enlightening my daily living? If so, can I count the ways?

january 8–14

Something to think and pray about each day this week:

Finding Joy in Christ

Christian joy stems from being able to see the good around us, as Jesus did: in Pilate, Magdalene, Judas, Peter, the women of Jerusalem, Thomas. It is a joy based on Christ's infinitely compassionate presence. The risen Christ enters as one bringing peace, yet realistic. Everyone he met was interesting to him. This was the presence round which the Christian community grew, a consoling presence, and also dynamic. Blessed are those who hunger and thirst after justice. We will not live in the perfect society in this life. We are like Abraham, on a pilgrimage of faith, facing the huge risks of the Christian, moving from one piece of Holy Ground to another, seeking God—"You would not seek me if you had not already found me." The apostasy is to stop seeking.

The Presence of God
The world is charged with the grandeur of God (Gerard Manley Hopkins).
I dwell for a moment on the presence of God
around me, in every part of my body,
and deep within my being.

Freedom
"In these days, God taught me
as a schoolteacher teaches a pupil" (St. Ignatius).
I remind myself that there are things God has to teach me yet,
and ask for the grace to hear them and let them change me.

Consciousness
How do I find myself today?
Where am I with God? With others?
Do I have something to be grateful for? Then I give thanks.
Is there something I am sorry for? Then I ask forgiveness.

The Word
I read the Word of God slowly, a few times over, and I listen to what God is saying to me. (Please turn to your scripture on the following pages. Inspiration points are there should you need them. When you are ready, return here to continue.)

Conversation
Sometimes I wonder what I might say
if I were to meet You in person, Lord.
I might say "Thank You, Lord" for always being there for me.
I know with certainty there were times when You carried me.
when through your strength I got through the dark times in my life.

Conclusion
Glory be to the Father, and to the Son, and to the Holy Spirit,
As it was in the beginning, is now, and ever shall be,
World without end. Amen.

Sunday 8th January,
The Epiphany of the Lord   Matthew 2:1–2, 7–12

In the time of King Herod, after Jesus was born in Bethlehem of Judea, wise men from the East came to Jerusalem, asking, "Where is the child who has been born king of the Jews? For we observed his star at its rising, and have come to pay him homage." Herod secretly called for the wise men and learned from them the exact time when the star had appeared. Then he sent them to Bethlehem, saying, "Go and search diligently for the child; and when you have found him, bring me word so that I may also go and pay him homage." When they had heard the king, they set out; and there, ahead of them, went the star that they had seen at its rising, until it stopped over the place where the child was. When they saw that the star had stopped, they were overwhelmed with joy. On entering the house, they saw the child with Mary his mother; and they knelt down and paid him homage. Then, opening their treasure chests, they offered him gifts of gold, frankincense, and myrrh. And having been warned in a dream not to return to Herod, they left for their own country by another road.

- Matthew presents the wise men, the astrologers or magi, as representatives of the Gentile world in all its racial diversity coming from the East—Persia, Syria, Arabia—just as many Gentiles did when they joined Matthew's community. The wise men, in gratitude, offer the child Jesus gifts fit for a king, gold, frankincense, and myrrh.
- The deepest obstacle to honest gratitude is the refusal to accept the fact that I am gifted by God in so many ways, often beyond imagining! It is pride, not humility, to refuse to acknowledge the gifts that God has endowed me with.
- Today I wish to express my gratitude to God for his many gifts.

Monday 9th January,
The Baptism of the Lord   Mark 1:7–11

John proclaimed, "The one who is more powerful than I is
coming after me; I am not worthy to stoop down and untie
the thong of his sandals. I have baptized you with water; but he
will baptize you with the Holy Spirit." In those days Jesus came
from Nazareth of Galilee and was baptized by John in the Jordan.
And just as he was coming up out of the water, he saw the heavens torn apart and the Spirit descending like a dove on him. And
a voice came from heaven, "You are my Son, the Beloved; with
you I am well pleased."

- Mark begins his gospel not with the birth of Jesus but his baptism.
- To be baptised with the Holy Spirit is to be immersed in and live
  by God's powerful love. I pray for a deep realization of this mystery.

Tuesday 10th January   Mark 1:21–28

Jesus entered the synagogue and taught. They were astounded
at his teaching, for he taught them as one having authority,
and not as the scribes. Just then there was in their synagogue a
man with an unclean spirit, and he cried out, "What have you
to do with us, Jesus of Nazareth? Have you come to destroy us?
I know who you are, the Holy One of God." But Jesus rebuked
him, saying, "Be silent, and come out of him!" And the unclean
spirit, convulsing him and crying with a loud voice, came out of
him. They were all amazed, and they kept on asking one another,
"What is this? A new teaching—with authority! He commands
even the unclean spirits, and they obey him." At once his fame
began to spread throughout the surrounding region of Galilee.

- In speaking about Jesus casting out demons, one has to keep in
  mind that Jesus was a man of his time, like us in all things but sin.
  So, like his contemporaries, he could well have understood mental

or psychosomatic illnesses to be forms of demonic possession. It was quite natural for Mark to speak of casting out an evil spirit.

- What "demons" do I carry around? Can I be honest with myself and bring them before the Lord?

Wednesday 11th January   Mark 1:35–39

In the morning, while it was still very dark, he got up and went out to a deserted place, and there he prayed. And Simon and his companions hunted for him. When they found him, they said to him, "Everyone is searching for you." He answered, "Let us go on to the neighboring towns, so that I may proclaim the message there also; for that is what I came out to do." And he went throughout Galilee, proclaiming the message in their synagogues and casting out demons.

- Daily prayer in the early morning was part of Jewish piety. Jesus gets up and goes to a place to be by himself to pray, to commune with his Father. However, Simon Peter and his companions soon come looking for him. "Everybody is searching for you," they say. Perhaps they thought Jesus was missing the chance to perform more miracles in Capernaum!
- I may wonder whether I spend too much time expecting Jesus to do miracles on my behalf.

Thursday 12th January   Mark 1:40–45

A leper came to Jesus begging him, and kneeling he said to him, "If you choose, you can make me clean." Moved with pity, Jesus stretched out his hand and touched him, and said to him, "I do choose. Be made clean!" Immediately the leprosy left him, and he was made clean. After sternly warning him he sent him away at once, saying to him, "See that you say nothing to anyone; but go, show yourself to the priest, and offer for your cleansing what Moses commanded, as a testimony to them." But he went out and began to proclaim it freely, and to spread the word, so that Jesus could no longer go into a town openly, but stayed out in the country; and people came to him from every quarter.

- Leprosy in the New Testament could mean any type of skin disease. Having cured someone, Jesus declares: "See that you say nothing to anyone." He does not want people to think that he has come to bring about political change. Jesus is not a revolutionary in that sense.
- There are many aspects of my life that need to be "made clean." I bring these to Jesus for healing.

Friday 13th January   Mark 2:3–7

Then some people came, bringing to him a paralyzed man, carried by four of them. And when they could not bring him to Jesus because of the crowd, they removed the roof above him; and after having dug through it, they let down the mat on which the paralytic lay. When Jesus saw their faith, he said to the paralytic, "Son, your sins are forgiven." Now some of the scribes were sitting there, questioning in their hearts, "Why does this fellow speak in this way? It is blasphemy! Who can forgive sins but God alone?"

- The scribes, rightly, assert that only God can forgive sins. No wonder they feel that Jesus is blaspheming. They fail to perceive that Jesus is God's Son, and so can clearly and unambiguously declare that he has the authority to forgive sins—mine included!
- Where can I find forgiveness for my sins?

Saturday 14th January   Mark 2:13–17

Jesus went out again beside the sea; the whole crowd gathered around him, and he taught them. As he was walking along, he saw Levi son of Alphaeus sitting at the tax booth, and he said to him, "Follow me." And he got up and followed him. And as he sat at dinner in Levi's house, many tax collectors and sinners were also sitting with Jesus and his disciples—for there were many who followed him. When the scribes of the Pharisees saw that he was eating with sinners and tax collectors, they said to his disciples, "Why does he eat with tax collectors and sinners?" When Jesus heard this, he said to them, "Those who are well have no need of a physician, but those who are sick; I have come to call not the righteous but sinners."

- The scribes and Pharisees regarded themselves as righteous because they carefully observed various customs that had been added to the Law of Moses, the so-called "traditions of the elders." When Jesus says that he has come not to call the righteous but sinners, he is referring ironically to the scribes and Pharisees who see obedience to custom as superior to love of God and neighbour.
- Jesus shocked these men with his choice of companions at dinner. Do I shock anyone, in Jesus' name?

january 15–21

Something to think and pray about each day this week:

Growing Together

"I appeal that there be no dissensions among you" (1 Corinthians 1:10).

We live with the scandal of a divided Christendom; but we can make it better or worse. We make it worse if we focus on the differences between Christians, better if we keep our eyes on what unites us. We are all baptised in the name of the Father, Son, and Holy Spirit. In worship, belief, morality, and in the love of Jesus, we share great areas of agreement; and we are travelling in hope towards one flock and one shepherd.

Jesus thinks and speaks in parables and images which he draws from the world around him. He reaches especially for symbols of life and growth. From a tiny seed grows a mighty tree. From Mary, the twelve apostles, and the holy women have grown the largest body of believers on the planet, a Church of every colour and culture. We are not uniform or cloned—all sorts of birds can make nests in our shade—but united in our recognition of Jesus as the revelation and Son of God.

The Presence of God
As I sit here, God is present,
breathing life into me and into everything around me.
For a few moments, I sit silently,
and become aware of God's loving presence.

Freedom
If God were trying to tell me something, would I know?
If God were reassuring me or challenging me, would I notice?
I ask for the grace to be free of my own preoccupations
and open to what God may be saying to me.

Consciousness
In God's loving presence I unwind the past day,
starting from now and looking back, moment by moment.
I gather in all the goodness and light, in gratitude.
I attend to the shadows and what they say to me,
seeking healing, courage, forgiveness.

The Word
I take my time to read the Word of God, slowly, a few times, allowing myself to dwell on anything that strikes me. (Please turn to your scripture on the following pages. Inspiration points are there should you need them. When you are ready, return here to continue.)

Conversation
What is stirring in me as I pray?
Am I consoled, troubled, left cold?
I imagine Jesus himself standing or sitting at my side,
and share my feelings with him.

Conclusion
Glory be to the Father, and to the Son, and to the Holy Spirit,
As it was in the beginning, is now, and ever shall be,
World without end. Amen.

Sunday 15th January,
Second Sunday in Ordinary Time   John 1:35–42

The next day John again was standing with two of his disciples, and as he watched Jesus walk by, he exclaimed, "Look, here is the Lamb of God!" The two disciples heard him say this, and they followed Jesus. When Jesus turned and saw them following, he said to them, "What are you looking for?" They said to him, "Rabbi" (which translated means Teacher), "where are you staying?" He said to them, "Come and see." They came and saw where he was staying, and they remained with him that day. It was about four o'clock in the afternoon. One of the two who heard John speak and followed him was Andrew, Simon Peter's brother. He first found his brother Simon and said to him, "We have found the Messiah" (which is translated Anointed). He brought Simon to Jesus, who looked at him and said, "You are Simon son of John. You are to be called Cephas" (which is translated Peter).

- Jesus looked hard at the disciples—looked right into them—and called them. They were affirmed and loved in that look. Prayer can start with you looking at God looking at you. Take in the look; allow the look to warm you and invite you. The look of Jesus says in its own way, "Come and see."

- Prayer is time to come and see who the Lord is, and who we are ourselves.

Monday 16th January   Mark 2:18–22

Now John's disciples and the Pharisees were fasting; and people came and said to him, "Why do John's disciples and the disciples of the Pharisees fast, but your disciples do not fast?" Jesus said to them, "The wedding-guests cannot fast while the bridegroom is with them, can they? As long as they have the bridegroom with them, they cannot fast. The days will come when the bridegroom is taken away from them, and then they will fast on that day. "No one sews a piece of unshrunk cloth on an old cloak; otherwise, the patch pulls away from it, the new from the old, and a worse tear is made. And no one puts new wine into old wineskins; otherwise, the wine will burst the skins, and the wine is lost, and so are the skins; but one puts new wine into fresh wineskins."

- Jesus is referring to old and new forms of religious practice: the old ways of the scribes and Pharisees with their many "traditions," which they patched onto the Mosaic Law, and which Jesus condemned, and the new "wine" of Jesus' teaching poured out on his disciples.
- Do I sometimes prefer to cling to old traditions rather than face the challenges presented by Jesus?

Tuesday 17th January   **Mark 2:23–28**

One sabbath Jesus was going through the grainfields; and as they made their way his disciples began to pluck heads of grain. The Pharisees said to him, "Look, why are they doing what is not lawful on the sabbath?" And he said to them, "Have you never read what David did when he and his companions were hungry and in need of food? He entered the house of God, when Abiathar was high priest, and ate the bread of the Presence, which it is not lawful for any but the priests to eat, and he gave some to his companions." Then he said to them, "The sabbath was made for humankind, and not humankind for the sabbath; so the Son of Man is lord even of the sabbath."

- The Pharisees object to what Jesus' disciples are doing on the Sabbath. Jesus replies with an extraordinarily radical statement, "The Sabbath was made for humankind and not humankind for the

Sabbath; so the Son of Man (Jesus) is Lord even of the Sabbath." Jesus' saying is not in opposition to Jewish teaching but a reminder of God's original purpose which recognized serious human needs as good reasons for sometimes setting aside Sabbath regulations.

- By claiming that he is "Lord even of the Sabbath," Jesus is claiming divine authority.

Wednesday 18th January   **Mark 3:1–6**

Again he entered the synagogue, and a man was there who had a withered hand. They watched him to see whether he would cure him on the sabbath, so that they might accuse him. And he said to the man who had the withered hand, "Come forward." Then he said to them, "Is it lawful to do good or to do harm on the sabbath, to save life or to kill?" But they were silent. He looked around at them with anger; he was grieved at their hardness of heart and said to the man, "Stretch out your hand." He stretched it out, and his hand was restored. The Pharisees went out and immediately conspired with the Herodians against him, how to destroy him.

- Good people often seem to provoke jealousy and even hostility in others. As I enter into the story in today's gospel, I allow myself to become aware of how Jesus provoked opposition and hostility.
- Are there any parallels in my own life?

Thursday 19th January   **Mark 3:7–12**

Jesus departed with his disciples to the sea, and a great multitude from Galilee followed him; hearing all that he was doing, they came to him in great numbers from Judea, Jerusalem, Idumea, beyond the Jordan, and the region around Tyre and Sidon. He told his disciples to have a boat ready for him because of the crowd, so that they would not crush him; for he had cured many, so that all who had diseases pressed upon him to touch him.

Whenever the unclean spirits saw him, they fell down before him and shouted, "You are the Son of God!" But he sternly ordered them not to make him known.

- As his popularity grows, people come to Jesus from far and wide. What are they looking for?
- When I approach Jesus, what am I looking for?

Friday 20th January   **Mark 3:13–19**

He went up the mountain and called to him those whom he wanted, and they came to him. And he appointed twelve, whom he also named apostles, to be with him, and to be sent out to proclaim the message, and to have authority to cast out demons. So he appointed the twelve: Simon (to whom he gave the name Peter); James son of Zebedee and John the brother of James (to whom he gave the name Boanerges, that is, Sons of Thunder); and Andrew, and Philip, and Bartholomew, and Matthew, and Thomas, and James son of Alphaeus, and Thaddaeus, and Simon the Cananaean, and Judas Iscariot, who betrayed him.

- When Jesus asked someone to "follow" him, he meant it literally, physically accompanying him on his preaching tours, and therefore leaving behind home, parents, and livelihood—just as Jesus himself had done. Abandoning home and livelihood could well result in hostility and suffering, even at the hands of one's family, as Jesus knew from his own experience.
- Jesus' call to follow him was radical and absolute. Following him was far different from merely following him as part of a crowd.

Saturday 21st January   **Mark 3:20–21**

And the crowd came together again, so that they could not even eat. When his family heard it, they went out to restrain him, for people were saying, "He has gone out of his mind."

- Jesus' family tries to restrain him because of what people are saying about him. Even those closest to him misunderstood Jesus and his mission.
- How do I react to being misunderstood?

january 22–28

Something to think and pray about each day this week:

Staying Close

Shame on my thoughts, how they stray from me! I fear great danger from this on the day of eternal judgment. During the psalms they wander on a path that is not right: they run, they distract, they misbehave before the eyes of the great God. Through eager assemblies, through companies of lewd women, through woods, through cities—swifter they are than the wind. One moment they follow ways of loveliness, and the next ways of riotous shame—no lie!

O beloved, truly chaste Christ, to whom every eye is clear, may the grace of the sevenfold spirit come to keep them, to hold them in check. Rule this heart of mine, O swift God of the elements, that you may be my love, and that I may do your will! That I may reach Christ with his chosen companions, that we may be together: they are neither fickle nor inconstant—they are not as I am (Irish prayer, ninth century).

The Presence of God
As I sit here with my book, God is here—
around me, in my sensations, in my thoughts, and deep within me.
I pause for a moment, and become aware
of God's life-giving presence.

Freedom
I need to close out the noise, to rise above the noise—
the noise that interrupts, that separates,
the noise that isolates.
I need to listen to God again.

Consciousness
I remind myself that I am in the presence of the Lord.
I will take refuge in His loving heart.
He is my strength in times of weakness.
He is my comforter in times of sorrow.

The Word
God speaks to each one of us individually. I need to listen to what
he is saying to me. (Please turn to your scripture on the following
pages. Inspiration points are there should you need them. When
you are ready, return here to continue.)

Conversation
Do I notice myself reacting as I pray with the Word of God?
Do I feel challenged, comforted, angry?
Imagining Jesus sitting or standing by me,
I speak out my feelings, as one trusted friend to another.

Conclusion
Glory be to the Father, and to the Son, and to the Holy Spirit,
As it was in the beginning, is now, and ever shall be,
World without end. Amen.

Sunday 22nd January,
Third Sunday in Ordinary Time   Mark 1:14–20

Now after John was arrested, Jesus came to Galilee, proclaiming the good news of God, and saying, "The time is fulfilled, and the kingdom of God has come near; repent, and believe in the good news." As Jesus passed along the Sea of Galilee, he saw Simon and his brother Andrew casting a net into the sea—for they were fishermen. And Jesus said to them, "Follow me and I will make you fish for people." And immediately they left their nets and followed him. As he went a little farther, he saw James son of Zebedee and his brother John, who were in their boat mending the nets. Immediately he called them; and they left their father Zebedee in the boat with the hired men, and followed him.

- Jesus called his disciples at their ordinary work. He involved himself in their lives, and they knew he had something relevant to offer. They seemed to think that they could take part in this project called "the kingdom of God."
- We also find the call of God to be people of the Gospel among the ordinary moments of life. We are invited to be people for whom the love of others is a motivation of all we do and say.

Monday 23rd January   Mark 3:22–30

And the scribes who came down from Jerusalem said, "He has Beelzebul, and by the ruler of the demons he casts out demons." And he called them to him, and spoke to them in parables, "How can Satan cast out Satan? If a kingdom is divided against itself, that kingdom cannot stand. And if a house is divided against itself, that house will not be able to stand. And if Satan has risen up against himself and is divided, he cannot stand, but his end has come. But no one can enter a strong man's house and plunder his property without first tying up the strong man; then indeed the house can be plundered. "Truly I tell you, people will be forgiven for their sins and whatever blasphemies they utter; but whoever blasphemes against the Holy Spirit can never have forgiveness, but is guilty of an eternal sin"—for they had said, "He has an unclean spirit."

- Jesus' response to these scribes is both logical and from the depths of his being: what he proclaims is the universal forgiveness of the kingdom which he preaches, and his healing is through God's Spirit.
- We are called to live through the same Spirit. Each one of us has that choice to make.

Tuesday 24th January — Mark 3:31–35

Then the mother and brothers of Jesus came; and standing outside, they sent to him and called him. A crowd was sitting around him; and they said to him, "Your mother and your brothers and sisters are outside, asking for you." And he replied, "Who are my mother and my brothers?" And looking at those who sat around him, he said, "Here are my mother and my brothers! Whoever does the will of God is my brother and sister and mother."

- Jesus highlights that the primary relationship is to God. The deepest, most natural bonds are created within this primary love.
- Mother and family were important to Jesus, but the real call was within this family relationship to hear and keep the Word of God.

Wednesday 25th January, Conversion of St. Paul, Apostle — Acts 22:6–10a

Paul said: "While I was on my way and approaching Damascus, about noon a great light from heaven suddenly shone about me. I fell to the ground and heard a voice saying to me, 'Saul, Saul, why are you persecuting me?' I answered, 'Who are

64

you, Lord?' Then he said to me, 'I am Jesus of Nazareth whom you are persecuting.' Now those who were with me saw the light but did not hear the voice of the one who was speaking to me. I asked, 'What am I to do, Lord?'"

- Out of this conversation on the way to Damascus, Paul undergoes an astonishing and instantaneous conversion.
- When I bully or malign others, spread false rumors or malicious gossip about them, I too am persecuting Jesus.

Thursday 26th January   Mark 4:21–25

He said to them, "Is a lamp brought in to be put under the bushel basket, or under the bed, and not on the lampstand? For there is nothing hidden, except to be disclosed; nor is any-thing secret, except to come to light. Let anyone with ears to hear listen!" And he said to them, "Pay attention to what you hear; the measure you give will be the measure you get, and still more will be given you. For to those who have, more will be given; and from those who have nothing, even what they have will be taken away."

- Jesus is saying that the person who seeks to gain some spiritual insight into what he is saying will have that insight increased by exposure to his parables, whereas whoever does not listen to Jesus will end up in spiritual ignorance.
- I need to let myself be puzzled by and challenged by Jesus' parables.

Friday 27th January   Mark 4:26–32

Jesus said to the crowd, "The kingdom of God is as if someone would scatter seed on the ground, and would sleep and rise night and day, and the seed would sprout and grow, he does not know how. The earth produces of itself, first the stalk, then the head, then the full grain in the head. But when the grain is ripe, at once he goes in with his sickle, because the harvest has come."

He also said, "With what can we compare the kingdom of God, or what parable will we use for it? It is like a mustard seed, which, when sown upon the ground, is the smallest of all the seeds on earth; yet when it is sown it grows up and becomes the greatest of all shrubs, and puts forth large branches, so that the birds of the air can make nests in its shade."

• The kingdom of God, God's rule or reign in human hearts, comes about when people truly listen to Jesus. The beginnings of the kingdom may be small, but God will reign in all human hearts in due course.

• Lord, I get so discouraged when I see all the evil and injustice in the world. I will pray for patience and for hope.

Saturday 28th January   Mark 4:35–41

On that day, when evening had come, he said to them, "Let us go across to the other side." And leaving the crowd behind, they took him with them in the boat, just as he was. Other boats were with him. A great windstorm arose, and the waves beat into the boat, so that the boat was already being swamped. But he was in the stern, asleep on the cushion; and they woke him up and said to him, "Teacher, do you not care that we are perishing?" He woke up and rebuked the wind, and said to the sea, "Peace! Be still!" Then the wind ceased, and there was a dead calm. He said to them, "Why are you afraid? Have you still no faith?" And they were filled with great awe and said to one another, "Who then is this, that even the wind and the sea obey him?"

• In the trials and troubles we face, Jesus often seems to be "asleep."

• God does not solve our problems. In prayer, I will call out to him and, no doubt, I will hear his voice saying, "Peace! Be still! Why are you afraid? Have you no faith?"

january 29–february 4

Something to think and pray about each day this week:

Making Yes Mean Yes

"Do not swear. All you need to say is 'Yes' if you mean yes, or 'No' if you mean no. Anything more than this comes from the evil one" (Matthew 5:37). The Sermon on the Mount speaks with a simplicity that has been lost in the complications of Church life and theology. St. Benedict is equally simple in his Rule for monks. Here is a piece that echoes Jesus' words and can serve as an examination of conscience for anyone: "I do not act in anger or nurse a grudge. I rid my heart of all deceit. I never give a hollow greeting of peace, and I never turn away when somebody needs my love. I speak the truth with heart and tongue."

The Presence of God

At any time of the day or night we can call on Jesus.
He is always waiting, listening for our call.
What a wonderful blessing.
No phone needed, no e-mails, just a whisper.

Freedom

I will ask God's help,
to be free from my own preoccupations,
to be open to God in this time of prayer,
to come to love and serve him more.

Consciousness

How am I really feeling? Light-hearted? Heavy-hearted?
I may be very much at peace, happy to be here.
Equally, I may be frustrated, worried, or angry.
I acknowledge how I really am. It is the real me that the Lord loves.

The Word

I read the Word of God slowly, a few times over, and I listen to what God is saying to me. (Please turn to your scripture on the following pages. Inspiration points are there should you need them. When you are ready, return here to continue.)

Conversation

Remembering that I am still in God's presence,
I imagine Jesus himself standing or sitting beside me,
and say whatever is on my mind, whatever is in my heart,
speaking as one friend to another.

Conclusion

Glory be to the Father, and to the Son, and to the Holy Spirit,
As it was in the beginning, is now, and ever shall be,
World without end. Amen.

Sunday 29th January,
Fourth Sunday in Ordinary Time
Mark 1:21–28

They came to Capernaum and on the sabbath Jesus entered the synagogue and taught. They were astounded at his teaching, for he taught them as one having authority, and not as the scribes. Just then there was in their synagogue a man with an unclean spirit, and he cried out, "What have you to do with us, Jesus of Nazareth? Have you come to destroy us? I know who you are, the Holy One of God." But Jesus rebuked him, saying, "Be silent, and come out of him!" And the unclean spirit, convulsing him and crying with a loud voice, came out of him. They were all amazed, and they kept on asking one another, "What is this? A new teaching—with authority! He commands even the unclean spirits, and they obey him." At once his fame began to spread throughout the surrounding region of Galilee.

- For the people present at this strange event, the exorcising of an unclean spirit identified Jesus as an agent of God. The battle here is between Jesus and the evil spirit, between good and evil. What happened in this conflict at the beginning of Jesus' ministry made him famous in Galilee.

- The very presence of Jesus challenged all that was contrary to him. Does my way of living call people beyond where they are?

Monday 30th January
Mark 5:16–20

As he was getting into the boat, the man who had been possessed by demons begged him that he might be with him. But Jesus refused, and said to him, "Go home to your friends, and tell them how much the Lord has done for you, and what mercy he has shown you." And he went away and began to proclaim in the Decapolis how much Jesus had done for him; and everyone was amazed.

- The healed man had asked to go with Jesus but, at Jesus' request, he stays in his own place to announce the Gospel. Our call to work with Jesus and our partnership with him is at Jesus' initiative. As disciples we wait to be told what to do and where to minister.
- Our daily call will be to announce in word and in our way of life the Gospel of Jesus, in the places and among people that are part of our ordinary life.

Tuesday 31st January   Mark 5:21–24

When Jesus had crossed again in the boat to the other side, a great crowd gathered around him; and he was by the sea. Then one of the leaders of the synagogue named Jairus came and, when he saw him, fell at his feet and begged him repeatedly, "My little daughter is at the point of death. Come and lay your hands on her, so that she may be made well, and live." So he went with him. And a large crowd followed him and pressed in on him.

- We can identify with people who ask for what we really want from the Lord. The synagogue official was out of his mind with worry about his child.
- In prayer we can be afraid to be really honest and hopeful in asking God for what we want. Ask now this day for God's real and strong intervention where you really want this in your life.

Wednesday 1st February   Mark 6:1–6

Jesus went on to his hometown, and his disciples followed him. On the sabbath he began to teach in the synagogue, and many who heard him were astounded. They said, "Where did this man get all this? What is this wisdom that has been given to him? What deeds of power are being done by his hands! Is not this the carpenter, the son of Mary and brother of James and Joses and Judas and Simon, and are not his sisters here with us?" And they took offense at him. Then Jesus said to them, "Prophets are not without honor, except in their hometown, and among their own kin, and in their own house." And he could do no deed of power there, except that he laid his hands on a few sick people and cured them. And he was amazed at their unbelief. Then he went about among the villages teaching.

- Jesus returns to his hometown of Nazareth only to be met with skepticism—in spite of all the miracles he has performed. It is both Jesus' wisdom and his mighty works that puzzle his relatives and the people of his native place.
- We often judge others because we think we know them. Perhaps we really don't.

Thursday 2nd February, Presentation of the Lord   Luke 2:25–30

Now there was a man in Jerusalem whose name was Simeon; this man was righteous and devout, looking forward to the consolation of Israel, and the Holy Spirit rested on him. It had been revealed to him by the Holy Spirit that he would not see death before he had seen the Lord's Messiah. Guided by the Spirit, Simeon came into the temple; and when the parents brought in the child Jesus, to do for him what was customary under the law, Simeon took him in his arms and praised God, saying, "Master, now you are dismissing your servant in peace, according to your word; for my eyes have seen your salvation, which you have prepared in the presence of all peoples, a light for revelation to the Gentiles and for glory to your people Israel." And the child's father and mother were amazed at what was being said about him.

- Sometimes we feel in prayer as if we've said it all to God; our problems, sins, failings seem the same today as last year. We may feel God is tired of it all, tired of us. But Simeon didn't tire of praising and thanking.

- Maybe that's part of the prayer of old age, and perhaps there are times when that is all God wants of us. A lot of prayer is letting the past go, whether it is only yesterday, a generation ago, or almost a lifetime ago.

Friday 3rd February   Psalm 17 (18):31, 47, 50–51

This God—his way is perfect; the promise of the Lord proves true; he is a shield for all who take refuge in him. The Lord lives! Blessed be my rock, and exalted be the God of my salvation. For this I will extol you, O Lord, among the nations, and sing praises to your name. Great triumphs he gives to his king, and shows steadfast love to his anointed, to David and his descendants for ever.

- The psalms portray David as the ideal king; David puts his trust in God who gives strength to his arm. This is the rock on whom David relies, the God on whom he calls in prayer.
- Do I know this God in my life? How do I give praise to God?

Saturday 4th February   Mark 6:30–31

The apostles gathered around Jesus, and told him all that they had done and taught. He said to them, "Come away to a deserted place all by yourselves and rest a while."

- It is good, indeed essential, to go apart to a "deserted" place from time to time to rest and feed one's heart by listening for the voice of God. The human heart is restless.
- Some assuage this human hunger by grasping for more and more money, fame, sex, power. To be fully human is to seek. We seek not just for food, facts, or things but for meaning. We want a purpose, a motive to go on. Jesus provides us with such a purpose.

february 5–11

Something to think and pray about each day this week:

Taking Time to Look

Critics of Christianity caricature us as gabbling pray-ers, rushing through the Rosary, uttering formulas about God without any lifting of the mind and heart. It is true that from the beginnings of the Church we have learned prayers like the Our Father. It is also true that not all prayer involves saying prayers. Those who follow a religious vocation often gather to pray together in words, such as the Divine Office and the Rosary. They also meet God in silence, like the old farmer who spent hours in the parish church of Ars and, when questioned, explained to Jean Vianney, the Curé of Ars, "I look at the good God and the good God looks at me."

The Presence of God
I pause for a moment
and think of the love and the grace that God showers on me,
creating me in His image and likeness, making me His temple.

Freedom
Lord, grant me the grace to be free from the excesses of this life.
Let me not get caught up with the desire for wealth.
Keep my heart and mind free to love and serve You.

Consciousness
In the presence of my loving Creator,
I look honestly at my feelings over the last day,
the highs, the lows, and the level ground.
Can I see where the Lord has been present?

The Word
God speaks to each one of us individually. I need to listen to what
he is saying to me. (Please turn to your scripture on the following
pages. Inspiration points are there should you need them. When
you are ready, return here to continue.)

Conversation
Sometimes I wonder what I might say
if I were to meet You in person, Lord.
I might say "Thank You, Lord" for always being there for me.
I know with certainty there were times when You carried me,
when through your strength I got through the dark times in my life.

Conclusion
Glory be to the Father, and to the Son, and to the Holy Spirit,
As it was in the beginning, is now, and ever shall be,
World without end. Amen.

Sunday 5th February,
Fifth Sunday in Ordinary Time   Mark 1:29–39

As soon as they left the synagogue, they entered the house of Simon and Andrew, with James and John. Now Simon's mother-in-law was in bed with a fever, and they told him about her at once. He came and took her by the hand and lifted her up. Then the fever left her, and she began to serve them. That evening, at sundown, they brought to him all who were sick or possessed with demons. And the whole city was gathered around the door. And he cured many who were sick with various diseases, and cast out many demons; and he would not permit the demons to speak, because they knew him. In the morning, while it was still very dark, he got up and went out to a deserted place, and there he prayed. And Simon and his companions hunted for him. When they found him, they said to him, "Everyone is searching for you." He answered, "Let us go on to the neighboring towns, so that I may proclaim the message there also; for that is what I came out to do." And he went throughout Galilee, proclaiming the message in their synagogues and casting out demons.

- In this time of his life Jesus seems busy with many people—his disciples, their families, and whole cities looking for him. Faith for him, as for us, is always in the midst of life, in the middle of the cares and concerns. It is amidst the difficulties and joys of ordinary life and with all the people who are part of our lives that our faith comes to life.

- All this is part of prayer, as we pray with and for others. Who might come into your prayer now that you can talk to the Lord about?

Monday 6th February   Mark 6:53–56

When Jesus and the disciples had crossed over, they came to land at Gennesaret and moored the boat. When they got out of the boat, people at once recognized him, and rushed about that whole region and began to bring the sick on mats to wherever they heard he was. And wherever he went, into villages or cities or farms, they laid the sick in the marketplaces, and begged him that they might touch even the fringe of his cloak; and all who touched it were healed.

- Mark's references to concrete terms like "mats," "begging," and "touching the fringe of his cloak," remind us of earlier miracles of Jesus. Mark's story is replete with actions and movements: a boat is moored, people run, they bring the sick to any place where Jesus is.
- Enter meditatively into the scene: see the persons, watch what they do, see what the Lord is saying to you.

Tuesday 7th February   Mark 7:1–2, 5–8

Now when the Pharisees and some of the scribes who had come from Jerusalem gathered around him, they noticed that some of his disciples were eating with defiled hands, that is, without washing them. So the Pharisees and the scribes asked him, "Why do your disciples not live according to the tradition of the elders, but eat with defiled hands?" He said to them, "Isaiah prophesied rightly about you hypocrites, as it is written, 'This people honors me with their lips, but their hearts are far from me; in vain do they worship me, teaching human precepts as doctrines.' You abandon the commandment of God and hold to human tradition."

- Washing one's hands before meals would seem like a good idea. However what is at stake for the Pharisees is not merely hygiene but ritual purification. "The traditions of the elders" were those injunctions and practices that the Pharisees added to the Law of Moses. Jesus is criticising his opponents for substituting human traditions for divine commandments.

- We know whether prayer is fruitful or sincere by the way we live our lives.

Wednesday 8th February — Mark 7:14–15, 20–23

Then he called the crowd again and said to them, "Listen to me, all of you, and understand: there is nothing outside a person that by going in can defile, but the things that come out are what defile." Then Jesus said to the disciples, "It is what comes out of a person that defiles. For it is from within, from the human heart, that evil intentions come: fornication, theft, murder, adultery, avarice, wickedness, deceit, licentiousness, envy, slander, pride, folly. All these evil things come from within, and they defile a person."

- These sayings of Jesus would strike his listeners as paradoxical or strange. In Jewish culture, concerned as it was about food laws, just the opposite of what Jesus says would seem to be true: the eating of certain foods such as pork causes ritual defilement.
- What is in the heart is at the core of our relationship with God; this is our moral core from which all else flows.

Thursday 9th February — Mark 7:24–30

From there Jesus set out and went away to the region of Tyre. He entered a house and did not want anyone to know he was there. Yet he could not escape notice, but a woman whose little daughter had an unclean spirit immediately heard about him, and she came and bowed down at his feet. Now the woman was a Gentile, of Syrophoenician origin. She begged him to cast the demon out of her daughter. He said to her, "Let the children be fed first, for it is not fair to take the children's food and throw it to the dogs." But she answered him, "Sir, even the dogs under the table eat the children's crumbs." Then he said to her, "For saying that, you may go—the demon has left your daughter." So she went home, found the child lying on the bed, and the demon gone.

- Jesus' words can seem harsh, but it is important to realize that Jewish writers sometimes described Gentiles, unflatteringly, as "little dogs." However, the Gentile woman is not put off by what Jesus says. She is able to best Jesus in verbal repartee, adapting Jesus' response to suit her desire to have her daughter cured.
- The story of the Gentile woman, an "outsider," warns us against setting limits on those who can be called sons and daughters of God.

Friday 10th February   **Mark 7:31–37**

Then Jesus returned from the region of Tyre, and went by way of Sidon towards the Sea of Galilee, in the region of the Decapolis. They brought to him a deaf man who had an impediment in his speech; and they begged him to lay his hand on him. He took him aside in private, away from the crowd, and put his fingers into his ears, and he spat and touched his tongue. Then looking up to heaven, he sighed and said to him, "Ephphatha," that is, "Be opened." And immediately his ears were opened, his tongue was released, and he spoke plainly. Then Jesus ordered them to tell no one; but the more he ordered them, the more zealously they proclaimed it. They were astounded beyond measure, saying, "He has done everything well; he even makes the deaf to hear and the mute to speak."

- There are several instances in Mark's gospel where Jesus commands people to be silent about his identity. The Messiah expected by the Jews was a political-military figure as well as a religious figure, so

Jesus was probably unwilling to use such a title to avoid provoking the Roman authorities.

- We remember those who live in communities where it is illegal or dangerous to tell the story of Jesus.

Saturday 11th February   Mark 8:1–8

In those days when there was again a great crowd without anything to eat, Jesus called his disciples and said to them, "I have compassion for the crowd, because they have been with me now for three days and have nothing to eat. If I send them away hungry to their homes, they will faint on the way—and some of them have come from a great distance." His disciples replied, "How can one feed these people with bread here in the desert?" He asked them, "How many loaves do you have?" They said, "Seven." Then he ordered the crowd to sit down on the ground; and he took the seven loaves, and after giving thanks he broke them and gave them to his disciples to distribute; and they distributed them to the crowd. They had also a few small fish; and after blessing them, he ordered that these too should be distributed. They ate and were filled; and they took up the broken pieces left over, seven baskets full.

- This scene is reminiscent of the story of the feeding of five thousand in Mark 6, but here Jesus only breaks seven loaves and two fish. Some scholars see in this number "seven" a reference to the mission to the Gentiles undertaken by the seven "deacons" mentioned in the Acts of the Apostles (Acts 6:1–7).
- All Christians are called to be missionaries in the sense of sharing God's unconditional love with others.

february 12–18

Something to think and pray about each day this week:

Taking Nourishment

The four stages of lectio divina are beautifully summarised by a Carthusian Prior, Guigo: "We **read** a text of scripture or serious poetry or religious writing. We **meditate** to enter deeply into the text's meaning. In **prayer** we respond to God in the light of this meaning. In **contemplation** we rest simply in the presence of God, needing no further words. Reading, as it were, puts the food into the mouth. Meditation chews it and breaks it up. Prayer extracts its flavour. Contemplation is the sweetness itself which gladdens and refreshes."

The Presence of God
As I sit here with my book, God is here—
around me, in my sensations, in my thoughts, and deep within me.
I pause for a moment, and become aware
of God's life-giving presence.

Freedom
A thick and shapeless tree-trunk would never believe
that it could become a statue, admired as a miracle of sculpture,
and would never submit itself to the chisel of the sculptor,
who sees by her genius what she can make of it (St. Ignatius).
I ask for the grace to let myself be shaped by my loving Creator.

Consciousness
How am I really feeling? Light-hearted? Heavy-hearted?
I may be very much at peace, happy to be here.
Equally, I may be frustrated, worried, or angry.
I acknowledge how I really am. It is the real me that the Lord loves.

The Word
God speaks to each one of us individually. I need to listen to what
he is saying to me. (Please turn to your scripture on the following
pages. Inspiration points are there should you need them. When
you are ready, return here to continue.)

Conversation
Do I notice myself reacting as I pray with the Word of God?
Do I feel challenged, comforted, angry?
Imagining Jesus sitting or standing by me,
I speak out my feelings, as one trusted friend to another.

Conclusion
Glory be to the Father, and to the Son, and to the Holy Spirit,
As it was in the beginning, is now, and ever shall be,
World without end. Amen.

82

Sunday 12th February,
Sixth Sunday in Ordinary Time
Mark 1:40–45

A leper came to Jesus begging him, and kneeling he said to him, "If you choose, you can make me clean." Moved with pity, Jesus stretched out his hand and touched him, and said to him, "I do choose. Be made clean!" Immediately the leprosy left him, and he was made clean. After sternly warning him he sent him away at once, saying to him, "See that you say nothing to anyone; but go, show yourself to the priest, and offer for your cleansing what Moses commanded, as a testimony to them." But he went out and began to proclaim it freely, and to spread the word, so that Jesus could no longer go into a town openly, but stayed out in the country; and people came to him from every quarter.

- To touch a leper was unthinkable in Jesus' time. A physical danger of contagion had become a religious taboo. Yet again Jesus cuts through religious taboo and harsh judgments on people with his own loving healing.
- What can be more personal than touch? Surely the leper was cleansed from more than physical illness by this touch—he was assured of personal human dignity.

Monday 13th February
Mark 8:11–13

The Pharisees came and began to argue with Jesus, asking him for a sign from heaven, to test him. And he sighed deeply in his spirit and said, "Why does this generation ask for a sign? Truly I tell you, no sign will be given to this generation." And he left them, and getting into the boat again, he went across to the other side.

- The Pharisees approach Jesus demanding some authenticating sign from God, some spectacular public display, to test whether he is the true Messiah. But, with a sigh that comes straight from the heart, Jesus says, "No sign will be given to this generation."

- Today, some people look to strengthen their faith by miraculous signs such as moving statues, revolutions of the sun, or some other spectacular display of God's power. The only sign that Jesus gives is his own life, death, and resurrection.

Tuesday 14th February,
Sts. Cyril and Methodius   Mark 8:14–17

Now the disciples had forgotten to bring any bread; and they had only one loaf with them in the boat. And he cautioned them, saying, "Watch out—beware of the yeast of the Pharisees and the yeast of Herod." They said to one another, "It is because we have no bread." And becoming aware of it, Jesus said to them, "Why are you talking about having no bread? Do you still not perceive or understand?"

- "Yeast" here symbolises the evil influences of both the religious and the political leaders of Israel who were at odds with Jesus. Their teaching and their politics could infest the minds and hearts of the disciples.
- Today's culture, with its rampant consumerism and commercial greed, can easily infest the hearts and minds of Christians.

Wednesday 15th February   Mark 8:22–26

They came to Bethsaida. Some people brought a blind man to Jesus and begged him to touch him. He took the blind man by the hand and led him out of the village; and when he had put saliva on his eyes and laid his hands on him, he asked him, "Can you see anything?" And the man looked up and said, "I can see people, but they look like trees, walking." Then Jesus laid his hands on his eyes again; and he looked intently and his sight was restored, and he saw everything clearly. Then he sent him away to his home, saying, "Do not even go into the village."

- This story, rich in human detail, only occurs in Mark's gospel. It is the only miracle that happens in stages.
- The journey of faith is usually a gradual, even a faltering process. There are many times our vision may be blurred. We can always take Jesus' hand; he will lead us on.

Thursday 16th February   Mark 8:31–33

Then Jesus began to teach them that the Son of Man must undergo great suffering, and be rejected by the elders, the chief priests, and the scribes, and be killed, and after three days rise again. He said all this quite openly. And Peter took him aside and began to rebuke him. But turning and looking at his disciples, he rebuked Peter and said, "Get behind me, Satan! For you are setting your mind not on divine things but on human things."

- Jesus indicates that his death and great suffering will not be final; he will rise again. At times the apostles must have talked about this statement and wondered what he meant.
- Prayer can be a time of mulling over what Jesus meant. As we admit we don't know, and that there is much about him we do not know, we can repeat, as Peter did, that he is the Messiah, the One to come, and that there is nobody else to whom we can go.

Friday 17th February   Mark 8:34–9:1

Jesus called the crowd with his disciples, and said to them, "If any want to become my followers, let them deny themselves and take up their cross and follow me. For those who want to save their life will lose it, and those who lose their life for my sake, and for the sake of the gospel, will save it. For what will it profit them to gain the whole world and forfeit their life? Indeed, what can they give in return for their life? Those who are ashamed of me and of my words in this adulterous and sinful generation, of them the Son of Man will also be ashamed when he comes in the glory of his Father with the holy angels." And he said to them, "Truly I tell you, there are some standing here who will not taste death until they see that the kingdom of God has come with power."

- To be asked to take up a cross would have been really shameful. In Jesus' time, the cross had not yet become the sign of victory and resurrection. Going with Jesus means often going against the tides of opinion, values, behaviour, or thought. The cross was a real symbol of losing life, both physical and spiritual.
- Prayer gives courage and strength to live like Jesus, to listen with a disciple's openness, and to share his life in our world.

Saturday 18th February **Mark 9:2–8**

Six days later, Jesus took with him Peter and James and John, and led them up a high mountain apart, by themselves. And he was transfigured before them, and his clothes became dazzling white, such as no one on earth could bleach them. And there appeared to them Elijah with Moses, who were talking with Jesus. Then Peter said to Jesus, "Rabbi, it is good for us to be here; let us make three dwellings, one for you, one for Moses, and one for Elijah." He did not know what to say, for they were terrified. Then a cloud overshadowed them, and from the cloud there came a voice, "This is my Son, the Beloved; listen to him!" Suddenly when they looked around, they saw no one with them any more, but only Jesus.

- Rest awhile in prayer and just say, "It's good to be here." Prayer is not always like that, but it includes the mystery of just being with

God. It is relaxing into the mystery of being loved, and of being called. It is good to pray, even if it sometimes seems like a waste of time. The apostles may have thought this mountain walk was a waste of time, yet, centuries later, it continues to inspire us.

- You never know where your prayer or goodness will be operative. Offer all that you are to the Lord in prayer; that in itself is good.

february 19–25

Something to think and pray about each day this week:

Taking the Cross
Wednesday is the start of Lent, the season that leads to our commemoration of the Passion and Resurrection of Jesus. He said, "Take up your cross" (Mark 8:34, Luke 9:23). It is not something you go looking for in faraway places. Sooner or later the Lord hands us a cross, and our job is to recognize it. For each of us there are events that make a difference. The sorrowful mysteries are different for each of us. Maybe it is a meeting with a friend, a lover, or an enemy. Maybe it is a sickness, or a triumph. We try to see our life through the eyes of faith, with a confidence that God in his providence can draw good out of the most awful and unwelcome happenings.

The Presence of God

"I stand at the door and knock," says the Lord.
What a wonderful privilege
that the Lord of all creation desires to come to me.
I welcome His presence.

Freedom

Lord, grant me the grace to be free from the excesses of this life.
Let me not get caught up with the desire for wealth.
Keep my heart and mind free to love and serve You.

Consciousness

"There is a time and place for everything," as the saying goes.
Lord, grant that I may always desire
to spend time in your presence, to hear your call.

The Word

God speaks to each one of us individually. I need to listen to what
he is saying to me. (Please turn to your scripture on the following
pages. Inspiration points are there should you need them. When
you are ready, return here to continue.)

Conversation

The gift of speech is a wonderful gift.
May I use this gift with kindness.
May I be slow to utter harsh words,
hurtful words, and words spoken in anger.

Conclusion

Glory be to the Father, and to the Son, and to the Holy Spirit,
As it was in the beginning, is now, and ever shall be,
World without end. Amen.

Sunday 19th February,
Seventh Sunday in Ordinary Time   Mark 2:1–5

When he returned to Capernaum after some days, it was reported that he was at home. So many gathered around that there was no longer room for them, not even in front of the door; and he was speaking the word to them. Then some people came, bringing to him a paralyzed man, carried by four of them. And when they could not bring him to Jesus because of the crowd, they removed the roof above him; and after having dug through it, they let down the mat on which the paralytic lay. When Jesus saw their faith, he said to the paralytic, "Son, your sins are forgiven."

- Faith opens a door to a living relationship with God in Jesus. Faith was the door opening to the forgiveness of sins and then to the cure of the sick man. The faith of all helped the sick man—he was healed by "their" faith.
- Our faithful time of prayer may help people we know or do not know. All Christian prayer reaches out to many.

Monday 20th February   Mark 9:17–24

Someone from the crowd answered Jesus, "Teacher, I brought you my son; he has a spirit that makes him unable to speak; and whenever it seizes him, it dashes him down; and he foams and grinds his teeth and becomes rigid; and I asked your disciples to cast it out, but they could not do so." Jesus said: "Bring him to me." And they brought the boy to him. When the spirit saw him, immediately it convulsed the boy, and he fell on the ground and rolled about, foaming at the mouth. Jesus asked the father, "How long has this been happening to him?" And he said, "From childhood. It has often cast him into the fire and into the water, to destroy him; but if you are able to do anything, have pity on us and help us." Jesus said to him, "If you are able! All things can be done for the one who believes." Immediately the father of the child cried out, "I believe; help my unbelief!"

- The last words of the this story have been a common prayer for so many people. We pray from a combination of faith and doubt. On some days faith is dry and prayer seems useless.
- We can ask for help; we come as we are and we will be heard. John Henry Cardinal Newman prayed, "The night is dark and I am far from home, lead thou me on."

Tuesday 21st February   Mark 9:30–32

They went on from there and passed through Galilee. He did not want anyone to know it; for he was teaching his disciples, saying to them, "The Son of Man is to be betrayed into human hands, and they will kill him, and three days after being killed, he will rise again." But they did not understand what he was saying and were afraid to ask him.

- In welcoming Jesus Christ into our lives, we welcome the Father and the Spirit. We welcome the Divine. With him, we are part of a total world, of heaven and earth, reaching out to all people.
- Prayer is part of that mystery. Prayer touches into the links of heaven and earth. It links us also to all of humanity. When we pray we join the whole human race in their prayer to God, and we join Jesus in his prayer for us.

Wednesday 22nd February, Ash Wednesday   Matthew 6:1–6

Jesus said to his disciples, "Beware of practicing your piety before others in order to be seen by them; for then you have no reward from your Father in heaven. So whenever you give alms, do not sound a trumpet before you, as the hypocrites do in the synagogues and in the streets, so that they may be praised by others. Truly I tell you, they have received their reward. But when you give alms, do not let your left hand know what your right hand is doing, so that your alms may be done in secret; and your Father who sees in secret will reward you. And whenever you pray, do not be like the hypocrites; for they love to stand and pray in the synagogues and at the street corners, so that they may be seen by others. Truly I tell you, they have received their reward. But whenever you pray, go into your room and shut the door and pray to your Father who is in secret; and your Father who sees in secret will reward you."

- Given the very different climate that exists in today's world, Jesus might well say the opposite, "Pray in public. Let your light shine before others so that, seeing you pray, they might be drawn to God!"

Thursday 23rd February   Luke 9:22–25

Jesus said to his disciples: "The Son of Man must undergo great suffering, and be rejected by the elders, chief priests, and scribes, and be killed, and on the third day be raised." Then he said to them all, "If any want to become my followers, let them deny themselves and take up their cross daily and follow me. For those who want to save their life will lose it, and those who lose their life for my sake will save it. What does it profit them if they gain the whole world, but lose or forfeit themselves?"

- Taking up one's cross is not a matter of simply putting up with the headaches and ordinary troubles of life, but of not being ashamed of Jesus, and being prepared to be true followers with all the dangers, even possible martyrdom, that that implies.
- Trying to save one's own skin by denying Jesus will only result in the loss of eternal life, of intimate union with God.

Friday 24th February   **Matthew 9:14–15**

Then the disciples of John came to him, saying, "Why do we and the Pharisees fast often, but your disciples do not fast?" And Jesus said to them, "The wedding guests cannot mourn as long as the bridegroom is with them, can they? The days will come when the bridegroom is taken away from them, and then they will fast."

- Matthew understands fasting to be a sign of mourning. Jesus compares his disciples to wedding guests who rejoice while he, the bridegroom, is still with them.
- But after he leaves them they will experience many tribulations, and therefore they will have good reasons for fasting.

Saturday 25th February   **Luke 5:27–32**

After this he went out and saw a tax collector named Levi, sitting at the tax booth; and he said to him, "Follow me." And he got up, left everything, and followed him. Then Levi gave a great banquet for him in his house; and there was a large crowd of tax collectors and others sitting at the table with them. The Pharisees and their scribes were complaining to his disciples, saying, "Why do you eat and drink with tax collectors and sinners?" Jesus answered, "Those who are well have no need of a physician, but those who are sick; I have come to call not the righteous but sinners to repentance."

- Jesus refers in an ironic tone to the scribes and Pharisees as "righteous"; by contrast, Jesus is the "doctor" who brings true righteousness (union with God) through his teaching and healings.
- Self-righteousness is not confined to people who lived at the time of Christ!

february 26–march 3

Something to think and pray about each day this week:

Strength of the Desert

Jesus went into the desert an unknown young carpenter from Nazareth, with thirty years of hidden life behind him. After the desert he returned to Galilee "with power of the Spirit in him," and started to preach. Quickly he became a public figure, but he loved to withdraw to desert or mountain to recharge his energies by prayer. He moved forward like any of us, with no sure knowledge of what was to happen to him. His life was shaped by the Spirit driving him forward, but shaped also by the accidents of his life, the enthusiasm of some of his listeners, and the resistance of others. He had a sense of where God was calling him—"I am sent to cast fire on the earth"—and of the joy he felt in this vocation—"My meat is to do the will of him who sent me." After the quiet life of Nazareth, Jesus' public life was tumultuous. If we are to do justice to his humanity, we must accept that he did not know what would happen next, only that this was where God wanted him to be.

The Presence of God
Jesus waits silent and unseen to come into my heart.
I will respond to His call.
He comes with His infinite power and love.
May I be filled with joy in His presence.

Freedom
I ask for the grace
to let go of my own concerns
and be open to what God is asking of me,
to let myself be guided and formed by my loving Creator.

Consciousness
Knowing that God loves me unconditionally,
I can afford to be honest about how I am.
How has the last day been, and how do I feel now?
I share my feelings openly with the Lord.

The Word
I read the Word of God slowly, a few times over, and I listen
to what God is saying to me. (Please turn to your scripture on
the following pages. Inspiration points are there should you need
them. When you are ready, return here to continue.)

Conversation
Remembering that I am still in God's presence,
I imagine Jesus himself standing or sitting beside me,
and say whatever is on my mind, whatever is in my heart,
speaking as one friend to another.

Conclusion
Glory be to the Father, and to the Son, and to the Holy Spirit,
As it was in the beginning, is now, and ever shall be,
World without end. Amen.

Sunday 26th February,
First Sunday of Lent   Mark 1:12–15

And the Spirit immediately drove him out into the wilderness. He was in the wilderness forty days, tempted by Satan; and he was with the wild beasts; and the angels waited on him. Now after John was arrested, Jesus came to Galilee, proclaiming the good news of God, and saying, "The time is fulfilled, and the kingdom of God has come near; repent, and believe in the good news."

- The wilderness is the place of destruction and danger, of being tempted off one's path, and also of meeting God. Jesus finds God's path for him in the wilderness.
- Prayer is a wilderness time. It can be dangerous for it brings us in touch with the evil as well as with the good in ourselves. With practice, it introduces us to the peace of God in Christ—the harmony of the desert of Jesus. It is also the place of rededication to God and of finding the strength of God.

Monday 27th February   Matthew 25:34–40

Jesus said to his disciples, "When the Son of Man comes in his glory, and all the angels with him, then he will sit on the throne of his glory. All the nations will be gathered before him, and he will separate people one from another as a shepherd separates the sheep from the goats, and he will put the sheep at his right hand and the goats at the left. Then the king will say to those at his right hand, 'Come, you that are blessed by my Father, inherit the kingdom prepared for you from the foundation of the world; for I was hungry and you gave me food, I was thirsty and you gave me something to drink, I was a stranger and you welcomed me, I was naked and you gave me clothing, I was sick and you took care of me, I was in prison and you visited me.'

Then the righteous will answer him, 'Lord, when was it that we saw you hungry and gave you food, or thirsty and gave you something to drink? And when was it that we saw you a stranger and welcomed you, or naked and gave you clothing? And when was it that we saw you sick or in prison and visited you?' And the king will answer them, 'Truly I tell you, just as you did it to one of the least of these who are members of my family, you did it to me.'"

- I can reflect on my life and see that whatever I did not do—and could have done—for others has also been neglect of Jesus. What I did for others is help for Jesus.
- Prayer gives an awareness of Jesus' presence and need in ordinary circumstances. Allow yesterday or last week to come into prayer, simply by asking where today or yesterday or last week did I answer or ignore a legitimate call of Jesus for help.
- See the scene in prayer, and try to sense or picture that Jesus is there saying, "This is me, here and now."

Tuesday 28th February　　　　　　**Matthew 6:7–15**

Jesus said, "When you are praying, do not heap up empty phrases as the Gentiles do; for they think that they will be heard because of their many words. Do not be like them, for your Father knows what you need before you ask him. Pray then in this way: 'Our Father in heaven, hallowed be your name. Your kingdom come. Your will be done, on earth as it is in heaven. Give us this day our daily bread. And forgive us our debts, as we also have forgiven our debtors. And do not bring us to the time of trial, but rescue us from the evil one.' For if you forgive others their trespasses, your heavenly Father will also forgive you; but if you do not forgive others, neither will your Father forgive your trespasses."

98

- Jesus gives a model for prayer in the Our Father. I pray for those who taught it to me, for all who helped me to understand it.
- I take the prayer in the words that are familiar to me and pray that God's way of being and seeing be evident in me.

Wednesday 29th February — Luke 11:29–30

When the crowds were increasing, he began to say, "This generation is an evil generation; it asks for a sign, but no sign will be given to it except the sign of Jonah. For just as Jonah became a sign to the people of Nineveh, so the Son of Man will be to this generation."

- Jesus sees that the people looked for great signs of God's presence and action and missed noticing that God's Spirit was among them. I acknowledge that too often I am easily distracted and take note of where I might attend to God's presence.
- Where have I found true consolation and encouragement? Do I value the nourishment that may be available to me?

Thursday 1st March — Matthew 7:9–12

Jesus said to the disciples, "Is there anyone among you who, if your child asks for bread, will give a stone? Or if the child asks for a fish, will give a snake? If you then, who are evil, know how to give good gifts to your children, how much more will your Father in heaven give good things to those who ask him! In everything do to others as you would have them do to you; for this is the law and the prophets."

- Aware of being in God's presence, I consider how my prayers have been answered in the past. As I note that not everything worked out as I initially wanted, I also realize that I have been blessed in many different ways.

- What do those around me need from me? Might I be blessing to them as I answer their prayers and consider their needs?

Friday 2nd March   Matthew 5:20–24

Jesus said to his disciples, "For I tell you, unless your righteousness exceeds that of the scribes and Pharisees, you will never enter the kingdom of heaven. You have heard that it was said to those of ancient times, 'You shall not murder'; and 'whoever murders shall be liable to judgment.' But I say to you that if you are angry with a brother or sister, you will be liable to judgment; and if you insult a brother or sister, you will be liable to the council; and if you say, 'You fool,' you will be liable to the hell of fire. So when you are offering your gift at the altar, if you remember that your brother or sister has something against you, leave your gift there before the altar and go; first be reconciled to your brother or sister, and then come and offer your gift."

- Jesus calls us not to be neutral, but to use our energies for the healing of relationships.
- Are there hurts that hold me back, that cause resentment? If so, I ask for healing and pray for those who have caused me pain. If not, I give thanks to God that I do not carry burdens of this kind.

Saturday 3rd March   Matthew 5:43–48

Jesus said to the disciples, "You have heard that it was said, 'You shall love your neighbor and hate your enemy.' But I say to you, love your enemies and pray for those who persecute you, so that you may be children of your Father in heaven; for he makes his sun rise on the evil and on the good, and sends rain on the righteous and on the unrighteous. For if you love those who love you, what reward do you have? Do not even the tax collectors do the same? And if you greet only your brothers and sisters, what more are you doing than others? Do not even the Gentiles do the same? Be perfect, therefore, as your heavenly Father is perfect."

- As I pray for those who bring blessings to me, I pray that I may include others in a widening circle of compassion.
- If being like God seems too ambitious, I recall that Jesus wants nothing less for me. He calls me to the fullness of life.

march 4–10

Something to think and pray about each day this week:

Discerning the Call

Lord, I believe you are calling me in all the circumstances of my life, but there are times when your hand is difficult to recognize. The calling can sometimes come in a disagreeable shape, a sickness, bereavement, betrayal, loss of a job, a bout of insecurity. It does not look like a vocation but rather an unfortunate accident, or a failure on my part. But success is what I do with my failures. Each step on the way is part of God's calling. How do I handle deep distress?

The Presence of God

For a few moments, I think of God's veiled presence in things:
in the elements, giving them existence;
in plants, giving them life; in animals, giving them sensation;
and finally, in me, giving me all this and more,
making me a temple, a dwelling-place of the Spirit.

Freedom

God is not foreign to my freedom.
Instead the Spirit breathes life into my most intimate desires,
gently nudging me towards all that is good.
I ask for the grace to let myself be enfolded by the Spirit.

Consciousness

Knowing that God loves me unconditionally,
I can afford to be honest about how I am.
How has the last day been, and how do I feel now?
I share my feelings openly with the Lord.

The Word

The Word of God comes down to us through the scriptures.
May the Holy Spirit enlighten my mind and my heart to respond
to the gospel teachings. (Please turn to your scripture on the following pages. Inspiration points are there should you need them.
When you are ready, return here to continue.)

Conversation

How has God's Word moved me? Has it left me cold?
Has it consoled me or moved me to act in a new way?
I imagine Jesus standing or sitting beside me;
I turn and share my feelings with him.

Conclusion

Glory be to the Father, and to the Son, and to the Holy Spirit,
As it was in the beginning, is now, and ever shall be,
World without end. Amen.

march 2012

Sunday 4th March,
Second Sunday of Lent   Mark 9:2–10

Six days later, Jesus took with him Peter and James and John, and led them up a high mountain apart, by themselves. And he was transfigured before them, and his clothes became dazzling white, such as no one on earth could bleach them. And there appeared to them Elijah with Moses, who were talking with Jesus. Then Peter said to Jesus, "Rabbi, it is good for us to be here; let us make three dwellings, one for you, one for Moses, and one for Elijah." He did not know what to say, for they were terrified. Then a cloud overshadowed them, and from the cloud there came a voice, "This is my Son, the Beloved; listen to him!" Suddenly when they looked around, they saw no one with them any more, but only Jesus. As they were coming down the mountain, he ordered them to tell no one about what they had seen, until after the Son of Man had risen from the dead. So they kept the matter to themselves, questioning what this rising from the dead could mean.

- The apostles saw into the real Jesus—hours on the mountains which they would never forget. When later they would see the disfigured face and the dying body on the cross, Peter and James and John would remember this day, and would remember it for the rest of their lives. They saw Jesus as the Son of God, and saw a glimpse in him of our humanity at its best.
- The glory of Jesus is the glory of love—his love unto death, and the love in him of Father and Spirit.

Monday 5th March   Luke 6:36–38

Be merciful, just as your Father is merciful. Do not judge, and you will not be judged; do not condemn, and you will not be condemned. Forgive, and you will be forgiven; give, and it will be given to you. A good measure, pressed down, shaken together, running over, will be put into your lap; for the measure you give will be the measure you get back."

- I ask God to continue to soften my heart to make me more compassionate, more merciful. I recognize that I am already able to show some forgiveness and ask God's help with this.
- "Forgive us our sins as we forgive those. . . ." As I ask God for forgiveness, I make room in my heart not just by letting go of hurts but by wishing well to any who may have brought me pain.

Tuesday 6th March   **Matthew 23:9–12**

Then Jesus said to the crowds and to his disciples, "Call no one your father on earth, for you have one Father—the one in heaven. Nor are you to be called instructors, for you have one instructor, the Messiah. The greatest among you will be your servant. All who exalt themselves will be humbled, and all who humble themselves will be exalted."

- It is easy to be distracted by fame, celebrity, or royalty. I think of how my real dignity—my true identity—lies in my being a child of God. I consider how I might live in a way that brings others to the fullness of their dignity.
- Jesus took on the role of servant and continues to serve me. I ask for the grace I need to serve humbly.

Wednesday 7th March   **Matthew 20:20–28**

Then the mother of the sons of Zebedee came to him with her sons, and kneeling before him, she asked a favor of him. And he said to her, "What do you want?" She said to him, "Declare that these two sons of mine will sit, one at your right hand and one at your left, in your kingdom." But Jesus answered, "You do not know what you are asking. Are you able to drink the cup that

I am about to drink?" They said to him, "We are able." He said to them, "You will indeed drink my cup, but to sit at my right hand and at my left, this is not mine to grant, but it is for those for whom it has been prepared by my Father." When the ten heard it, they were angry with the two brothers. But Jesus called them to him and said, "You know that the rulers of the Gentiles lord it over them, and their great ones are tyrants over them. It will not be so among you; but whoever wishes to be great among you must be your servant, and whoever wishes to be first among you must be your slave; just as the Son of Man came not to be served but to serve, and to give his life a ransom for many."

- Even though the disciples lives closely with Jesus, it took some a long time to grow into an understanding of his vision. I realize that Jesus recognizes that I too can be slow to understand, and allow myself to experience his compassionate, loving gaze.
- As I realize how the other apostles were angry with James and John, I ask Jesus to help me to be patient and forgiving of those disciples who do not see things as I do.

Thursday 8th March   Luke 16:19–31

Jesus said to the Pharisees, "There was a rich man who was dressed in purple and fine linen and who feasted sumptuously every day. And at his gate lay a poor man named Lazarus, covered with sores, who longed to satisfy his hunger with what fell from the rich man's table; even the dogs would come and lick his sores. The poor man died and was carried away by the angels to be with Abraham. The rich man also died and was buried. In Hades, where he was being tormented, he looked up and saw Abraham far away with Lazarus by his side. He called out, 'Father Abraham, have mercy on me, and send Lazarus to dip the tip of his finger in water and cool my tongue; for I am in agony in these flames.' But Abraham said, 'Child, remember that during your lifetime you received your good things, and Lazarus in like manner evil things; but now he is comforted here, and you are in agony. Besides all this, between you and us a great chasm has been fixed, so that those who might want to pass from here to you cannot do so, and no one can cross from there to us.' He said, 'Then, father, I beg you to send him to my father's house—for I have five brothers—that he may warn them, so that they will not also come into this place of torment.' Abraham replied, 'They have Moses and the prophets; they should listen to them.' He said, 'No, father Abraham; but if someone goes to them from the dead, they will repent.' He said to him, 'If they do not listen to Moses and the prophets, neither will they be convinced even if someone rises from the dead.'"

- During Lent, I try to hear the call to come back home to God. I join the great pilgrimage of people who, throughout the ages, have been called by Moses and the prophets to listen to the Word of the Lord.
- I ask for a greater sensitivity to those who live with nothing, and I think of how I might show some compassion to those whose need is greater than mine.

Friday 9th March   Matthew 21:33–41

Jesus said, "Listen to another parable. There was a landowner who planted a vineyard, put a fence around it, dug a wine press in it, and built a watch-tower. Then he leased it to tenants and went to another country. When the harvest time had come, he sent his slaves to the tenants to collect his produce. But the tenants seized his slaves and beat one, killed another, and stoned another. Again he sent other slaves, more than the first; and they treated them in the same way. Finally he sent his son to them, saying, 'They will respect my son.' But when the tenants saw the son, they said to themselves, 'This is the heir; come, let us kill him and get his inheritance.' So they seized him, threw him out of the vineyard, and killed him. Now when the owner of the vineyard comes, what will he do to those tenants?" They said to him, "He will put those wretches to a miserable death, and lease the vineyard to other tenants who will give him the produce at the harvest time."

- Just as the landlord planted, protected, nourished, and guarded his property, so has God attended to my needs.
- I think of how I am made to give glory to God. I give thanks as I realize that the goodness of God can be seen in my life. I ask forgiveness as I acknowledge that I, like the tenants in the parable, sometimes prefer to run things in my own way.

Saturday 10th March   Luke 15:21–24

Then the son said to him, "Father, I have sinned against heaven and before you; I am no longer worthy to be called your son." But the father said to his slaves, "Quickly, bring out a robe—the best one—and put it on him; put a ring on his finger and sandals on his feet. And get the fatted calf and kill it, and let us eat and celebrate; for this son of mine was dead and is alive again; he was lost and is found!" And they began to celebrate.

- Jesus was criticised for associating with sinners and the unworthy. I remind myself that I do not earn Jesus' grace by my prayer or by my action. Jesus wants to be with me to bring me fullness of life.
- Even though I may not feel worthy, I listen for the voice of God recognizing me, welcoming me, loving me, lavishing me with the best of gifts: the ring reminds me of my dignity and the sandals tell me that I am free.

march 11–17

Something to think and pray about each day this week:

The Mystery of Conversion
There is a legend of how St. Patrick, when preaching to some soon-to-be converted heathens, was shown a sacred standing stone marked with a circle that was symbolic of the moon goddess. Patrick made the mark of a Latin cross through the circle and blessed the stone, making the first Celtic cross. This legend implies that the saint was willing to make ideas and practices that were formerly Druid into Christian ideas and practices. The circle of the Celtic cross is a symbol of eternity that emphasizes the endlessness of God's love as shown through Christ's sacrifice on the cross—or the circle may be seen as a halo. The crucifixion is important, and not just as an event at a certain point in time. The circle symbolises the unending mystery of how, through the crucifixion and resurrection, Christ continues to offer the hope of salvation to the faithful throughout all time.

The Presence of God
Dear Jesus, today I call on You in a special way.
Mostly I come asking for favors.
Today I'd like just to be in Your presence.
Let my heart respond to Your love.

Freedom
"I am free."
When I look at these words in writing
they seem to create in me a feeling of awe—
yes, a wonderful feeling of freedom.
Thank You, God.

Consciousness
Lord, You gave me the night to rest in sleep.
In my waking hours may I not forget your goodness to me.
Guide me to share your blessings with others.

The Word
I read the Word of God slowly, a few times over, and I listen to what God is saying to me. (Please turn to your scripture on the following pages. Inspiration points are there should you need them. When you are ready, return here to continue.)

Conversation
Dear Jesus, I can open up my heart to You.
I can tell You everything that troubles me.
I know You care about all the concerns in my life.
Teach me to live in the knowledge
that You who care for me today
will care for me tomorrow and all the days of my life.

Conclusion
Glory be to the Father, and to the Son, and to the Holy Spirit,
As it was in the beginning, is now, and ever shall be,
World without end. Amen.

112

Sunday 11th March, Third Sunday of Lent — John 2:13–17

The Passover of the Jews was near, and Jesus went up to Jerusalem. In the temple he found people selling cattle, sheep, and doves, and the money changers seated at their tables. Making a whip of cords, he drove all of them out of the temple, both the sheep and the cattle. He also poured out the coins of the money changers and overturned their tables. He told those who were selling the doves, "Take these things out of here! Stop making my Father's house a marketplace!" His disciples remembered that it was written, "Zeal for your house will consume me."

- Lent gives us new insights into how Jesus lived his life, always within the shadow of his death. The glory of God here is Jesus fully alive to the exploitation of the poor, the mistreatment of the house of God, and fully alive to the faith that was beginning to grow in his disciples.
- Our prayer today might remember all who suffer and are endangered in their commitment to justice and right religion.

Monday 12th March — Luke 4:24–30

And he said, "Truly I tell you, no prophet is accepted in the prophet's hometown. But the truth is, there were many widows in Israel in the time of Elijah, when the heaven was shut up three years and six months, and there was a severe famine over all the land; yet Elijah was sent to none of them except to a widow at Zarephath in Sidon. There were also many lepers in Israel in the time of the prophet Elisha, and none of them was cleansed except Naaman the Syrian." When they heard this, all in the synagogue were filled with rage. They got up, drove him out of the town, and led him to the brow of the hill on which their town was built, so that they might hurl him off the cliff. But he passed through the midst of them and went on his way.

- The people of Jesus' hometown had come to their conclusions; they left no room for Jesus to work in a new way.
- I bring my fixed ideas before God, that I may let go of them, praying that they not blind me to the movement of God's Spirit.

Tuesday 13th March **Matthew 18:21–22**

Then Peter came and said to him, "Lord, if another member of the church sins against me, how often should I forgive? As many as seven times?" Jesus said to him, "Not seven times, but, I tell you, seventy-seven times."

- As Jesus continues to emphasize forgiveness, I humbly bring myself before God who forgives me everything, who loves me beyond any sin. The forgiveness that God gives is often difficult for me to receive.
- I pray for those who have caused me hurt and, even if I can't wish them well now, I pray that one day I might.

Wednesday 14th March **Matthew 5:17–19**

Jesus said to his disciples, "Do not think that I have come to abolish the law or the prophets; I have come not to abolish but to fulfill. For truly I tell you, until heaven and earth pass away, not one letter, not one stroke of a letter, will pass from the law until all is accomplished. Therefore, whoever breaks one of the least of these commandments, and teaches others to do the same, will be called least in the kingdom of heaven; but whoever does them and teaches them will be called great in the kingdom of heaven."

- I consider my way of living and my influence on others. I pray in thanksgiving for those places in my life in which I can imagine that I have a good influence.
- I ask for God's help in the areas that my example and inspiration might be better.

Thursday 15th March   Luke 11:14–20

Jesus was casting out a demon that was mute; when the demon had gone out, the one who had been mute spoke, and the crowds were amazed. But some of them said, "He casts out demons by Beelzebul, the ruler of the demons." Others, to test him, kept demanding from him a sign from heaven. But he knew what they were thinking and said to them, "Every kingdom divided against itself becomes a desert, and house falls on house. If Satan also is divided against himself, how will his kingdom stand?—for you say that I cast out the demons by Beelzebul. Now if I cast out the demons by Beelzebul, by whom do your exorcists cast them out? Therefore they will be your judges. But if it is by the finger of God that I cast out the demons, then the kingdom of God has come to you.

- The people who criticise Jesus focused on the demons, not on the One who sought to banish them. Sometimes I become preoccupied by negative details, by failures and disappointments. I ask Jesus to help me during this Lent to realize that he calls me away from any ill that holds me back.
- As I realize how I need to reform my life during Lent, I remember not to depend on my own efforts but to learn to rely on Jesus who gathers me together.

Friday 16th March   Mark 12:28–34

One of the scribes came near and heard them disputing with one another, and seeing that he answered them well, he asked him, "Which commandment is the first of all?" Jesus answered, "The first is, 'Hear, O Israel: the Lord our God, the Lord is one; you shall love the Lord your God with all your heart, and with all your soul, and with all your mind, and with all your strength.' The second is this, 'You shall love your neighbor as yourself.' There is no other commandment greater than these." Then the scribe said to him, "You are right, Teacher; you have truly said that 'he is one, and besides him there is no other'; and 'to love him with all the heart, and with all the understanding, and with all the strength,' and 'to love one's neighbor as oneself,' —this is much more important than all whole burnt offerings and sacrifices." When Jesus saw that he answered wisely, he said to him, "You are not far from the kingdom of God." After that no one dared to ask him any question.

• Jesus recites the "Shema Israel," the prayer that he knew from his earliest years. As I am at prayer, I give God thanks for my own history of prayer, recalling those who taught me and giving thanks for all who have helped me to hear the voice of the Lord.

• I consider how my love for myself and my love for my neighbour might be brought into a better balance this Lent.

Saturday 17th March,
St. Patrick   Luke 10:1–6

After this the Lord appointed seventy others and sent them on ahead of him in pairs to every town and place where he himself intended to go. He said to them, "The harvest is plentiful, but the laborers are few; therefore ask the Lord of the harvest to send out laborers into his harvest. Go on your way. See, I am sending you out like lambs into the midst of wolves. Carry no purse, no bag, no sandals; and greet no one on the road. Whatever house you enter, first say, 'Peace to this house!' And if anyone

116

is there who shares in peace, your peace will rest on that person; but if not, it will return to you."

- Jesus sent the disciples out to be joyful presences in a troubled world. I am sent in the same way.
- The disciples were sent in a spirit of trust; they were to learn to rely on Jesus and not be distracted. I pray that I may be able to keep my focus and to trust in the presence of God's Spirit as I am sent out on the mission of peace.

march 18–24

Something to think and pray about each day this week:

Learning in Life

This week the Church remembers St. Joseph, husband of Mary and foster-father of Jesus. Jean-Paul Sartre, in his Christmas play *Barjona,* tries to picture Joseph in the stable at Bethlehem. "I would not paint Joseph. I would show no more than a shadow at the back of the stable, and two shining eyes. For I do not know what to say about Joseph, and Joseph does not know what to say about himself. He adores, and is happy to adore, and he feels himself slightly out of it. I believe he suffers without admitting it. He suffers because he sees how much this woman whom he loves resembles God; how she is already at the side of God. For God has burst like a bomb into the intimacy of this family. Joseph and Mary are separated forever by this explosion of light. And I imagine that all through his life Joseph will be learning to accept this."

The Presence of God
I pause for a moment
and think of the love and the grace that God showers on me,
creating me in His image and likeness, making me His temple.

Freedom
Everything has the potential to draw forth from me a fuller love
and life.
Yet my desires are often fixed, caught, on illusions of fulfillment.
I ask that God, through my freedom, may orchestrate
my desires in a vibrant, loving melody rich in harmony.

Consciousness
In the presence of my loving Creator,
I look honestly at my feelings over the last day,
the highs, the lows, and the level ground.
Can I see where the Lord has been present?

The Word
God speaks to each one of us individually. I need to listen to what
he is saying to me. (Please turn to your scripture on the following
pages. Inspiration points are there should you need them. When
you are ready, return here to continue.)

Conversation
What feelings are rising in me
as I pray and reflect on God's Word?
I imagine Jesus himself sitting or standing beside me,
and open my heart to him.

Conclusion
Glory be to the Father, and to the Son, and to the Holy Spirit,
As it was in the beginning, is now, and ever shall be,
World without end. Amen.

Sunday 18th March,
Fourth Sunday of Lent   **John 3:14–21**

Jesus said to Nicodemus, "And just as Moses lifted up the serpent in the wilderness, so must the Son of Man be lifted up, that whoever believes in him may have eternal life. For God so loved the world that he gave his only Son, so that everyone who believes in him may not perish but may have eternal life. Indeed, God did not send the Son into the world to condemn the world, but in order that the world might be saved through him. Those who believe in him are not condemned; but those who do not believe are condemned already, because they have not believed in the name of the only Son of God. And this is the judgment, that the light has come into the world, and people loved darkness rather than light because their deeds were evil. For all who do evil hate the light and do not come to the light, so that their deeds may not be exposed. But those who do what is true come to the light, so that it may be clearly seen that their deeds have been done in God."

- The divine spark or presence is in each of us, often called the light of God. Prayer is the time when we "switch on" this light and allow ourselves to become aware of the light of God filling us with love, forgiveness, and healing.
- The light of God in each of us spreads to others, and it is through God's people that God's light shines in the world.

Monday 19th March,
St. Joseph   **Matthew 1:18–25**

Now the birth of Jesus the Messiah took place in this way. When his mother Mary had been engaged to Joseph, but before they lived together, she was found to be with child from the Holy Spirit. Her husband Joseph, being a righteous man and unwilling to expose her to public disgrace, planned to dismiss her quietly. But just when he had resolved to do this, an angel of the Lord appeared to him in a dream and said, "Joseph, son of David, do not be afraid to take Mary as your wife, for the child conceived in her is from the Holy Spirit. She will bear a son, and you are to name him Jesus, for he will save his people from their sins." All this took place to fulfill what had been spoken by the Lord through the prophet: "Look, the virgin shall conceive and bear a son, and they shall name him Emmanuel," which means, "God is with us." When Joseph awoke from sleep, he did as the angel of the Lord commanded him; he took her as his wife, but had no marital relations with her until she had borne a son; and he named him Jesus.

- We see Joseph as a sensitive person, careful not to bring dishonour on Mary and attending to the message of his dreams. There may be situations I need to avoid and conditions I need to create to become more sensitive to the quiet movements of God's Spirit.
- Joseph did not have much to go on but trusted his intuition, discerning in it the hand of God. I consider where in my life I have been blessed by trusting in God.

Tuesday 20th March   **John 5:2–9**

Now in Jerusalem by the Sheep Gate there is a pool, called in Hebrew Beth-zatha, which has five porticoes. In these lay many invalids—blind, lame, and paralyzed. One man was there who had been ill for thirty-eight years. When Jesus saw him lying there and knew that he had been there a long time, he said to him, "Do you want to be made well?" The sick man answered him, "Sir, I have no one to put me into the pool when the water is stirred up; and while I am making my way, someone else steps down ahead of me." Jesus said to him, "Stand up, take your mat

122

and walk." At once the man was made well, and he took up his mat and began to walk.

- The sick man did not answer Jesus' question, but told the familiar story of his troubles.
- As Jesus now speaks to me, I do my best to answer what he asks, being careful not to rehearse any disempowering message.

Wednesday 21st March   John 5:24–25

Jesus said to the Jews, "Very truly, I tell you, anyone who hears my word and believes him who sent me has eternal life, and does not come under judgment, but has passed from death to life. Very truly, I tell you, the hour is coming, and is now here, when the dead will hear the voice of the Son of God, and those who hear will live."

- Here Jesus is letting me in on the secret. As well as being the man who heals and teaches, he is much more.
- Am I open to the knowledge that Jesus is the way to eternal life? If I have difficulty understanding it, I can ask for insight.

Thursday 22nd March   John 5:31–36

Jesus said to the Jews, "If I testify about myself, my testimony is not true. There is another who testifies on my behalf, and I know that his testimony to me is true. You sent messengers to John, and he testified to the truth. Not that I accept such human testimony, but I say these things so that you may be saved. He was a burning and shining lamp, and you were willing to rejoice for a while in his light. But I have a testimony greater than John's."

- Jesus appeals to the minds of those who seek to disregard him. He reminds them of what they have seen, of the witnesses they have heard, and of the words of the prophets.

- I pray that I be blessed with deeper faith as I "review the evidence" to which Jesus draws my attention.
- As I believe in Jesus who was sent by God, the Word of God is alive in me. I can give witness to this Word in my deeds and speech.

Friday 23rd March   **John 7:25–27**

Now some of the people of Jerusalem were saying, "Is not this the man whom they are trying to kill? And here he is, speaking openly, but they say nothing to him! Can it be that the authorities really know that this is the Messiah? Yet we know where this man is from; but when the Messiah comes, no one will know where he is from."

- They want an excuse not to believe. They want to be able to say, "This is not the Christ." So they focus on where he came from and say that the Christ will come from where nobody knows.
- "They" are "we"! It is human to find excuses not to believe, not to accept, not to follow God in Jesus. We bring these blocks within ourselves to prayer, and ask that hardness of heart may be softened by faith. Teach us that we do not have to have an answer to everything.

Saturday 24th March   **John 7:40–44**

When they heard these words, some in the crowd said, "This is really the prophet." Others said, "This is the Messiah." But some asked, "Surely the Messiah does not come from Galilee, does he? Has not the scripture said that the Messiah is descended from David and comes from Bethlehem, the village where David lived?" So there was a division in the crowd because of him. Some of them wanted to arrest him, but no one laid hands on him.

- Some people who heard Jesus could not believe that God might work powerfully in such ordinary and familiar circumstances. I pray that I may look again at my own situation, realizing that God is already at work even as I pray for an increase in God's grace.

march 25–31

Something to think and pray about each day this week:

At the Tipping Point

We have just passed the equinox: night is as long as day, and we are halfway to summer or winter, depending on where we live. Where am I in my life? Past the equinox? In Andrew Marvell's words:

> But at my back I always hear
> Time's wingèd chariot hurrying near.

Lord, I cannot find you in time past or time future; only in this present moment. Teach me to use it to the full. That use may be writing or sleeping or loving or talking or playing or working—or praying. It is no use looking before and after and pining for what is not. The now is all I have. It is a sacrament, a sign of inward grace. A friend who came close to death once said that as she felt God's love sweep irresistibly over her, all the past, its achievements and its failures, became irrelevant. It is only in this moment that I can come close to God.

The Presence of God

I reflect for a moment on God's presence around me and in me.
Creator of the universe, the sun and the moon, the earth,
every molecule, every atom, everything that is—
God is in every beat of my heart. God is with me, now.

Freedom

A thick and shapeless tree-trunk would never believe
that it could become a statue, admired as a miracle of sculpture,
and would never submit itself to the chisel of the sculptor,
who sees by her genius what she can make of it (St. Ignatius).
I ask for the grace to let myself be shaped by my loving Creator.

Consciousness

Knowing that God loves me unconditionally,
I look honestly over the last day, its events, and my feelings.
Do I have something to be grateful for? Then I give thanks.
Is there something I am sorry for? Then I ask forgiveness.

The Word

I read the Word of God slowly, a few times over, and I listen
to what God is saying to me. (Please turn to your scripture on
the following pages. Inspiration points are there should you need
them. When you are ready, return here to continue.)

Conversation

What is stirring in me as I pray?
Am I consoled, troubled, left cold?
I imagine Jesus himself standing or sitting at my side,
and share my feelings with him.

Conclusion

Glory be to the Father, and to the Son, and to the Holy Spirit,
As it was in the beginning, is now, and ever shall be,
World without end. Amen.

128

Sunday 25th March, Fifth Sunday of Lent — John 12:20–26

Now among those who went up to worship at the festival were some Greeks. They came to Philip, who was from Bethsaida in Galilee, and said to him, "Sir, we wish to see Jesus." Philip went and told Andrew; then Andrew and Philip went and told Jesus. Jesus answered them, "The hour has come for the Son of Man to be glorified. Very truly, I tell you, unless a grain of wheat falls into the earth and dies, it remains just a single grain; but if it dies, it bears much fruit. Those who love their life lose it, and those who hate their life in this world will keep it for eternal life. Whoever serves me must follow me, and where I am, there will my servant be also. Whoever serves me, the Father will honor."

- In every death, there is life—this is the big message of Lent and of Easter. The grain of wheat will die and will through death nourish us with food.
- In the death of relationships, of health, of faith, and of all that may be dear to us, there is always the invitation to deeper life. In our final death is the call to everlasting life.

Monday 26th March, Annunciation of the Lord — Luke 1:26–33

In the sixth month the angel Gabriel was sent by God to a town in Galilee called Nazareth, to a virgin whose name was Mary. And he came to her and said, "Greetings, favored one! The Lord is with you." But she was much perplexed by his words and pondered what sort of greeting this might be. The angel said to her, "Do not be afraid, Mary, for you have found favor with God. And now, you will conceive in your womb and bear a son, and you will name him Jesus. He will be great, and will be called the Son of the Most High, and the Lord God will give to him the throne of his ancestor David. He will reign over the house of Jacob forever, and of his kingdom there will be no end."

- Mary was "much perplexed" by the words of the angel. Her inspiration points were her trust and her faith. She had to rely on her experience of the working of God as she pondered this other direction of her life.
- I hear the Word of God addressed to me, "Do not be afraid, you have found favour with God." I remain alert to any habit of hearing that robs this message of its power.

Tuesday 27th March   **John 8:21–30**

Again Jesus said to them, "I am going away, and you will search for me, but you will die in your sin. Where I am going, you cannot come." Then the Jews said, "Is he going to kill himself? Is that what he means by saying, 'Where I am going, you cannot come'?" He said to them, "You are from below, I am from above; you are of this world, I am not of this world. I told you that you would die in your sins, for you will die in your sins unless you believe that I am he." They said to him, "Who are you?" Jesus said to them, "Why do I speak to you at all? I have much to say about you and much to condemn; but the one who sent me is true, and I declare to the world what I have heard from him." They did not understand that he was speaking to them about the Father. Jesus said to them, "When you have lifted up the Son of Man, then you will realize that I am he, and that I do nothing on my own, but I speak these things as the Father instructed me. And the one who sent me is with me; he has not left me alone, for I always do what is pleasing to him." As he was saying these things, many believed in him.

- The people who heard Jesus' message often took in just the words on the surface. His meaning was hidden from them when they failed to listen on a deeper level, to reflect about what his words might mean for them.

- This is the work of our prayer: to receive the Word of God into our hearts, to go beyond superficial—even important —meanings.

Wednesday 28th March — John 8:31–42

Then Jesus said to the Jews who had believed in him, "If you continue in my word, you are truly my disciples; and you will know the truth, and the truth will make you free." They answered him, "We are descendants of Abraham and have never been slaves to anyone. What do you mean by saying, 'You will be made free'?" Jesus answered them, "Very truly, I tell you, everyone who commits sin is a slave to sin. The slave does not have a permanent place in the household; the son has a place there forever. So if the Son makes you free, you will be free indeed. I know that you are descendants of Abraham; yet you look for an opportunity to kill me, because there is no place in you for my word. I declare what I have seen in the Father's presence; as for you, you should do what you have heard from the Father." They answered him, "Abraham is our father." Jesus said to them, "If you were Abraham's children, you would be doing what Abraham did, but now you are trying to kill me, a man who has told you the truth that I heard from God. This is not what Abraham did. You are indeed doing what your father does." They said to him, "We are not illegitimate children; we have one father, God himself." Jesus said to them, "If God were your Father, you would love me, for I came from God and now I am here. I did not come on my own, but he sent me."

- Jesus' hearers were stuck in their sense of themselves, in the pride they took in their heritage. Perhaps I can admit that I too have sometimes climbed the wrong heights, have congratulated myself mistakenly. I know that my true dignity lives in my being a child of God.

- I pray that I may show my true worth in how I live and call others to a deeper and richer sense of themselves.

Thursday 29th March   **John 8:54–59**

Jesus said to the Jews, "If I glorify myself, my glory is nothing. It is my Father who glorifies me, he of whom you say, 'He is our God,' though you do not know him. But I know him; if I were to say that I do not know him, I would be a liar like you. But I do know him and I keep his word. Your ancestor Abraham rejoiced that he would see my day; he saw it and was glad." Then the Jews said to him, "You are not yet fifty years old, and have you seen Abraham?" Jesus said to them, "Very truly, I tell you, before Abraham was, I am." So they picked up stones to throw at him, but Jesus hid himself and went out of the temple.

- We keep the words of loved ones in our hearts, like their photos in a precious place. Or when we see them on a DVD or a video, we find love and memories coming alive. The Word of God is the same; it enlivens our souls and our convictions about what is best in life.
- Prayer brings us deeply into the words of God that mean a lot to us. God's word in Jesus keeps our faith alive, and his Word, who is Jesus, will be with us forever.

Friday 30th March   **John 10:31–40**

The Jews took up stones again to stone him. Jesus replied, "I have shown you many good works from the Father. For which of these are you going to stone me?" The Jews answered, "It is not for a good work that we are going to stone you, but for blasphemy, because you, though only a human being, are making yourself God." Jesus answered, "Is it not written in your law, 'I said, you are gods'? If those to whom the Word of God came were called 'gods'—and the scripture cannot be annulled—can you say that the one whom the Father has sanctified and sent into the world is blaspheming because I said, 'I am God's Son'? If I am not doing the works of my Father, then do not believe me. But if I do them, even though you do not believe me, believe the works, so that you may know and understand that the Father is in me and I am in the Father."

- Jesus was not putting himself above the people, but was calling them to realize their true worth.
- I think of how Jesus was born and became like me so that I may know myself truly as he accompanies me.

Saturday 31st March
John 11:47–52

So the chief priests and the Pharisees called a meeting of the council, and said, "What are we to do? This man is performing many signs. If we let him go on like this, everyone will believe in him, and the Romans will come and destroy both our holy place and our nation." But one of them, Caiaphas, who was high priest that year, said to them, "You know nothing at all! You do not understand that it is better for you to have one man die for the people than to have the whole nation destroyed." He did not say this on his own, but being high priest that year he prophesied that Jesus was about to die for the nation, and not for the nation only, but to gather into one the dispersed children of God.

- As we approach Holy Week, we consider how Jesus faced the prospect of arrest and condemnation.
- I pray that I may always do as Jesus did, considering how he took time in quiet, was with his friends, and chose the times in which to speak and those in which to stay silent. Lord, help me find the proper balance, neither complicating issues nor thinking everything simple.

april 1–7

Something to think and pray about each day this week:

Calvary's Victory

Holy Week is unlike any other week in the Church's year. It begins with the illusory triumph of Palm Sunday, when Jesus is hailed as a celebrity in his own city of Jerusalem. It leads through the betrayal of Judas (remembered on Spy Wednesday) and the farewells of Thursday (called Maundy Thursday after the *Mandatum,* the command to love one another), the humiliations, tortures and death on Good Friday, to the victory over death on Resurrection Morning. Nearly every human life will include some of those experiences. This week we can identify with the Lord each step of the way from the Mount of Olives to Calvary. When it comes to the resurrection, the imagination boggles, yet it is the centre of our faith. Lord, teach me to love my face and body, my temple of the Holy Spirit. It will grow old and die with me, but that is not the end. My body is sacred, and Easter opens a window for it and me onto a mysterious but endless vista.

The Presence of God

In the silence of my innermost being,
in the fragments of my yearned-for wholeness,
can I hear the whispers of God's presence?
Can I remember when I felt God's nearness?
When we walked together and I let myself be embraced by
God's love.

Freedom

There are very few people
who realize what God would make of them
if they abandoned themselves into his hands,
and let themselves be formed by his grace (St. Ignatius).
I ask for the grace to trust myself totally to God's love.

Consciousness

How do I find myself today?
Where am I with God? With others?
Do I have something to be grateful for? Then I give thanks.
Is there something I am sorry for? Then I ask forgiveness.

The Word

I take my time to read the Word of God, slowly, a few times, allowing myself to dwell on anything that strikes me. (Please turn to your scripture on the following pages. Inspiration points are there should you need them. When you are ready, return here to continue.)

Conversation

Do I notice myself reacting as I pray with the Word of God?
Do I feel challenged, comforted, angry?
Imagining Jesus sitting or standing by me,
I speak out my feelings, as one trusted friend to another.

Conclusion

Glory be to the Father, and to the Son, and to the Holy Spirit,
As it was in the beginning, is now, and ever shall be,
World without end. Amen.

april 2012

Sunday 1st April,
Palm Sunday of the Lord's Passion   Mark 14:1–9

It was two days before the Passover and the festival of Unleavened Bread. The chief priests and the scribes were looking for a way to arrest Jesus by stealth and kill him; for they said, "Not during the festival, or there may be a riot among the people." While he was at Bethany in the house of Simon the leper, as he sat at the table, a woman came with an alabaster jar of very costly ointment of nard, and she broke open the jar and poured the ointment on his head. But some were there who said to one another in anger, "Why was the ointment wasted in this way? For this ointment could have been sold for more than three hundred denarii, and the money given to the poor." And they scolded her. But Jesus said, "Let her alone; why do you trouble her? She has performed a good service for me. For you always have the poor with you, and you can show kindness to them whenever you wish; but you will not always have me. She has done what she could; she has anointed my body beforehand for its burial. Truly I tell you, wherever the good news is proclaimed in the whole world, what she has done will be told in remembrance of her.

- This woman put her own reputation and safety on the line to comfort the one she loved, to give thanks for his compassion. Her action would be remembered forever, and the scent of her ointment is the scent of resurrection. This nard would soothe the spirits of those who would always miss Jesus.
- Part of our prayer is missing Jesus when he seems so absent, when prayerful feelings seem so distant. The scent of the Lord in our lives keeps us going.

Monday 2nd April   John 12:1–6

Six days before the Passover Jesus came to Bethany, the home of Lazarus, whom he had raised from the dead. There they gave a dinner for him. Martha served, and Lazarus was one of those at the table with him. Mary took a pound of costly perfume made of pure nard, anointed Jesus' feet, and wiped them with her hair. The house was filled with the fragrance of the perfume. But Judas Iscariot, one of his disciples (the one who was about to betray him), said, "Why was this perfume not sold for three hundred denarii and the money given to the poor?" (He said this not because he cared about the poor, but because he was a thief; he kept the common purse and used to steal what was put into it.)

- Mary was able to be extravagant and generous and was not held back by the opinions of those around her. I can reflect her generosity and God's goodness to me by how I share my property, my goodwill, my love, and my forgiveness.
- I picture the house filled with perfume and imagine the fragrance of the good that I do permeating my surroundings.

Tuesday 3rd April　　　　　　　　**John 13:31–33, 36–38**

When Judas had gone out, Jesus said, "Now the Son of Man has been glorified, and God has been glorified in him. If God has been glorified in him, God will also glorify him in himself and will glorify him at once. Little children, I am with you only a little longer. You will look for me; and as I said to the Jews so now I say to you, 'Where I am going, you cannot come.'" Simon Peter said to him, "Lord, where are you going?" Jesus answered, "Where I am going, you cannot follow me now; but you will follow afterwards." Peter said to him, "Lord, why can I not follow you now? I will lay down my life for you." Jesus answered, "Will you lay down your life for me? Very truly, I tell you, before the cock crows, you will have denied me three times."

138

- Enthusiasm did not allow Peter to be calculating or measured. I pray for the same willingness to follow Jesus boldly, even as I know that I also need the courage and resolve that would fail Peter in the difficult hour.
- Peter's denials were matched by his professions of faith. I prepare myself to walk with Jesus on his way of the cross by recalling how I have been strong and by asking for forgiveness for my weakness.

Wednesday 4th April   **Matthew 26:14–16, 20–25**

Then one of the twelve, who was called Judas Iscariot, went to the chief priests and said, "What will you give me if I betray him to you?" They paid him thirty pieces of silver. And from that moment he began to look for an opportunity to betray him. When it was evening, Jesus took his place with the twelve; and while they were eating, he said, "Truly I tell you, one of you will betray me." And they became greatly distressed and began to say to him one after another, "Surely not I, Lord?" He answered, "The one who has dipped his hand into the bowl with me will betray me. The Son of Man goes as it is written of him, but woe to that one by whom the Son of Man is betrayed! It would have been better for that one not to have been born." Judas, who betrayed him, said, "Surely not I, Rabbi?" He replied, "You have said so."

- I ask for compassion for all who, like Judas, have been brought to a point of denial. I linger on the response of Jesus during these days of his trial.
- Aware of my own fragility, I ask Jesus for the strength that I need to give witness to his Spirit in difficult moments.

**Thursday 5th April,
Holy Thursday**   John 13:2–15

During supper Jesus, knowing that the Father had given all things into his hands, and that he had come from God and was going to God, got up from the table, took off his outer robe, and tied a towel around himself. Then he poured water into a basin and began to wash the disciples' feet and to wipe them with the towel that was tied around him. He came to Simon Peter, who said to him, "Lord, are you going to wash my feet?" Jesus answered, "You do not know now what I am doing, but later you will understand." Peter said to him, "You will never wash my feet." Jesus answered, "Unless I wash you, you have no share with me." Simon Peter said to him, "Lord, not my feet only but also my hands and my head!" Jesus said to him, "One who has bathed does not need to wash, except for the feet, but is entirely clean. And you are clean, though not all of you." For he knew who was to betray him; for this reason he said, "Not all of you are clean." After Jesus had washed their feet, had put on his robe, and had returned to the table, he said to them, "Do you know what I have done to you? You call me Teacher and Lord— and you are right, for that is what I am. So if I, your Lord and Teacher, have washed your feet, you also ought to wash one another's feet. For I have set you an example, that you also should do as I have done to you."

- Jesus knows who he is—where he has come from, where he is going. He is teaching his disciples that their true identity is to be servants of one another in his image. I ask to learn what I need to learn from this scene.
- How do I feel as I see him rise from table and approach me, kneel before me, and prepare to wash my feet?

140

Friday 6th April,
Good Friday   John 19:25–30

Meanwhile, standing near the cross of Jesus were his mother, and his mother's sister, Mary the wife of Clopas, and Mary Magdalene. When Jesus saw his mother and the disciple whom he loved standing beside her, he said to his mother, "Woman, here is your son." Then he said to the disciple, "Here is your mother." And from that hour the disciple took her into his own home. After this, when Jesus knew that all was now finished, he said (in order to fulfill the scripture), "I am thirsty." A jar full of sour wine was standing there. So they put a sponge full of the wine on a branch of hyssop and held it to his mouth. When Jesus had received the wine, he said, "It is finished." Then he bowed his head and gave up his spirit.

- There are four "acts" in the passion of Jesus: his arrest, his interrogation by the High Priest, his trial before Pilate, his crucifixion and burial. I watch him as he moves through these scenes. I observe how he seems gentle and calm. I look at the impact he has on others.
- I watch him subjected to disgraceful injustice and unspeakable torture and humiliation as he moves through his passion. He does not protest or cry out. How do I respond to injustice, ill-treatment, humiliation in my own life? What can I learn from him?

Saturday 7th April,
Holy Saturday   Matthew 27:57–66

When it was evening, there came a rich man from Arimathea, named Joseph, who was also a disciple of Jesus. He went to Pilate and asked for the body of Jesus; then Pilate ordered it to be given to him. So Joseph took the body and wrapped it in a clean linen cloth and laid it in his own new tomb, which he had hewn in the rock. He then rolled a great stone to the door of the tomb and went away. Mary Magdalene and the other Mary were there, sitting opposite the tomb. The next day, that is, after the day of Preparation, the chief priests and the Pharisees gathered before Pilate and said, "Sir, we remember what that impostor said while he was still alive, 'After three days I will rise again.' Therefore command that the tomb be made secure until the third day; otherwise his disciples may go and steal him away, and tell the people, 'He has been raised from the dead', and the last deception would be worse than the first." Pilate said to them, "You have a guard of soldiers; go, make it as secure as you can." So they went with the guard and made the tomb secure by sealing the stone.

- I think of Pilate and Joseph of Arimathea in the presence of that dead body. Pilate had known Jesus was innocent but, fearing for his own position, handed him over to death. Joseph had come to believe and hope in him as a disciple. Pilate wants to get rid of the body. Joseph receives it with deep reverence. I watch him place the body with great love and care in the tomb he had prepared for himself.
- Joseph goes away. I remain with Mary Magdalene and the other Mary, watching, waiting, and reflecting on what has happened over the past days.

april 8–14

Something to think and pray about each day this week:

The Words of Love
Lord, I envy the enthusiasm of the early disciples. They could not keep from speaking about what they had seen and heard. But I have not seen or heard it, and when I speak about your love, it sometimes sounds as though I have learned it out of a book. Yet I have felt you: sometimes in moments of anguish and incompleteness when I know that I am made for something beyond this; sometimes in moments of transcending joy, when I feel the glory of being loved. Give me words to do justice to my own experience.

The Presence of God

God is with me, but more,
God is within me, giving me existence.
Let me dwell for a moment on God's life-giving presence
in my body, my mind, my heart,
and in the whole of my life.

Freedom

Many countries are at this moment suffering
the agonies of war.
I bow my head in thanksgiving for my freedom.
I pray for all prisoners and captives.

Consciousness

I remind myself that I am in the presence of the Lord.
I will take refuge in His loving heart.
He is my strength in times of weakness.
He is my comforter in times of sorrow.

The Word

I read the Word of God slowly, a few times over, and I listen
to what God is saying to me. (Please turn to your scripture on
the following pages. Inspiration points are there should you need
them. When you are ready, return here to continue.)

Conversation

How has God's Word moved me? Has it left me cold?
Has it consoled me or moved me to act in a new way?
I imagine Jesus standing or sitting beside me;
I turn and share my feelings with him.

Conclusion

Glory be to the Father, and to the Son, and to the Holy Spirit,
As it was in the beginning, is now, and ever shall be,
World without end. Amen.

144

Sunday 8th April,
Easter Sunday   John 20:1–9

Early on the first day of the week, while it was still dark, Mary Magdalene came to the tomb and saw that the stone had been removed from the tomb. So she ran and went to Simon Peter and the other disciple, the one whom Jesus loved, and said to them, "They have taken the Lord out of the tomb, and we do not know where they have laid him." Then Peter and the other disciple set out and went toward the tomb. The two were running together, but the other disciple outran Peter and reached the tomb first. He bent down to look in and saw the linen wrappings lying there, but he did not go in. Then Simon Peter came, following him, and went into the tomb. He saw the linen wrappings lying there, and the cloth that had been on Jesus' head, not lying with the linen wrappings but rolled up in a place by itself. Then the other disciple, who reached the tomb first, also went in, and he saw and believed; for as yet they did not understand the scripture, that he must rise from the dead.

- It is the "first day of the week." Mary Magdalene is the first witness of an event which marks not just the beginning of a new week but the transformation of human history. But "it is still dark" and she does not yet understand what has happened. I ponder the mystery.
- Peter and the other disciple, who had stood faithfully beneath the cross, run to the tomb. The other disciple saw and believed. Peter, whose last recorded action was to deny Jesus, still does not believe. What blocks me from fuller faith?

Monday 9th April   Matthew 28:8–10

So the women left the tomb quickly with fear and great joy, and ran to tell his disciples. Suddenly Jesus met them and said, "Greetings!" And they came to him, took hold of his feet,

april 2012

and worshiped him. Then Jesus said to them, "Do not be afraid; go and tell my brothers to go to Galilee; there they will see me."

- It has been said that joy is the sure sign of God's presence. The women experience joy at an absence which is an overwhelming presence. When I experience this liberating, creative movement of joy in my own life, I can be sure the Risen Jesus is at work in me.
- The women bring the good news of their transforming encounter; the guards bring the bad news that the body of Jesus is gone. The news that Jesus has risen is, in the end, the only news that matters. Am I a light-bringer, a bearer of good news, a reflection of the Resurrection in the lives of others?

Tuesday 10th April   **John 20:11–18**

But Mary stood weeping outside the tomb. As she wept, she bent over to look into the tomb; and she saw two angels in white, sitting where the body of Jesus had been lying, one at the head and the other at the feet. They said to her, "Woman, why are you weeping?" She said to them, "They have taken away my Lord, and I do not know where they have laid him." When she had said this, she turned around and saw Jesus standing there, but she did not know that it was Jesus. Jesus said to her, "Woman, why are you weeping? Whom are you looking for?" Supposing him to be the gardener, she said to him, "Sir, if you have carried him away, tell me where you have laid him, and I will take him away." Jesus said to her, "Mary!" She turned and said to him in Hebrew, "Rabbouni!" (which means Teacher). Jesus said to her, "Do not hold on to me, because I have not yet ascended to the Father. But go to my brothers and say to them, 'I am ascending to my Father and your Father, to my God and your God.'" Mary Magdalene went and announced to the disciples, "I have seen the Lord"; and she told them that he had said these things to her.

- "Woman, why are you weeping?" the angels ask. Why is Mary weeping? For her own loss or, rather, the thought of what her friend has had to suffer?

- Jesus said his sheep would know him when he called their names. Mary knows Jesus when he speaks her name to her. Can I hear him speak mine to me? What do I experience in this precious moment of encounter?

Wednesday 11th April   Luke 24:13–19, 25–29

Now on that same day two of them were going to a village called Emmaus, about seven miles from Jerusalem, and talking with each other about all these things that had happened. While they were talking and discussing, Jesus himself came near and went with them, but their eyes were kept from recognizing him. And he said to them, "What are you discussing with each other while you walk along?" They stood still, looking sad. Then one of them, whose name was Cleopas, answered him, "Are you the only stranger in Jerusalem who does not know the things that have taken place there in these days?" He asked them, "What things?" They replied, "The things about Jesus of Nazareth, who was a prophet mighty in deed and word before God and all the people. . . . Then Jesus said to them, "Oh, how foolish you are, and how slow of heart to believe all that the prophets have declared! Was it not necessary that the Messiah should suffer these things and then enter into his glory?" Then beginning with Moses and all the prophets, he interpreted to them the things about himself in all the scriptures. As they came near the village to which they were going, he walked ahead as if he were going on. But they urged him strongly, saying, "Stay with us, because it is almost evening and the day is now nearly over." So he went in to stay with them.

- The disappointed disciples ask the stranger who walks with them if he is the only one who does not know "the things that have taken place in these days." In fact, he is the only one who does truly know. But, like a good counselor, he lets them pour out their feelings and tell their story. In prayer, he invites me to do the same.
- The disciples were "stuck" in a big way, unable to see what had happened in the light of God's Word. Jesus is present in his word, accompanying me in the experiences of my life, making sense of what happens. Do I search for him? Can I recognize him?

Thursday 12th April   Luke 24:35–40

Then the disciples told what had happened on the road, and how he had been made known to them in the breaking of the bread. While they were talking about this, Jesus himself stood among them and said to them, "Peace be with you." They were startled and terrified, and thought that they were seeing a ghost. He said to them, "Why are you frightened, and why do doubts arise in your hearts? Look at my hands and my feet; see that it is I myself. Touch me and see; for a ghost does not have flesh and bones as you see that I have." And when he had said this, he showed them his hands and his feet.

- In our relationship with Jesus, we too are tempted to think of him as a ghost. But, as he tells the disciples, he has flesh and blood as we do. He knows of what we are made. He shares everything we experience and offers us a share in everything he experiences, including his resurrection.
- Jesus had told his disciples that, when they gathered in his name, he would be in their midst. His presence brings peace, casts out fear. Do I let him give me his peace? Do I recognize fear as the counter-sign that it is?

148

Friday 13th April — John 21:4–14

Just after daybreak, Jesus stood on the beach; but the disciples did not know that it was Jesus. Jesus said to them, "Children, you have no fish, have you?" They answered him, "No." He said to them, "Cast the net to the right side of the boat, and you will find some." So they cast it, and now they were not able to haul it in because there were so many fish. That disciple whom Jesus loved said to Peter, "It is the Lord!" When Simon Peter heard that it was the Lord, he put on some clothes, for he was naked, and jumped into the sea. But the other disciples came in the boat, dragging the net full of fish, for they were not far from the land, only about a hundred yards off. When they had gone ashore, they saw a charcoal fire there, with fish on it, and bread. Jesus said to them, "Bring some of the fish that you have just caught." So Simon Peter went aboard and hauled the net ashore, full of large fish, a hundred fifty-three of them; and though there were so many, the net was not torn. Jesus said to them, "Come and have breakfast." Now none of the disciples dared to ask him, "Who are you?" because they knew it was the Lord. Jesus came and took the bread and gave it to them, and did the same with the fish. This was now the third time that Jesus appeared to the disciples after he was raised from the dead.

- This is "the morning after." The disciples think they are back to square one. They revert to their old occupations, the adventure with Jesus apparently over. In our times of rejection, he is present, waiting for us to recognize him and find new hope, a new beginning.
- Often in the gospels, Jesus shares meals with his friends. We see him here as host, solicitous of the disciples' need—for food but, more deeply, for his companionship. This is what he offers in the nourishment of prayer and in the Eucharist.

Saturday 14th April Mark 16:9–15

Now after he rose early on the first day of the week, he appeared first to Mary Magdalene, from whom he had cast out seven demons. She went out and told those who had been with him, while they were mourning and weeping. But when they heard that he was alive and had been seen by her, they would not believe it. After this he appeared in another form to two of them, as they were walking into the country. And they went back and told the rest, but they did not believe them. Later he appeared to the eleven themselves as they were sitting at the table; and he upbraided them for their lack of faith and stubbornness, because they had not believed those who saw him after he had risen. And he said to them, "Go into all the world and proclaim the good news to the whole creation."

- Mary is a witness for the disciples but they "who had been with him" thought they knew better and would not believe her. How often do we disregard the witness of others in our daily lives?
- Often, like the disciples, we hold on to our sadness and our negative feelings, refusing to believe. Jesus upbraids the eleven for their stubbornness. "Today, if you should hear his voice, harden not your hearts," Psalm 94 says. Where is the stubbornness and hardness of heart in my life that prevents me from giving myself more completely to faith in him today?

april 15–21

Something to think and pray about each day this week:

The Tomb Is Empty

The angels upbraided the holy women at the tomb: "Why do you look for the living among the dead?" You are not in any tomb, Lord. The tomb is empty. You are not a dead hero to be studied in retrospect. You are alive, and meeting me, at my side, in my heart, sustaining me in the Eucharist. The report brought by the good women, dismissed by the apostles as an idle tale, is the creed by which I live.

The Presence of God
To be present is to arrive as one is and open up to the other.
At this instant, as I arrive here, God is present waiting for me.
God always arrives before me, desiring to connect with me
even more than my most intimate friend.
I take a moment and greet my loving God.

Freedom
"In these days, God taught me
as a schoolteacher teaches a pupil" (St. Ignatius).
I remind myself that there are things God has to teach me yet,
and ask for the grace to hear them and let them change me.

Consciousness
How am I really feeling? Lighthearted? Heavyhearted?
I may be very much at peace, happy to be here.
Equally, I may be frustrated, worried, or angry.
I acknowledge how I really am. It is the real me that the Lord loves.

The Word
I take my time to read the Word of God, slowly, a few times, allowing myself to dwell on anything that strikes me. (Please turn to your scripture on the following pages. Inspiration points are there should you need them. When you are ready, return here to continue.)

Conversation
What feelings are rising in me
as I pray and reflect on God's Word?
I imagine Jesus himself sitting or standing beside me,
and open my heart to him.

Conclusion
Glory be to the Father, and to the Son, and to the Holy Spirit,
As it was in the beginning, is now, and ever shall be,
World without end. Amen.

152

Sunday 15th April, Second Sunday of Easter   John 20:24–29

But Thomas (who was called the Twin), one of the twelve, was not with them when Jesus came. So the other disciples told him, "We have seen the Lord." But he said to them, "Unless I see the mark of the nails in his hands, and put my finger in the mark of the nails and my hand in his side, I will not believe." A week later his disciples were again in the house, and Thomas was with them. Although the doors were shut, Jesus came and stood among them and said, "Peace be with you." Then he said to Thomas, "Put your finger here and see my hands. Reach out your hand and put it in my side. Do not doubt but believe." Thomas answered him, "My Lord and my God!" Jesus said to him, "Have you believed because you have seen me? Blessed are those who have not seen and yet have come to believe."

- In community, the disciples found faith in the risen Christ. Thomas, for some reason, was not with them when the Lord came. Separated from the community, he found faith more difficult.
- Faith in the Lord, while personal, is not a private affair. In the faith of one, the faith of another may be strengthened.

Monday 16th April   John 3:1–8

Now there was a Pharisee named Nicodemus, a leader of the Jews. He came to Jesus by night and said to him, "Rabbi, we know that you are a teacher who has come from God; for no one can do these signs that you do apart from the presence of God." Jesus answered him, "Very truly, I tell you, no one can see the kingdom of God without being born from above." Nicodemus said to him, "How can anyone be born after having grown old? Can one enter a second time into the mother's womb and be born?" Jesus answered, "Very truly, I tell you, no one can enter the kingdom of God without being born of water and Spirit. What is born of the flesh is flesh, and what is born of the Spirit is spirit. Do not be astonished that I said to you, 'You must be born from above.' The wind blows where it chooses, and you hear the sound of it, but you do not know where it comes from or where it goes. So it is with everyone who is born of the Spirit."

- Nicodemus approaches Jesus with great caution, "by night." He does not commit himself openly. In what ways do I hold back from full commitment to him?
- Jesus always knew what was in people, what their real agenda was. What did he see when he looked at Nicodemus? What does he see when he looks at me?

Tuesday 17th April   John 3:7–10

Jesus said to Nicodemus, "Do not be astonished that I said to you, 'You must be born from above.' The wind blows where it chooses, and you hear the sound of it, but you do not know where it comes from or where it goes. So it is with everyone who is born of the Spirit." Nicodemus said to him, "How can these things be?" Jesus answered him, "Are you a teacher of Israel, and yet you do not understand these things?"

- Jesus opens the scripture to this "teacher of Israel," referring to his death which will scandalize Nicodemus's fellow-Pharisees.
- What is he trying to make me aware of through this scripture today?

Wednesday 18th April   John 3:16–18

Jesus said to Nicodemus, "For God so loved the world that he gave his only Son, so that everyone who believes in him may not perish but may have eternal life. "Indeed, God did not send the Son into the world to condemn the world, but in order that the world might be saved through him. Those who believe in him are not condemned; but those who do not believe are condemned already, because they have not believed in the name of the only Son of God."

- God loves the world, loves each one of us, loves me. This is the whole message of Jesus, expressed in his words and embodied, directly or indirectly, in the whole of his life. As one theologian has said about his message, "There just isn't anything else."
- Am I convinced of this myself? Thinking of myself in the presence of Jesus, one on one, do I experience myself as found wanting, condemned, or, even in my darkness, loved through and through and invited into the light?

Thursday 19th April   John 3:31–36

John the Baptist said to his disciples, "The one who comes from above is above all; the one who is of the earth belongs to the earth and speaks about earthly things. The one who comes from heaven is above all. He testifies to what he has seen and heard, yet no one accepts his testimony. Whoever has accepted his testimony has certified this, that God is true. He whom God has sent speaks the words of God. The Father loves the Son and has placed all things in his hands. Whoever believes in the Son has eternal life; whoever disobeys the Son will not see life, but must endure God's wrath."

- Jesus' whole mission was to give the living water of truth to the men and women of every age. He knew that he was offering them not some restrictive teaching but the eternal life for which they were created. He longs to offer this to me now.
- God gives the Spirit without measure, but my heart is small. I pray so that my capacity to receive God's unbounded Spirit may grow and keep growing.

Friday 20th April   **John 6:1–13**

After this Jesus went to the other side of the Sea of Galilee, also called the Sea of Tiberias. A large crowd kept following him, because they saw the signs that he was doing for the sick. Jesus went up the mountain and sat down there with his disciples. Now the Passover, the festival of the Jews, was near. When he looked up and saw a large crowd coming toward him, Jesus said to Philip, "Where are we to buy bread for these people to eat?" He said this to test him, for he himself knew what he was going to do. Philip answered him, "Six months' wages would not buy enough bread for each of them to get a little." One of his disciples, Andrew, Simon Peter's brother, said to him, "There is a boy here who has five barley loaves and two fish. But what are they among so many people?" Jesus said, "Make the people sit down." Now there was a great deal of grass in the place; so they sat down, about five thousand in all. Then Jesus took the loaves, and when he had given thanks, he distributed them to those who were seated; so also the fish, as much as they wanted. When they were satisfied, he told his disciples, "Gather up the fragments left over, so that nothing may be lost." So they gathered them up, and from the fragments of the five barley loaves, left by those who had eaten, they filled twelve baskets.

- The Passover, recalling how the Israelites were fed with manna in the desert, is "near." Jesus is giving a sign here of who he is, the new Moses, leading those with faith in him into true freedom.
- I mingle with the crowd, observing what happens around me, accepting his overwhelming bounty, watching him relate to each individual person.

Saturday 21st April   **John 6:16–21**

When evening came, his disciples went down to the sea, got into a boat, and started across the sea to Capernaum. It was now dark, and Jesus had not yet come to them. The sea became rough because a strong wind was blowing. When they had rowed about three or four miles, they saw Jesus walking on the sea and coming near the boat, and they were terrified. But he said to them, "It is I; do not be afraid." Then they wanted to take him into the boat, and immediately the boat reached the land toward which they were going.

- Jesus echoes the Passover again as he crosses the sea by his own mysterious power. Once the disciples want him with them again on their journey, the storms around them subside and they get safely to their destination.

- I ask him to be with me and to master the storms around me or within me, which sometimes threaten to engulf me.

april 22–28

Something to think and pray about each day this week:

Our True Vocation

If you have ever worked in a large organisation, you know what it is like if you meet a senior manager by accident, and his or her face lights up and they greet you, "Hello, Anne, how are you?" It matters a lot to us to be known. Jesus says, "*I know my own and mine know me.*" Not only does he know us, but we believe that his providence shapes our lives. He calls us by name. We are, each of us, called—we have a vocation. It may be to an obviously important job like rearing children, or caring for a sick or elderly person. It may be a full-time vocation in the religious life or priesthood. It may be the calling of those who only stand and wait. It is not a pigeon-hole sort of call, fixed for our lifetime, but rather something dynamic, that changes as we grow older, grow stronger, and then grow weaker with age. Lord, may I hear your call.

The Presence of God
What is present to me is what has a hold on my becoming.
I reflect on the presence of God always there in love,
amidst the many things that have a hold on me.
I pause and pray that I may let God
affect my becoming in this precise moment.

Freedom
If God were trying to tell me something, would I know?
If God were reassuring me or challenging me, would I notice?
I ask for the grace to be free of my own preoccupations
and open to what God may be saying to me.

Consciousness
Knowing that God loves me unconditionally,
I can afford to be honest about how I am.
How has the last day been, and how do I feel now?
I share my feelings openly with the Lord.

The Word
God speaks to each one of us individually. I need to listen to what
he is saying to me. (Please turn to your scripture on the following
pages. Inspiration points are there should you need them. When
you are ready, return here to continue.)

Conversation
What is stirring in me as I pray?
Am I consoled, troubled, left cold?
I imagine Jesus himself standing or sitting at my side,
and share my feelings with him.

Conclusion
Glory be to the Father, and to the Son, and to the Holy Spirit,
As it was in the beginning, is now, and ever shall be,
World without end. Amen.

Sunday 22nd April,
Third Sunday of Easter   Luke 24:35–48

Then they told what had happened on the road, and how he had been made known to them in the breaking of the bread. While they were talking about this, Jesus himself stood among them and said to them, "Peace be with you." They were startled and terrified, and thought that they were seeing a ghost. He said to them, "Why are you frightened, and why do doubts arise in your hearts? Look at my hands and my feet; see that it is I myself. Touch me and see; for a ghost does not have flesh and bones as you see that I have." And when he had said this, he showed them his hands and his feet. While in their joy they were disbelieving and still wondering, he said to them, "Have you anything here to eat?" They gave him a piece of broiled fish, and he took it and ate in their presence. Then he said to them, "These are my words that I spoke to you while I was still with you—that everything written about me in the law of Moses, the prophets, and the psalms must be fulfilled." Then he opened their minds to understand the scriptures, and he said to them, "Thus it is written, that the Messiah is to suffer and to rise from the dead on the third day, and that repentance and forgiveness of sins is to be proclaimed in his name to all nations, beginning from Jerusalem. You are witnesses of these things."

- Take this journey in prayer. Walk with the disciples, and feel their fear and anxiety and sense of being let down. Feel their hope also that maybe his promise to rise will be fulfilled. What might this bring up in you? The darkness and the light, shared on the journey, hour by hour, with the Lord of light.
- Walk and listen; let Jesus remind you of the scripture that brings trust, peace, and confidence.

Monday 23rd April　　　　　　　　　　**John 6:22–27**

The next day the crowd that had stayed on the other side of the lake saw that there had been only one boat there. They also saw that Jesus had not got into the boat with his disciples, but that his disciples had gone away alone. Then some boats from Tiberias came near the place where they had eaten the bread after the Lord had given thanks. So when the crowd saw that neither Jesus nor his disciples were there, they themselves got into the boats and went to Capernaum looking for Jesus. When they found him on the other side of the lake, they said to him, "Rabbi, when did you come here?" Jesus answered them, "Very truly, I tell you, you are looking for me, not because you saw signs, but because you ate your fill of the loaves. Do not work for the food that perishes, but for the food that endures for eternal life, which the Son of Man will give you."

- Jesus is always leading us beyond where we are, beyond our hunger for physical food to the "the food that endures for eternal life." He reveals what this means step by step. The key task we must perform is to believe in him as the One sent by the Father. Have we really taken that step?
- Believing is "the work of God." It is what God wants of us. It is also what God works in us. God nourishes the roots of faith in us when we pray.

Tuesday 24th April　　　　　　　　　　**John 6:30–35**

So they said to him, "What sign are you going to give us then, so that we may see it and believe you? What work are you performing? Our ancestors ate the manna in the wilderness; as it is written, 'He gave them bread from heaven to eat.'" Then Jesus said to them, "Very truly, I tell you, it was not Moses who gave you the bread from heaven, but it is my Father who gives you the true bread from heaven. For the bread of God is that which comes down from heaven and gives life to the world." They said to him, "Sir, give us this bread always." Jesus said to them, "I am the bread of life. Whoever comes to me will never be hungry, and whoever believes in me will never be thirsty."

- Those challenging Jesus for a sign have failed to recognize what he has done. Above all, they have failed to recognize that he is, in himself, the sign. He invites, but does not compel, faith in himself. We too look for signs. Jesus is the sign.
- He is "the bread of life," the bread "which comes down from heaven and gives life to the word." Am I in touch with the hunger within myself which is for God and nothing less? This is the hunger Jesus came to satisfy.

Wednesday 25th April,
St. Mark, Evangelist   Mark 16:15–20

And Jesus said to the disciples, "Go into all the world and proclaim the good news to the whole creation. The one who believes and is baptized will be saved; but the one who does not believe will be condemned. And these signs will accompany those who believe: by using my name they will cast out demons; they will speak in new tongues; they will pick up snakes in their hands, and if they drink any deadly thing, it will not hurt them; they will lay their hands on the sick, and they will recover." So then the Lord Jesus, after he had spoken to them, was taken up into heaven and sat down at the right hand of God. And they went out and proclaimed the good news everywhere, while the Lord worked with them and confirmed the message by the signs that accompanied it.

- The words of Jesus at the end of his Easter appearances link heaven and earth. From his place in heaven, the Lord works with us and is a companion in the work of proclaiming Good News. His friendship with each of us is good news for us. We are to share that in different situations.

- Prayer deepens in us the sense that the message of Jesus is good news in our own lives and, through us, in the lives of others.

Thursday 26th April   John 6:45–51

Jesus said to the people: "It is written in the prophets: 'They will all be taught by God'; everyone who has listened to the Father and learned from him comes to me. Not that anyone has seen the Father except the one who is from God; he has seen the Father. Very truly, I tell you, whoever believes has eternal life. I am the bread of life. Your ancestors ate the manna in the wilderness, and they died. This is the bread that comes down from heaven, so that one may eat of it and not die. I am the living bread that came down from heaven. Whoever eats of this bread will live for ever; and the bread that I will give for the life of the world is my flesh."

- We watch Jesus gradually inviting his hearers to understand what he means by saying that he is the bread of life. First, he opens them up to awareness of their need. Then he offers himself.
- Am I self-sufficient, or do I know my need? Do I hunger for this bread?

Friday 27th April   John 6:52–59

The Jews then disputed among themselves, saying, "How can this man give us his flesh to eat?" So Jesus said to them, "Very truly, I tell you, unless you eat the flesh of the Son of Man and drink his blood, you have no life in you. Those who eat my flesh and drink my blood have eternal life, and I will raise them up on the last day; for my flesh is true food and my blood is true drink. Those who eat my flesh and drink my blood abide in me,

164

and I in them. Just as the living Father sent me, and I live because of the Father, so whoever eats me will live because of me."

- The message of Jesus is that he is our life, he is the pathway leading to life, he is the inner truth of our existence, he is the very substance of eternal life.
- Only by embracing his message, consuming his words in the most profound sense as we try to do in prayer, and encountering him in the mystery of the Eucharist can we have true life in ourselves.

Saturday 28th April   **John 6:66–69**

Because of his teaching many of his disciples turned back and no longer went about with him. So Jesus asked the twelve, "Do you also wish to go away?" Simon Peter answered him, "Lord, to whom can we go? You have the words of eternal life. We have come to believe and know that you are the Holy One of God."

- Peter may not understand the full import of what Jesus is saying, but he knows what is essential: "You have the words of eternal life."
- To follow Jesus is to walk forward in faith, understanding that other would-be bearers of truth can never satisfy us. It is to say, whatever happens, "You have the words of eternal life."

april 29–may 5

Something to think and pray about each day this week:

Light and Life

In the Northern Hemisphere, May brings the special joy of brighter sunlight and longer days. Throughout the scriptures God is spoken of as the source of light, living in inaccessible light. Jesus is the light of the world, bringing sight to the sightless. We are to walk as children of the light. Light is more than just a condition to see by. Sunlight opens the world to us, nourishes our skin and our body, shows us we are still alive. Dylan Thomas's angry poem bids his sick father, "Rage, rage against the dying of the light."

Lord, I treasure your light, and the feeling of the sun on my back. May I never lose my gratitude for the sight of my eyes and the glory of sunlight. I need your light too in the dark hours, when I am baffled by the evil of the world. Be the light of my life.

The Presence of God

At any time of the day or night we can call on Jesus.
He is always waiting, listening for our call.
What a wonderful blessing.
No phone needed, no e-mail, just a whisper.

Freedom

I need to close out the noise, to rise above the noise—
the noise that interrupts, that separates,
the noise that isolates.
I need to listen to God again.

Consciousness

Help me, Lord, to be more conscious of your presence.
Teach me to recognize your presence in others.
Fill my heart with gratitude for the times your love
has been shown to me through the care of others.

The Word

I read the Word of God slowly, a few times over, and I listen
to what God is saying to me. (Please turn to your scripture on
the following pages. Inspiration points are there should you need
them. When you are ready, return here to continue.)

Conversation

Do I notice myself reacting as I pray with the Word of God?
Do I feel challenged, comforted, angry?
Imagining Jesus sitting or standing by me,
I speak out my feelings, as one trusted friend to another.

Conclusion

Glory be to the Father, and to the Son, and to the Holy Spirit,
As it was in the beginning, is now, and ever shall be,
World without end. Amen.

Sunday 29th April,
Fourth Sunday of Easter John 10:11–18

I am the good shepherd. The good shepherd lays down his life for the sheep. The hired hand, who is not the shepherd and does not own the sheep, sees the wolf coming and leaves the sheep and runs away—and the wolf snatches them and scatters them. The hired hand runs away because a hired hand does not care for the sheep. I am the good shepherd. I know my own and my own know me, just as the Father knows me and I know the Father. And I lay down my life for the sheep. I have other sheep that do not belong to this fold. I must bring them also, and they will listen to my voice. So there will be one flock, one shepherd. For this reason the Father loves me, because I lay down my life in order to take it up again. No one takes it from me, but I lay it down of my own accord. I have power to lay it down, and I have power to take it up again. I have received this command from my Father."

- The love of Jesus is the self-sacrificing love which we see on the cross. It is the love which can always see the resurrection ahead in some form or other.
- In caring for all people, Jesus knew something of the resurrection, for in love are the seeds of resurrection. We rise above the self-centredness that confines and narrows us, to the outgoing love which expands our hearts and minds, as our hearts and minds grow to be like the heart and mind of Jesus.

Monday 30th April John 10:1–10

Jesus said to the Pharisees, "Very truly, I tell you, anyone who does not enter the sheepfold by the gate but climbs in by another way is a thief and a bandit. The one who enters by the gate is the shepherd of the sheep. The gatekeeper opens the gate for him, and the sheep hear his voice. He calls his own sheep by name and leads them out. When he has brought out all his own, he goes ahead of them, and the sheep follow him because they know his voice. They will not follow a stranger, but they will run from him because they do not know the voice of strangers." Jesus used this figure of speech with them, but they did not understand what he was saying to them.

- We live in a world of discordant voices.
- To pray is to become increasingly sensitive to the voice of Jesus and to recognize in him the "way in" to God, the gate that opens out into the wide pastures where we encounter truth and life.

Tuesday 1st May   **John 10:22–30**

At that time the festival of the Dedication took place in Jerusalem. It was winter, and Jesus was walking in the temple, in the portico of Solomon. So the Jews gathered around him and said to him, "How long will you keep us in suspense? If you are the Messiah, tell us plainly." Jesus answered, "I have told you, and you do not believe. The works that I do in my Father's name testify to me; but you do not believe, because you do not belong to my sheep. My sheep hear my voice. I know them, and they follow me. I give them eternal life, and they will never perish. No one will snatch them out of my hand. What my Father has given me is greater than all else, and no one can snatch it out of the Father's hand. The Father and I are one."

- Jesus knows that those who have eyes to see will recognize the works he does and find faith in him.
- In our prayer, we watch him and listen to him, knowing in faith that we see and hear the Father. And this is what we desire.

170

Wednesday 2nd May   John 12:44–50

Then Jesus cried aloud: "Whoever believes in me believes not in me but in him who sent me. And whoever sees me sees him who sent me. I have come as light into the world, so that everyone who believes in me should not remain in the darkness. I do not judge anyone who hears my words and does not keep them, for I came not to judge the world, but to save the world. The one who rejects me and does not receive my word has a judge; on the last day the word that I have spoken will serve as judge, for I have not spoken on my own, but the Father who sent me has himself given me a commandment about what to say and what to speak. And I know that his commandment is eternal life. What I speak, therefore, I speak just as the Father has told me."

- Jesus cried aloud. He knows that the Father's commandment, which he is carrying out, "is eternal life," and he wants his voice to rise above the babble around him in the Temple portico. His voice is the voice of one who desires to save, not to judge.
- I listen for the saving voice of Jesus above the other voices that surround me.

Thursday 3rd May,
Sts. Philip and James, Apostles   John 14:7–14

Jesus said to his disciples, "If you know me, you will know my Father also. From now on you do know him and have seen him." Philip said to him, "Lord, show us the Father, and we will be satisfied." Jesus said to him, "Have I been with you all this time, Philip, and you still do not know me? Whoever has seen me has seen the Father. How can you say, 'Show us the Father'? Do you not believe that I am in the Father and the Father is in me? The words that I say to you I do not speak on my own; but the Father who dwells in me does his works. Believe me that I am in the Father and the Father is in me; but if you do not, then believe me because of the works themselves. Very truly, I tell you, the one who believes in me will also do the works that I do and, in fact, will do greater works than these, because I am going to the Father. I will do whatever you ask in my name, so that the Father may be glorified in the Son. If in my name you ask me for anything, I will do it."

- I recognize something of Philip in me: although he lived with and listened to Jesus every day, he still looked for something more.
- I take some time as I pray today to listen to where God has already been speaking to me. Before I ask for anything else, I consider the gifts that God gives to me.

Friday 4th May   John 14:1–6

Jesus said to his disciples, "Do not let your hearts be troubled. Believe in God, believe also in me. In my Father's house there are many dwelling places. If it were not so, would I have told you that I go to prepare a place for you? And if I go and prepare a place for you, I will come again and will take you to myself, so that where I am, there you may be also. And you know the way to the place where I am going." Thomas said to him, "Lord, we do not know where you are going. How can we know the way?" Jesus said to him, "I am the way, and the truth, and the life. No one comes to the Father except through me."

- Jesus brings inner peace. Even in face of his impending death and what they will have to endure in the world, he does not want their hearts to be troubled. He wants them to be at peace because he will not abandon them. He does not abandon us.
- He is the way: where he goes, we follow. He is the truth: all other claims to truth are measured by him. He is the life: we have

true life in us, the spring of water welling up into everlasting life, through him.

Saturday 5th May   John 14:11–14

Jesus said to his disciples, "Believe me that I am in the Father and the Father is in me; but if you do not, then believe me because of the works themselves. Very truly, I tell you, the one who believes in me will also do the works that I do and, in fact, will do greater works than these, because I am going to the Father. I will do whatever you ask in my name, so that the Father may be glorified in the Son. If in my name you ask me for anything, I will do it."

- One of the biggest mysteries in the life of Jesus is his relationship with his Father and the Holy Spirit. It is always presented in terms of deep closeness; they are "I" to each other. So that when we know and love Jesus, we know and love the Father and the Holy Spirit.
- We are immersed in a world of divine community and so are called to live in the world of human community.

may 6–12

Something to think and pray about each day this week:

Working in the Spirit

Jesus spoke of the Holy Spirit not merely as a comforter but as a breeze, blowing mysteriously. If we but put up our sails, the Holy Spirit will do a good deal of the work for us, help us to be open to the human condition and be creative in solutions to the myriad problems that are the stuff of many of our lives today—bad marriages, ungrateful children, loss of jobs, financial debts, sizeable moral flaws. For this we need to be open to the moment, ready to alter plans if we sense a need for immediate change. Religion becomes natural and organic, without any of the glad-handing, fixed-smile religiosity that often goes no deeper. It is desire, not guilt, that is the prime motivator.

The Presence of God
As I sit here, the beating of my heart,
the ebb and flow of my breathing, the movements of my mind
are all signs of God's ongoing creation of me.
I pause for a moment, and become aware
of this presence of God within me.

Freedom
I will ask God's help,
to be free from my own preoccupations,
to be open to God in this time of prayer,
to come to love and serve him more.

Consciousness
Knowing that God loves me unconditionally,
I look honestly over the last day, its events, and my feelings.
Do I have something to be grateful for? Then I give thanks.
Is there something I am sorry for? Then I ask forgiveness.

The Word
I take my time to read the Word of God, slowly, a few times, allowing myself to dwell on anything that strikes me. (Please turn
to your scripture on the following pages. Inspiration points are
there should you need them. When you are ready, return here to
continue.)

Conversation
Remembering that I am still in God's presence,
I imagine Jesus himself standing or sitting beside me,
and say whatever is on my mind, whatever is in my heart,
speaking as one friend to another.

Conclusion
Glory be to the Father, and to the Son, and to the Holy Spirit,
As it was in the beginning, is now, and ever shall be,
World without end. Amen.

Sunday 6th May,
Fifth Sunday of Easter   John 15:1–8

Jesus said to his disciples, "I am the true vine, and my Father is the vine-grower. He removes every branch in me that bears no fruit. Every branch that bears fruit he prunes to make it bear more fruit. You have already been cleansed by the word that I have spoken to you. Abide in me as I abide in you. Just as the branch cannot bear fruit by itself unless it abides in the vine, neither can you unless you abide in me. I am the vine, you are the branches. Those who abide in me and I in them bear much fruit, because apart from me you can do nothing. Whoever does not abide in me is thrown away like a branch and withers; such branches are gathered, thrown into the fire, and burned. If you abide in me, and my words abide in you, ask for whatever you wish, and it will be done for you. My Father is glorified by this, that you bear much fruit and become my disciples."

- The closeness of the relationship with ourselves and Jesus is like branch and tree. One gives life to the other and draws life from the other.
- A real relationship with Jesus is life-giving—it is loving, healing, and challenging. It brings life to the soul and energy to the body. The relationship itself bears fruit and brings to each of us a loving and energetic quality of life.

Monday 7th May   John 14:21–26

Jesus said to his disciples: "They who have my commandments and keep them are those who love me; and those who love me will be loved by my Father, and I will love them and reveal myself to them." Judas (not Iscariot) said to him, "Lord, how is it that you will reveal yourself to us, and not to the world?" Jesus answered him, "Those who love me will keep my word, and my

Father will love them, and we will come to them and make our home with them. Whoever does not love me does not keep my words; and the word that you hear is not mine, but is from the Father who sent me. I have said these things to you while I am still with you. The Advocate, the Holy Spirit, whom the Father will send in my name, will teach you everything, and remind you of all that I have said to you."

- Loving God and doing what God wants are essentially linked. "Love is proved in deeds not words" was the ending St. Ignatius gave to people after a thirty-day retreat.
- We love the Lord by keeping God's word, by doing what that word indicates to us. In times of prayer we can recall our working for God in the past and consider our working with God in the future.

Tuesday 8th May   John 14:27
Jesus said to his disciples, "Peace I leave with you; my peace I give to you. I do not give to you as the world gives. Do not let your hearts be troubled, and do not let them be afraid."

- I repeat Jesus' promise, making it my prayer for today, "Peace I leave with you; my peace I give to you."
- I quietly review my life, seeing what has helped my peace, recognizing what has broken it down. I think of what I need to do to preserve this gift of peace that Jesus has in his heart for me.

Wednesday 9th May   John 15:1–5
Jesus said to his disciples, "I am the true vine, and my Father is the vine-grower. He removes every branch in me that bears no fruit. Every branch that bears fruit he prunes to make it bear more fruit. You have already been cleansed by the word that I have spoken to you. Abide in me as I abide in you. Just as the

branch cannot bear fruit by itself unless it abides in the vine, neither can you unless you abide in me."

- I am now invited to abide—to be at home—with Jesus. I recall some of the places in which I have lived, places that I have called "home." I think of what helps me to feel at home.

- I am called to be at home with Jesus not to some comfortable end or for a cosy existence. Being at home with Jesus is to share in his life and to give glory to his Father. I am drawn into the very life of God.

Thursday 10th May   **John 15:9–11**

Jesus said to his disciples, "As the Father has loved me, so I have loved you; abide in my love. If you keep my command-ments, you will abide in my love, just as I have kept my Father's commandments and abide in his love. I have said these things to you so that my joy may be in you, and that your joy may be complete."

- Jesus wants to set me free. I realize that I do not have to earn anything and become aware that I cannot do so. As I come before God, I loosen my grip on my own intentions and plans. Praying for freedom, I share the joy of Jesus.

- Jesus gives freely of the love of God, holding nothing back. I think of those people and situations that I deal with. I ask for the help I need to bring God's love to bear on them.

Friday 11th May   **John 15:12–17**

Jesus said to his disciples: "This is my commandment, that you love one another as I have loved you. No one has greater love than this, to lay down one's life for one's friends. You are my friends if you do what I command you. I do not call you servants any longer, because the servant does not know what the master is doing; but I have called you friends, because I have made known to you everything that I have heard from my Father. You did not choose me but I chose you. And I appointed you to go and bear fruit, fruit that will last, so that the Father will give you whatever you ask him in my name. I am giving you these commands so that you may love one another."

- Even though I may be happy to be a servant of Jesus, I realize that he calls me a friend. He wants me to know what is most important to him, what is closest to his heart.
- I arrange, plan, and organise my life in many ways. Jesus reminds me that it is he who has chosen me. I allow my priorities to fade and give in to what Jesus tells me: "I have chosen you."

Saturday 12th May   **John 15:18–21**

Jesus said to his disciples: "If the world hates you, be aware that it hated me before it hated you. If you belonged to the world, the world would love you as its own. Because you do not belong to the world, but I have chosen you out of the world—therefore the world hates you. Remember the word that I said to you, 'Servants are not greater than their master.' If they persecuted me, they will persecute you; if they kept my word, they will keep yours also. But they will do all these things to you on account of my name, because they do not know him who sent me."

- Having the last word and winning the argument do not appear to be temptations. I listen to Jesus and consider his words.
- I realize that he accepted that not everyone would follow in his way. I pray for the humility that I need.

may 13–19

Something to think and pray about each day this week:

Fullness of Life

With any of the parables, we look for the central message. It does not help to seek meaning in all the little details—that is not how the Jews would have heard them or how Jesus intended them. He would want to convey one main lesson, as in the parable of the talents. Here you have three men with different gifts. A talent was originally a coin or a weight, but through this parable it acquired the general meaning of a gift or an aptitude with which each of us is endowed. Some have more gifts than others—that is obvious. People have different temperaments, some more optimistic than others, a more or less attractive personality, more or less brains, a stronger or sicklier body, more or less beautiful hair, skin, face, body, and so on. Jesus is saying: Use everything you are given. Live your life to the full. Do not hide away the gifts the Lord gave you, whether of personality or of brains or whatever. The biggest tragedy is a life unlived. The fact that you are endowed in a different way from your brother or sister or parents or friends does not mean that you should hide away the abilities and personality you have. Use it to the full for other people. The central message is the real explanation: use everything you are given.

The Presence of God

Dear Jesus, today I call on You in a special way.
Mostly I come asking for favors.
Today I'd like just to be in Your presence.
Let my heart respond to Your love.

Freedom

"I am free."
When I look at these words in writing
they seem to create in me a feeling of awe—
yes, a wonderful feeling of freedom.
Thank You, God.

Consciousness

Lord, You gave me the night to rest in sleep.
In my waking hours may I not forget your goodness to me.
Guide me to share your blessings with others.

The Word

I read the Word of God slowly, a few times over, and I listen
to what God is saying to me. (Please turn to your scripture on
the following pages. Inspiration points are there should you need
them. When you are ready, return here to continue.)

Conversation

Dear Jesus, I can open up my heart to You.
I can tell You everything that troubles me.
I know You care about all the concerns in my life.
Teach me to live in the knowledge
that You who care for me today
will care for me tomorrow and all the days of my life.

Conclusion

Glory be to the Father, and to the Son, and to the Holy Spirit,
As it was in the beginning, is now, and ever shall be,
World without end. Amen.

Sunday 13th May,
Sixth Sunday of Easter   John 15:9–14

Jesus said to his disciples, "As the Father has loved me, so I have loved you; abide in my love. If you keep my commandments, you will abide in my love, just as I have kept my Father's commandments and abide in his love. I have said these things to you so that my joy may be in you, and that your joy may be complete. This is my commandment, that you love one another as I have loved you. No one has greater love than this, to lay down one's life for one's friends. You are my friends if you do what I command you."

- Jesus' commands are not just our duty but our path to joy and love in life. The love he means us to have is the love that is welcoming, accepting, and forgiving of others—lived out as best we can. It is the love that joins his followers together.

- Without this love, the following of Jesus is empty and dry. His way of life is not just taught but shown to us by the way he lives.

Monday 14th May,
St. Matthias, Apostle   John 15:15–17

Jesus said to his disciples, "I do not call you servants any longer, because the servant does not know what the master is doing; but I have called you friends, because I have made known to you everything that I have heard from my Father. You did not choose me but I chose you. And I appointed you to go and bear fruit, fruit that will last, so that the Father will give you whatever you ask him in my name. I am giving you these commands so that you may love one another."

- Jesus has sent me to bear fruit. With him, I look at the fruit of my life, not as a servant making a report, but as with a friend who knows how I have lived, knows the desires of my heart, and loves me.

- I show my faith by my life. I believe in the words of Jesus. I accept that Jesus has chosen me and allow myself to be affirmed by his choice.

Tuesday 15th May   John 16:5–11

Jesus said to his disciples, "But now I am going to him who sent me; yet none of you asks me, 'Where are you going?' But because I have said these things to you, sorrow has filled your hearts. Nevertheless I tell you the truth: it is to your advantage that I go away, for if I do not go away, the Advocate will not come to you; but if I go, I will send him to you. And when he comes, he will prove the world wrong about sin and righteousness and judgment: about sin, because they do not believe in me; about righteousness, because I am going to the Father and you will see me no longer; about judgment, because the ruler of this world has been condemned."

- There is so much commentary on television, or radio, on the internet, and in print; there are many opinions, judgments, and values. I allow some time to take to heart Jesus' assurance that only the Holy Spirit, the Advocate, brings a true understanding of sin, righteousness, and judgment.
- As I look at my life, I pray for the grace of the Holy Spirit to shed light, to bring truth, and to be the consolation that Jesus promises.

Wednesday 16th May   John 16:12–15

Jesus said, "I still have many things to say to you, but you cannot bear them now. When the Spirit of truth comes, he will guide you into all the truth; for he will not speak on his own, but will speak whatever he hears, and will declare to you the things that are to come. He will glorify me, because he will take what is mine and declare it to you. All that the Father has is mine. For this reason I said that he will take what is mine and declare it to you."

184

- The Father, Son, and Spirit are one; they act of one accord, seeking the same good. I am invited to find myself in their relationship to one another. I pray that I may grow in appreciation of the fact that I am created, redeemed, and made holy by God's continuing action and presence.

- As he promises us the Holy Spirit and offers us all that the Father has, Jesus gives fully of himself. I pray for generosity.

Thursday 17th May — John 16:19–20

Jesus said to his disciples, "Are you discussing among yourselves what I meant when I said, 'A little while, and you will no longer see me, and again a little while, and you will see me'? Very truly, I tell you, you will weep and mourn, but the world will rejoice; you will have pain, but your pain will turn into joy."

- Jesus knew what was in the disciples' hearts; he realised what they wanted to ask him. As I pray now, I know that Jesus sees what is in my heart and ask for the will of God to be revealed a little more to me.

- Reflecting on my life, I realize that there have been times of light and shade. I pray for all of those who are in darkness just now, that they may draw hope from Jesus' promises. I pray that all who rejoice may give thanks for God's blessings.

Friday 18th May — John 16:20–23

Jesus said to his disciples, "Very truly, I tell you, you will weep and mourn, but the world will rejoice; you will have pain, but your pain will turn into joy. When a woman is in labor, she has pain, because her hour has come. But when her child is born, she no longer remembers the anguish because of the joy of having brought a human being into the world. So you have pain now; but I will see you again, and your hearts will rejoice, and no one will take your joy from you. On that day you will ask nothing of me. Very truly, I tell you, if you ask anything of the Father in my name, he will give it to you."

- There is a deep-down joy that nothing can take from us. Perhaps you noticed this in a time of doubt, confusion, pain, or fear. It is a conviction that God is near and does not abandon us, and it lasts.
- Prayer can confirm this deep-down joy, when we return to it in memory, and the joy goes deeper. It is a joy born in times of life we may never have chosen, but it may emerge, with the grace of God, in times of confusion, doubt, pain, and personal darkness.

Saturday 19th May   John 16:23–24

Jesus said to his disciples, "Very truly, I tell you, if you ask anything of the Father in my name, he will give it to you. Until now you have not asked for anything in my name. Ask and you will receive, so that your joy may be complete."

- I have often come to God with my prayer, asking for what I need and for the needs of others.
- I take some time to consider how God has answered my prayer, allowing my joy to be more complete by recognizing, appreciating, and giving thanks.

Something to think and pray about each day this week:

Dying to Give Life
Jesus' image of the wheatgrain dying, then bearing fruit, symbolises not just our mortal life but the many times we die a little before our death: with every parting, moving of house or job, loss of a friend or dear one, loss of property. Can I think of any experience of suffering and loss that has borne fruit because of God's grace? How did it happen? To cling to what we have lost is to bury our life in the past. Even the most painful loss can be a new beginning. Lord, when I was suffering pain, and the loss of people and things I loved, I believe you were somehow present to me. Show me how you were.

The Presence of God
I remind myself that, as I sit here now,
God is gazing on me with love and holding me in being.
I pause for a moment and think of this.

Freedom
I need to close out the noise, to rise above the noise—
the noise that interrupts, that separates,
the noise that isolates.
I need to listen to God again.

Consciousness
In God's loving presence I unwind the past day,
starting from now and looking back, moment by moment.
I gather in all the goodness and light, in gratitude.
I attend to the shadows and what they say to me,
seeking healing, courage, forgiveness.

The Word
I take my time to read the Word of God, slowly, a few times, allowing myself to dwell on anything that strikes me. (Please turn to your scripture on the following pages. Inspiration points are there should you need them. When you are ready, return here to continue.)

Conversation
Do I notice myself reacting as I pray with the Word of God?
Do I feel challenged, comforted, angry?
Imagining Jesus sitting or standing by me,
I speak out my feelings, as one trusted friend to another.

Conclusion
Glory be to the Father, and to the Son, and to the Holy Spirit,
As it was in the beginning, is now, and ever shall be,
World without end. Amen.

Sunday 20th May,
Ascension of the Lord   Mark 16:15–20

And Jesus said to the disciples, "Go into all the world and proclaim the good news to the whole creation. The one who believes and is baptized will be saved; but the one who does not believe will be condemned. And these signs will accompany those who believe: by using my name they will cast out demons; they will speak in new tongues; they will pick up snakes in their hands, and if they drink any deadly thing, it will not hurt them; they will lay their hands on the sick, and they will recover." So then the Lord Jesus, after he had spoken to them, was taken up into heaven and sat down at the right hand of God. And they went out and proclaimed the good news everywhere, while the Lord worked with them and confirmed the message by the signs that accompanied it.

- The final departure of Jesus and the coming of the Holy Spirit gave new strength and energy to the group of disciples.
- The new message seems to transcend boundaries like language among people and illness within people. From heaven the Lord continues his work on earth through his followers.

Monday 21st May   John 16:29–33

The disciples said to Jesus, "Yes, now you are speaking plainly, not in any figure of speech! Now we know that you know all things, and do not need to have anyone question you; by this we believe that you came from God." Jesus answered them, "Do you now believe? The hour is coming, indeed it has come, when you will be scattered, each one to his home, and you will leave me alone. Yet I am not alone because the Father is with me. I have said this to you, so that in me you may have peace. In the world you face persecution. But take courage; I have conquered the world!"

- The prospect of being alone was not daunting to Jesus; he knew that his Father was with him.
- I think of all those others who use *Sacred Space* today—book or website—thousands of people all over the world, each in her and his own place. I may be alone, but I'm united with them in prayer, encouraged by their invisible companionship. I draw strength from remembering that when I pray, I am never alone.

Tuesday 22nd May   John 17:1–3

After Jesus had spoken these words, he looked up to heaven and said, "Father, the hour has come; glorify your Son so that the Son may glorify you, since you have given him authority over all people, to give eternal life to all whom you have given him. And this is eternal life, that they may know you, the only true God, and Jesus Christ whom you have sent."

- Jesus wants me to have eternal life and describes what that life is: to know God and to know Jesus. As I grow in knowledge of God I begin to taste the eternal life Jesus promises.
- I thank God for the light I have, for the quiet revelations and for the personal inspirations that have been given to me.

Wednesday 23rd May   John 17:18–19

Jesus said to the disciples, "Sanctify them in the truth; your word is truth. As you have sent me into the world, so I have sent them into the world. And for their sakes I sanctify myself, so that they also may be sanctified in truth."

- The words and actions of Jesus were never just for himself. His prayer was so that we might be sanctified in truth.

- I take some time to let myself be prayed for by Jesus, to pray with him, that I may be made whole and holy by what is true, preserved from anything that is false, misleading, or diminishing.

Thursday 24th May   John 17:20–21

Jesus looked up to heaven and said, "Father, I ask not only on behalf of these, but also on behalf of those who will believe in me through their word, that they may all be one. As you, Father, are in me and I am in you, may they also be in us, so that the world may believe that you have sent me."

- I am one of those who, through the words handed down by the disciples, now believe in Jesus. Here Jesus speaks of me, he prays for me, that I may be one with him and with his Father.
- Jesus draws me into life with the Father so that I may give witness. I accept now the nourishment that I need for my spirit, prayerfully considering the ways in which I am called to witness.

Friday 25th May   John 21:15–17

When they had finished breakfast, Jesus said to Simon Peter, "Simon son of John, do you love me more than these?" He said to him, "Yes, Lord; you know that I love you." Jesus said to him, "Feed my lambs." A second time he said to him, "Simon son of John, do you love me?" He said to him, "Yes, Lord; you know that I love you." Jesus said to him, "Tend my sheep." He said to him the third time, "Simon son of John, do you love me?" Peter felt hurt because he said to him the third time, "Do you love me?" And he said to him, "Lord, you know everything; you know that I love you." Jesus said to him, "Feed my sheep."

- Jesus asked Peter the question three times. Perhaps it was not that he wanted the answer, but he wanted Peter to hear himself profess his love.

- Not all of my love is expressed in my words. My faith is sometimes stumbling and inarticulate. I give thanks to God who attends to me at a level that is deeper than my words, who looks even beyond my actions, who values what is in my heart. I pray that I may give expression to God's very presence in me.

Saturday 26th May   John 21:20–25

Peter turned and saw the disciple whom Jesus loved following them; he was the one who had reclined next to Jesus at the supper and had said, "Lord, who is it that is going to betray you?" When Peter saw him, he said to Jesus, "Lord, what about him?" Jesus said to him, "If it is my will that he remain until I come, what is that to you? Follow me!" So the rumor spread in the community that this disciple would not die. Yet Jesus did not say to him that he would not die, but, "If it is my will that he remain until I come, what is that to you?" This is the disciple who is testifying to these things and has written them, and we know that his testimony is true. But there are also many other things that Jesus did; if every one of them were written down, I suppose that the world itself could not contain the books that would be written.

- Even as John concludes his gospel, he is aware that the words of Jesus may be misunderstood. I pray that I may be preserved from any misinterpretation of Jesus' words as I take this time in prayer, asking God to speak directly to my heart.
- John had a sense that the works of Jesus were many, and that numerous books might be written. Before God, I consider the works of Jesus in my life, giving thanks for the hidden and evident ways in which I have come to life. I think of myself as a "gospel," a testament to God's loving presence and action.

may 27–june 2

Something to think and pray about each day this week:

Living with the Spirit

Sometimes people say, "It would have been marvellous to be in Palestine when Jesus was there—then I would have no difficulty believing or praying." Maybe they forget how unsteady in faith the disciples were—until the day of Pentecost. That was when everything changed for them.

At the Last Supper Jesus spoke about sending them a new gift, the Paraclete. The original Greek word means several things: consoler, helper, protector, intercessor, or defence lawyer. Indeed, Jesus says that the presence of the Spirit will be "another" Paraclete for us. In other words, Jesus himself was our first friend and defender, but now the Spirit will continue his work in an even more intimate way—both "with you" and "in you" in the words of John 14:17. It is as if all of us believers are on trial before the hostile court called the "world," but we are not left defenceless. The Paraclete will be beside us, like a good advocate. Even more importantly, the Spirit will be within us to keep our hearts in tune with Christ and able to pray in the different circumstances of life.

The Presence of God
What is present to me is what has a hold on my becoming.
I reflect on the presence of God always there in love,
amidst the many things that have a hold on me.
I pause and pray that I may let God
affect my becoming in this precise moment.

Freedom
There are very few people
who realize what God would make of them
if they abandoned themselves into his hands,
and let themselves be formed by his grace (St. Ignatius).
I ask for the grace to trust myself totally to God's love.

Consciousness
In the presence of my loving Creator,
I look honestly at my feelings over the last day,
the highs, the lows, and the level ground.
Can I see where the Lord has been present?

The Word
God speaks to each one of us individually. I need to listen to what
he is saying to me. (Please turn to your scripture on the following
pages. Inspiration points are there should you need them. When
you are ready, return here to continue.)

Conversation
What is stirring in me as I pray?
Am I consoled, troubled, left cold?
I imagine Jesus himself standing or sitting at my side,
and share my feelings with him.

Conclusion
Glory be to the Father, and to the Son, and to the Holy Spirit,
As it was in the beginning, is now, and ever shall be,
World without end. Amen.

Sunday 27th May,
Feast of Pentecost   John 20:19–23

When it was evening on that day, the first day of the week, and the doors of the house where the disciples had met were locked for fear of the Jews, Jesus came and stood among them and said, "Peace be with you." After he said this, he showed them his hands and his side. Then the disciples rejoiced when they saw the Lord. Jesus said to them again, "Peace be with you. As the Father has sent me, so I send you." When he had said this, he breathed on them and said to them, "Receive the Holy Spirit. If you forgive the sins of any, they are forgiven them; if you retain the sins of any, they are retained."

- A great gift of the risen Lord is the forgiveness of our sins. The claim that he could forgive sins was one of the reasons he was brought to death, for only God could forgive.
- Forgiveness is given day by day in various ways. Through the community of the Church we are given the forgiveness of our sins. We need this gift and the grace of knowing that God is always the God of another chance, never remembering our sins forever.

Monday 28th May   Mark 10:17–27

As he was setting out on a journey, a man ran up and knelt before him, and asked him, "Good Teacher, what must I do to inherit eternal life?" Jesus said to him, "Why do you call me good? No one is good but God alone. You know the commandments: 'You shall not murder; You shall not commit adultery; You shall not steal; You shall not bear false witness; You shall not defraud; Honor your father and mother.'" He said to him, "Teacher, I have kept all these since my youth." Jesus, looking at him, loved him and said, "You lack one thing; go, sell what you own, and give the money to the poor, and you will have treasure in heaven; then come, follow me." When he heard this, he was shocked and went away grieving, for he had many possessions. Then Jesus looked around and said to his disciples, "How hard it will be for those who have wealth to enter the kingdom of God!"

- The young man felt as if he had been asked too much. His thought was only of himself and of the things to which he was attached. He could not see himself as Jesus saw him.
- I pray that I may not be trapped by my own view of myself as Jesus invites me to a new freedom.

Tuesday 29th May   Mark 10:28–30

Peter began to say to him, "Look, we have left everything and followed you." Jesus said, "Truly I tell you, there is no one who has left house or brothers or sisters or mother or father or children or fields, for my sake and for the sake of the good news, who will not receive a hundredfold now in this age—houses, brothers and sisters, mothers and children, and fields, with persecutions—and in the age to come eternal life."

- Peter's experience as a fisherman told him that taking stock was necessary from time to time. Although he was often enthusiastic and spontaneous, now he seems to panic as he suddenly realises that he may be left with nothing.
- I pray for a deeper trust and faith in the message of Jesus, in his presence to me. Aware of anything that causes me to be too cautious and calculating, I ask for God's help.

Wednesday 30th May   Mark 10:32–34

They were on the road, going up to Jerusalem, and Jesus was walking ahead of them; they were amazed, and those who followed were afraid. He took the twelve aside again and began to tell them what was to happen to him, saying, "See, we are going up to Jerusalem, and the Son of Man will be handed over to the chief priests and the scribes, and they will condemn him to death; then they will hand him over to the Gentiles; they will mock him, and spit upon him, and flog him, and kill him; and after three days he will rise again."

- Jesus was never far from the disciples as they travelled. Although he may have walked ahead, he often stopped to take them aside and to help them understand his message and his presence.
- I pray that I may grow in awareness of my need for Jesus to call me aside, even as he shares my journey. Jesus knows that I need these times of intimacy if I am to grow in friendship.

Thursday 31st May,
Visitation of the Virgin Mary   Luke 1:39–45

In those days Mary set out and went with haste to a Judean town in the hill country, where she entered the house of Zechariah and greeted Elizabeth. When Elizabeth heard Mary's greeting, the child leaped in her womb. And Elizabeth was filled with the Holy Spirit and exclaimed with a loud cry, "Blessed are you among women, and blessed is the fruit of your womb. And why has this happened to me, that the mother of my Lord comes to me? For as soon as I heard the sound of your greeting, the child in my womb leaped for joy. And blessed is she who believed that there would be a fulfillment of what was spoken to her by the Lord."

- Elizabeth's joyful greeting of Mary must have come from years of thinking like this. Being familiar with counting her blessings and realizing their origin, she was able to recognize Mary and give thanks to God.

- I bring before the Lord in my prayer all the people who help me to be a disciple. I call to mind especially those who make me smile, giving thanks and praying for them.

Friday 1st June   Mark 11:15–18

They came to Jerusalem. And Jesus entered the temple and began to drive out those who were selling and those who were buying in the temple, and he overturned the tables of the money-changers and the seats of those who sold doves; and he would not allow anyone to carry anything through the temple. He was teaching and saying, "Is it not written, 'My house shall be called a house of prayer for all the nations'? But you have made it a den of robbers." And when the chief priests and the scribes heard it, they kept looking for a way to kill him; for they were afraid of him, because the whole crowd was spellbound by his teaching.

- Jesus resisted everything that came between God and people.
- I pray that I may really hear his message and be drawn into the very life of God, that I too may be spellbound by his teaching.

Saturday 2nd June   Mark 11:27–33

Again they came to Jerusalem. As he was walking in the temple, the chief priests, the scribes, and the elders came to him and said, "By what authority are you doing these things? Who gave you this authority to do them?" Jesus said to them, "I will ask you one question; answer me, and I will tell you by what authority I do these things. Did the baptism of John come from heaven, or was it of human origin? Answer me." They argued with one another, "If we say, 'From heaven', he will say, 'Why then did you not believe him?' But shall we say, 'Of human origin'?"—they were afraid of the crowd, for all regarded John as truly a prophet. So they answered Jesus, "We do not know." And

Jesus said to them, "Neither will I tell you by what authority I am doing these things."

- Jesus spoke openly to the disciples to help them to understand what he meant, but he was careful not to not become involved in refined argument meant to trap him.
- I take care to approach the Word of God with reverence, not looking for food for thought, not seeking a teaching for others, but taking time to listen to Jesus who wants to converse with me.

june 3–9

Something to think and pray about each day this week:

The Light of Jesus

Light remains bright even if nobody is seeing it. There were times when Christians needed the metaphor of the light of the world, the city on a hill, in times of persecution, for instance, when it gave us an identity and enabled us to survive. Now two things have changed: the global culture has grown more secular, and many religious leaders have been found to be masking crimes of others. One result: we may be afraid to put our heads above the parapet, or even to preach the Gospel, and when we do, we are liable to make fools of ourselves. Perhaps it is time for another image of the Church: yeast in the dough, working for good even when unseen.

Yeast is a less attractive image than light. If there is anything of the exhibitionist in us, this image will discover it. Young priests and religious can feel sad when their initial ambition to serve is rebuffed. Jesus showed the same disappointment over Jerusalem, over Nazareth and his own people, over the rich young man. His commitment did not waver, though he offered an option to his disciples, "Will you also go away?" Few of us could have improved on Peter's reply, "Lord, to whom should we go? You have the message of eternal life."

The Presence of God
"I stand at the door and knock," says the Lord.
What a wonderful privilege
that the Lord of all creation desires to come to me.
I welcome His presence.

Freedom
Lord, grant me the grace to be free from the excesses of this life.
Let me not get caught up with the desire for wealth.
Keep my heart and mind free to love and serve You.

Consciousness
"There is a time and place for everything," as the saying goes.
Lord, grant that I may always desire
to spend time in your presence, to hear your call.

The Word
God speaks to each one of us individually. I need to listen to what
he is saying to me. (Please turn to your scripture on the following
pages. Inspiration points are there should you need them. When
you are ready, return here to continue.)

Conversation
The gift of speech is a wonderful gift.
May I use this gift with kindness.
May I be slow to utter harsh words,
hurtful words, and words spoken in anger.

Conclusion
Glory be to the Father, and to the Son, and to the Holy Spirit,
As it was in the beginning, is now, and ever shall be,
World without end. Amen.

Sunday 3rd June, Trinity Sunday   Matthew 28:16–20

Now the eleven disciples went to Galilee, to the mountain to which Jesus had directed them. When they saw him, they worshiped him; but some doubted. And Jesus came and said to them, "All authority in heaven and on earth has been given to me. Go therefore and make disciples of all nations, baptizing them in the name of the Father and of the Son and of the Holy Spirit, and teaching them to obey everything that I have commanded you. And remember, I am with you always, to the end of the age."

- The name of God at our Baptism is the name of love—the Trinity exists in a community of love. Each time we make the Sign of the Cross, we place on our bodies the badge of love.
- Love has brought us into being, has introduced us into the community of Jesus in the Church, and love in Jesus Christ is with us all our days, and with God's world until the end of time.

Monday 4th June   Psalm 90 (91):1–2, 14–16

You who live in the shelter of the Most High, who abide in the shadow of the Almighty, will say to the Lord, "My refuge and my fortress; my God, in whom I trust." Those who love me, I will deliver; I will protect those who know my name. When they call to me, I will answer them; I will be with them in trouble, I will rescue them and honor them. With long life I will satisfy them, and show them my salvation.

- Trusting God is at the heart of our spiritual life, and "abiding" is an important expression of that trust in the psalms. The word marks a peaceful, confident, and enduring relationship with God.
- God is present with those who strive to be present with God; abiding with God is a mutual and not a one-sided relationship. As Jesus

said, "As the Father has loved me, so I have loved you; abide in my love" (John 15:9).

Tuesday 5th June   **Mark 12:13–17**

Then they sent to Jesus some Pharisees and some Herodians to trap him in what he said. And they came and said to him, "Teacher, we know that you are sincere, and show deference to no one; for you do not regard people with partiality, but teach the way of God in accordance with truth. Is it lawful to pay taxes to the emperor, or not? Should we pay them, or should we not?" But knowing their hypocrisy, he said to them, "Why are you putting me to the test? Bring me a denarius and let me see it." And they brought one. Then he said to them, "Whose head is this, and whose title?" They answered, "The emperor's." Jesus said to them, "Give to the emperor the things that are the emperor's, and to God the things that are God's." And they were utterly amazed at him.

- People have worked on this reply of Jesus, some hankering for revolution against an oppressive regime, some trying to bolster their conservatism. What is your answer, Lord?
- You hungered and thirsted for justice and heard the cry of the poor. In all your preaching you championed the cause of the destitute. But you sought change by peaceful means, even turning the other cheek to violence.

Wednesday 6th June   **2 Timothy 1:1–3, 6–8**

Paul, an apostle of Christ Jesus by the will of God, for the sake of the promise of life that is in Christ Jesus, To Timothy, my beloved child: Grace, mercy, and peace from God the Father and Christ Jesus our Lord. I am grateful to God—whom I worship with a clear conscience, as my ancestors did—when I remember you constantly in my prayers night and day. For this reason I remind you to rekindle the gift of God that is within you through the laying on of my hands; for God did not give us a spirit of cowardice, but rather a spirit of power and of love and of self-discipline.

- I bring the people who are in my heart and mind before God, as Paul brought Timothy.
- I give thanks for the gifts I have received. I consider the gifts I ask for in their names. I pray for a strengthening of the spirit of power, love, and self-discipline.

Thursday 7th June   2 Timothy 2:8–13

Remember Jesus Christ, raised from the dead, a descendant of David—that is my gospel, for which I suffer hardship, even to the point of being chained like a criminal. But the Word of God is not chained. Therefore I endure everything for the sake of the elect, so that they may also obtain the salvation that is in Christ Jesus, with eternal glory. The saying is sure: If we have died with him, we will also live with him; if we endure, we will also reign with him; if we deny him, he will also deny us; if we are faithless, he remains faithful—for he cannot deny himself.

- "The Word of God is not chained." I pray that I may not impose limits on God's word for me. I ask that I be able to let it lead me to freedom.
- Jesus identifies fully with us; he will never deny us. I think of how I might identify more closely with Jesus in my life now.

Friday 8th June   2 Timothy 3:16–17

All scripture is inspired by God and is useful for teaching, for reproof, for correction, and for training in righteousness, so that everyone who belongs to God may be proficient, equipped for every good work.

- Paul describes how the Word of God is alive and active working in many different ways.
- Do I listen to the Word of God for my comfort or assurance, or do I hear only what challenges me? When the prayer conversation is real, I will understand how God speaks to me in different ways—always for my good.

Saturday 9th June **2 Timothy 4:1–8**

In the presence of God and of Christ Jesus, who is to judge the living and the dead, and in view of his appearing and his kingdom, I solemnly urge you: proclaim the message; be persistent whether the time is favorable or unfavorable; convince, rebuke, and encourage, with the utmost patience in teaching. For the time is coming when people will not put up with sound doctrine, but having itching ears, they will accumulate for themselves teachers to suit their own desires, and will turn away from listening to the truth and wander away to myths. As for you, always be sober, endure suffering, do the work of an evangelist, carry out your ministry fully.

- Paul encourages me to think of myself as an evangelist. I consider how I bring good news to the people among whom I live.
- I sometimes have "itching ears," ready to hear messages that suit me. I bring what distracts me before God, that I may see more clearly what is liable to distract me and lead me away from the happiness God intends for me.

june 10–16

Something to think and pray about each day this week:

Mary, the Handmaid

Over the centuries, religious people have done strange things to Mary as she appears in the gospels. She is sometimes called a queen, a strange-sounding title today, when queens, where they exist, are largely decorative and symbolic figures. Queenship is a redundant job, as computer programming may be in a hundred years. It was a questionable way of managing a society, open to corruption, and unworthy of Mary. We find her words are spare, in the first and third chapter of Luke, and at Cana. She is the handmaid (not queen) in Nazareth and the wise mother at Cana, giving her son a push to start his public life. The second verse of the Angelus sums her up best, "Behold the handmaid of the Lord. Be it done to me according to your word." It speaks of how God can work through us if we allow his word to work in us.

The Presence of God
I remind myself that, as I sit here now,
God is gazing on me with love and holding me in being.
I pause for a moment and think of this.

Freedom
I need to close out the noise, to rise above the noise—
the noise that interrupts, that separates,
the noise that isolates.
I need to listen to God again.

Consciousness
In God's loving presence I unwind the past day,
starting from now and looking back, moment by moment.
I gather in all the goodness and light, in gratitude.
I attend to the shadows and what they say to me,
seeking healing, courage, forgiveness.

The Word
I take my time to read the Word of God, slowly, a few times, allowing myself to dwell on anything that strikes me. (Please turn to your scripture on the following pages. Inspiration points are there should you need them. When you are ready, return here to continue.)

Conversation
Do I notice myself reacting as I pray with the Word of God?
Do I feel challenged, comforted, angry?
Imagining Jesus sitting or standing by me,
I speak out my feelings, as one trusted friend to another.

Conclusion
Glory be to the Father, and to the Son, and to the Holy Spirit,
As it was in the beginning, is now, and ever shall be,
World without end. Amen.

Sunday 10th June,
Feast of the Body and Blood of Christ   Mark 14:12–16

On the first day of Unleavened Bread, when the Passover lamb is sacrificed, his disciples said to him, "Where do you want us to go and make the preparations for you to eat the Passover?" So he sent two of his disciples, saying to them, "Go into the city, and a man carrying a jar of water will meet you; follow him, and wherever he enters, say to the owner of the house, 'The Teacher asks, "Where is my guest room where I may eat the Passover with my disciples?"' He will show you a large room upstairs, furnished and ready. Make preparations for us there." So the disciples set out and went to the city, and found everything as he had told them; and they prepared the Passover meal.

- At this Passover meal, Jesus broke the bread and poured the wine which would be forever the action of his love among us. As he ate the Passover with the disciples, so now we eat and drink with him, the sacramental sign of his presence and his love among us.
- Faith nourished in prayer leads us to the Eucharist, the sign of unity and of mission in his people.

Monday 11th June   1 Kings 17:1–6

Now Elijah the Tishbite, of Tishbe in Gilead, said to Ahab, "As the Lord the God of Israel lives, before whom I stand, there shall be neither dew nor rain these years, except by my word." The word of the Lord came to him, saying, "Go from here and turn eastwards, and hide yourself by the Wadi Cherith, which is east of the Jordan. You shall drink from the wadi, and I have commanded the ravens to feed you there." So he went and did according to the word of the Lord; he went and lived by the Wadi Cherith, which is east of the Jordan. The ravens brought him bread and meat in the morning, and bread and meat in the evening; and he drank from the wadi.

- The image of the ravens bringing forward food to Elijah is often used as a sign of God's providence. I give thanks to God for the nourishment I receive.
- I think of the unexpected means and unlikely messengers that give me food on life's journey. Like Elijah, I listen for the Word of God, who wants to draw me to sources of life.

Tuesday 12th June   1 Kings 17:7–16

When Elijah came to the gate of the town, a widow was there gathering sticks; he called to her and said, "Bring me a little water in a vessel, so that I may drink." As she was going to bring it, he called to her and said, "Bring me a morsel of bread in your hand." But she said, "As the Lord your God lives, I have nothing baked, only a handful of meal in a jar, and a little oil in a jug; I am now gathering a couple of sticks, so that I may go home and prepare it for myself and my son, that we may eat it, and die." Elijah said to her, "Do not be afraid; go and do as you have said; but first make me a little cake of it and bring it to me, and afterwards make something for yourself and your son. For thus says the Lord the God of Israel: The jar of meal will not be emptied and the jug of oil will not fail until the day that the Lord sends rain on the earth." She went and did as Elijah said, so that she as well as he and her household ate for many days. The jar of meal was not emptied, neither did the jug of oil fail, according to the word of the Lord that he spoke by Elijah.

- I pray that I may continue to be generous, even when I see no immediate or obvious promise of reward.

- Elijah acknowledged and encouraged the woman's generosity. I consider how I might recognize and strengthen the presence of the Spirit of God in the people I encounter.

Wednesday 13th June,
St. Anthony of Padua   Psalm 16:5, 8, 11

The Lord is my chosen portion and my cup; you hold my lot. I keep the Lord always before me; because he is at my right hand, I shall not be moved. You show me the path of life. In your presence there is fullness of joy; in your right hand are pleasures for evermore.

- The psalmist rests in God, knowing a deep security in God's presence. I allow myself to be assured of God's presence and care.
- God holds blessings and goodness in store for me. I lay aside my preoccupations and requests so that I may receive what God has to offer to me.

Thursday 14th June   Psalm 65:10–11, 12–13

You water its furrows abundantly, settling its ridges, softening it with showers, and blessing its growth. You crown the year with your bounty; your wagon tracks overflow with richness. The pastures of the wilderness overflow, the hills gird themselves with joy, the meadows clothe themselves with flocks, the valleys deck themselves with grain, they shout and sing together with joy.

- The psalmist describes the abundance of creation, recognizing God as the source of goodness.
- I picture the bountifulness that the psalm describes, the abundance of grain, flocks, and flowers. I give thanks to God for the beauty of creation as I experience it, considering how my life depends on the fruits of the earth.

Friday 15th June,
Feast of the Sacred Heart   John 19:31–37

Since it was the day of Preparation, the Jews did not want the bodies left on the cross during the sabbath, especially because that sabbath was a day of great solemnity. So they asked Pilate to have the legs of the crucified men broken and the bodies removed. Then the soldiers came and broke the legs of the first and of the other who had been crucified with him. But when they came to Jesus and saw that he was already dead, they did not break his legs. Instead, one of the soldiers pierced his side with a spear, and at once blood and water came out. (He who saw this has testified so that you also may believe. His testimony is true, and he knows that he tells the truth.) These things occurred so that the scripture might be fulfilled, "None of his bones shall be broken." And again another passage of scripture says, "They will look on the one whom they have pierced."

- The flow of blood and water from the body of Jesus has always been seen as a picture of the birth of his new community, evoking the water of Baptism and the blood poured in the Eucharist.
- In the very body of death is the risen life of God in Jesus. Resurrection happens from the dead body—just as the life of Jesus is found in the ordinary, daily life of us all.

Saturday 16th June   Matthew 5:33–37

Jesus said to the crowds, "Again, you have heard that it was said to those of ancient times, 'You shall not swear falsely, but carry out the vows you have made to the Lord.' But I say to you, Do not swear at all, either by heaven, for it is the throne of God, or by the earth, for it is his footstool, or by Jerusalem, for it is the city of the great King. And do not swear by your head, for you

212

cannot make one hair white or black. Let your word be 'Yes, Yes' or 'No, No'; anything more than this comes from the evil one."

- Jesus shows us that calling on God as witness is something of great importance. This attitude may come into all our lives.
- There are times when we bow to the glory of God in life and in prayer, and know that we belong to Someone much greater than ourselves, the One who made heaven and earth.

june 17–23

Something to think and pray about each day this week:

Exposing the Power of Love

Look hard at a crucifix. It is sometimes fashioned to look beautiful, in precious materials that gloss over its obscenity: a human being nailed up to a wooden gibbet to die in public. To those who have suffered grievously, from pain or betrayal or other people's malice, the crucifix is precious precisely because it shows the Son of God exposed to irrational evil, to gross injustice, or to an agonising, lonely death, as so many people are exposed. There are times when it is the only religious image that makes sense. I think of a wife whose world was collapsing as she discovered the infidelity of her husband; she kept her sanity by clinging to the crucifix on her rosary and joining her agony to that of Jesus. His last words, "Father forgive them," are consoling because they show the power of love to overcome evil, a real triumph in contrast to the empty Hosannahs of Palm Sunday.

The Presence of God
For a few moments, I think of God's veiled presence in things:
in the elements, giving them existence;
in plants, giving them life; in animals, giving them sensation;
and finally, in me, giving me all this and more,
making me a temple, a dwelling-place of the Spirit.

Freedom
God is not foreign to my freedom.
Instead the Spirit breathes life into my most intimate desires,
gently nudging me towards all that is good.
I ask for the grace to let myself be enfolded by the Spirit.

Consciousness
Knowing that God loves me unconditionally,
I can afford to be honest about how I am.
How has the last day been, and how do I feel now?
I share my feelings openly with the Lord.

The Word
I take my time to read the Word of God, slowly, a few times, allowing myself to dwell on anything that strikes me. (Please turn to your scripture on the following pages. Inspiration points are there should you need them. When you are ready, return here to continue.)

Conversation
How has God's Word moved me? Has it left me cold?
Has it consoled me or moved me to act in a new way?
I imagine Jesus standing or sitting beside me;
I turn and share my feelings with him.

Conclusion
Glory be to the Father, and to the Son, and to the Holy Spirit,
As it was in the beginning, is now, and ever shall be,
World without end. Amen.

216

Sunday 17th June,
Eleventh Sunday in Ordinary Time   Mark 4:26–29

Jesus said to the crowd, "The kingdom of God is as if someone would scatter seed on the ground, and would sleep and rise night and day, and the seed would sprout and grow, he does not know how. The earth produces of itself, first the stalk, then the head, then the full grain in the head. But when the grain is ripe, at once he goes in with his sickle, because the harvest has come."

- Perhaps this parable of the seed tells us that Jesus has scattered the seed, the word, and though it may seem to us that nothing dramatic may seem to be happening, growth is taking place. The rest, the "harvest," happens in God's good time, not in ours.
- Does this bring to mind any frustrations I feel, with myself or with others? Can I speak with the Lord about this?

Monday 18th June   Matthew 5:38–42

Jesus said to the crowds, "You have heard that it was said, 'An eye for an eye and a tooth for a tooth.' But I say to you, do not resist an evildoer. But if anyone strikes you on the right cheek, turn the other also; and if anyone wants to sue you and take your coat, give your cloak as well; and if anyone forces you to go one mile, go also the second mile. Give to everyone who begs from you, and do not refuse anyone who wants to borrow from you."

- I try to listen to these words of Jesus not as law giving, perhaps not even as a sermon, but as a message that is given for my freedom.
- Jesus wants me to be free of limits that I may have set upon myself by imagining others wrongly. I pray that attitudes and actions may change by my acting in the freedom that Jesus gives.

Tuesday 19th June   Matthew 5:43–48

Jesus said to the crowds, "You have heard that it was said, 'You shall love your neighbor and hate your enemy.' But I say to you, love your enemies and pray for those who persecute you, so that you may be children of your Father in heaven; for he makes his sun rise on the evil and on the good, and sends rain on the righteous and on the unrighteous. For if you love those who love you, what reward do you have? Do not even the tax collectors do the same? And if you greet only your brothers and sisters, what more are you doing than others? Do not even the Gentiles do the same? Be perfect, therefore, as your heavenly Father is perfect."

- Inspired by the words of Jesus, I bring to mind those people I have learned to distrust. I place them before God. If I can, I ask God to bless them; if I cannot, I ask for the grace I need to wish them well.
- I think of the people in my community and pray for them. I look beyond them and consider who else might also need my prayer and action for their good.

Wednesday 20th June   Matthew 6:5–6

Jesus said to the disciples, "Whenever you pray, go into your room and shut the door and pray to your Father who is in secret; and your Father who sees in secret will reward you."

- I take this time in the room of my heart, assured that God is with me. I draw strength from Jesus' telling me that God sees what is in the secret of my heart.
- As I pray that I may receive the reward that God has in heart for me, I take care to consider if there are any blessings in the last few days that I may not have appreciated.
- I give thanks to God for this moment of prayer. I ask that I may grow in the love of God, serve others joyfully, and be blessed myself.

Thursday 21st June,
St. Aloysius Gonzaga   Matthew 6:7–15

Then Jesus looked around and said to his disciples, "How hard it will be for those who have wealth to enter the kingdom of God!" And the disciples were perplexed at these words. But Jesus said to them again, "Children, how hard it is to enter the kingdom of God! It is easier for a camel to go through the eye of a needle than for someone who is rich to enter the kingdom of God." They were greatly astounded and said to one another, "Then who can be saved?" Jesus looked at them and said, "For mortals it is impossible, but not for God; for God all things are possible."

- Jesus gives us a model of prayer in the Our Father. The prayer begins with a focus on God. I wonder if my prayer is sometimes focused on me, beginning with my situation, my wants, my perception.
- I pray that I may receive from God what I need and that I may be generous and free in my giving to others. I see that everything I give comes from God.

Friday 22nd June   Matthew 6:19–21

Jesus said to his disciples, "Do not store up for yourselves treasures on earth, where moth and rust consume and where thieves break in and steal; but store up for yourselves treasures in heaven, where neither moth nor rust consumes and where thieves do not break in and steal. For where your treasure is, there your heart will be also."

- The world often teaches me to want more, to gather and accumulate. In this time of prayer I can admit whether I am restless to have more. I take care to note whether my treasure is in the right place, and I ask for God's help.
- I think of what I admire, of what attracts my attention and arouses my desire. I bring this before God so that I may see whether this

is something that is for my true enlightenment or something from which I might turn away.

Saturday 23rd June   Matthew 6:25–34

J esus said to his disciples, "Therefore I tell you, do not worry about your life, what you will eat or what you will drink, or about your body, what you will wear. Is not life more than food, and the body more than clothing? Look at the birds of the air; they neither sow nor reap nor gather into barns, and yet your heavenly Father feeds them. Are you not of more value than they? And can any of you by worrying add a single hour to your span of life? And why do you worry about clothing? Consider the lilies of the field, how they grow; they neither toil nor spin, yet I tell you, even Solomon in all his glory was not clothed like one of these. But if God so clothes the grass of the field, which is alive today and tomorrow is thrown into the oven, will he not much more clothe you—you of little faith? Therefore do not worry, saying, 'What will we eat?' or 'What will we drink?' or 'What will we wear?' For it is the Gentiles who strive for all these things; and indeed your heavenly Father knows that you need all these things. But strive first for the kingdom of God and his righteousness, and all these things will be given to you as well. So do not worry about tomorrow, for tomorrow will bring worries of its own. Today's trouble is enough for today."

- I listen to Jesus' words not just as advice. I also take time to consider how he lived them out. I think of the difference his living freely made in the lives of others and continues to make in mine.
- Following Jesus' advice, I think of how I might take time to consider the natural world. I plan to spend some time with a plant or watching the birds.

Something to think and pray about each day this week:

The Gentle Presence

Jesus invites to himself all those who labor and are burdened. The phrase "comfort zone" is used of the state where we feel life is under control and satisfactory. Jesus is inviting those who are not in the comfort zone, who feel oppressed by anxiety and uncertainty. I am often weary, Lord, and my burden feels heavy on me. When I look at Christians, some of them indeed seem relaxed and easy in your company. Others appear uptight and driven, not restful people to be near. You are a gentle, humble presence. If I feel under pressure in prayer, something is wrong. It is a sign of your presence to me that my soul feels rested.

The Presence of God
At any time of the day or night we can call on Jesus.
He is always waiting, listening for our call.
What a wonderful blessing.
No phone needed, no e-mail, just a whisper.

Freedom
Lord, grant me the grace to be free from the excesses of this life.
Let me not get caught up with the desire for wealth.
Keep my heart and mind free to love and serve You.

Consciousness
I exist in a web of relationships—links to nature, people, God.
I trace out these links, giving thanks
for the life that flows through them.
Some links are twisted or broken:
I may feel regret, anger, disappointment.
I pray for the gift of acceptance and forgiveness.

The Word
God speaks to each one of us individually. I need to listen to what
he is saying to me. (Please turn to your scripture on the following
pages. Inspiration points are there should you need them. When
you are ready, return here to continue.)

Conversation
Remembering that I am still in God's presence,
I imagine Jesus himself standing or sitting beside me,
and say whatever is on my mind, whatever is in my heart,
speaking as one friend to another.

Conclusion
Glory be to the Father, and to the Son, and to the Holy Spirit,
As it was in the beginning, is now, and ever shall be,
World without end. Amen.

Sunday 24th June,
Birth of St. John the Baptist   Luke 1:57–66

Now the time came for Elizabeth to give birth, and she bore a son. Her neighbors and relatives heard that the Lord had shown his great mercy to her, and they rejoiced with her. On the eighth day they came to circumcise the child, and they were going to name him Zechariah after his father. But his mother said, "No; he is to be called John." They said to her, "None of your relatives has this name." Then they began motioning to his father to find out what name he wanted to give him. He asked for a writing tablet and wrote, "His name is John." And all of them were amazed. Immediately his mouth was opened and his tongue freed, and he began to speak, praising God. Fear came over all their neighbors, and all these things were talked about throughout the entire hill country of Judea. All who heard them pondered them and said, "What then will this child become?" For, indeed, the hand of the Lord was with him.

- Zechariah and Elizabeth were very much people of tradition, yet they were able to turn aside from the practiced and the usual to follow the prompting of God. As I bring my life before God I ask that I may recognize where my habits have dulled my awareness of God's prompting.
- My expectations of others and of myself are sometimes limiting. I pray for freedom and for courage.

Monday 25th June   Matthew 7:1–5

Jesus said to the disciples, "Do not judge, so that you may not be judged. For with the judgment you make you will be judged, and the measure you give will be the measure you get. Why do you see the speck in your neighbor's eye, but do not notice the log in your own eye? Or how can you say to your neighbor, 'Let me take the speck out of your eye,' while the log is in your own eye? You hypocrite, first take the log out of your own eye, and then you will see clearly to take the speck out of your neighbor's eye."

- As I ask God to look upon me lovingly and to judge me favorably, I try to do the same for others. I pray for forgiveness and ask God's help to be more forgiving myself.
- The world is complex: sometimes it seems easier to turn away from it, to switch it all off. I remember that, even with all the information that is made available, not everything is known. I pray with compassion for all who are judged hastily or harshly.

Tuesday 26th June   **Matthew 7:12–14**

Jesus said, "In everything do to others as you would have them do to you; for this is the law and the prophets. Enter through the narrow gate; for the gate is wide and the road is easy that leads to destruction, and there are many who take it. For the gate is narrow and the road is hard that leads to life, and there are few who find it."

- I bring to mind how I will spend my day and picture how I might keep this simple statement of Jesus before me. I know it is not just a billboard statement or an advertising motto. I pray that it may become my rule of life.
- Jesus asks me to follow through a narrow gate and on a hard road. Even as I consider what that means to me, I allow myself to hear Jesus invite me to be with him on this journey.

Wednesday 27th June   **Matthew 7:15–20**

Jesus told the crowds, "Beware of false prophets, who come to you in sheep's clothing but inwardly are ravenous wolves. You will know them by their fruits. Are grapes gathered from thorns, or figs from thistles? In the same way, every good tree bears good fruit, but the bad tree bears bad fruit. A good tree cannot bear bad fruit, nor can a bad tree bear good fruit. Every tree that does not bear good fruit is cut down and thrown into the fire. Thus you will know them by their fruits."

- Jesus promised me the Holy Spirit who enriches my life and is evident in my attitudes, words, and actions. As I turn away from false prophets and seek guidance of those who may truly help me, I ask the Spirit for guidance.
- I think of the fruits that I have prayed for in the past or pray for now. I ask God to help me to appreciate where these fruits may be budding, present now, or already given away. I pray that I may recognize fruits that I did not ask for but which God has generously given.

Thursday 28th June   Matthew 7:24–27

Jesus said to his disciples, "Everyone then who hears these words of mine and acts on them will be like a wise man who built his house on rock. The rain fell, the floods came, and the winds blew and beat on that house, but it did not fall, because it had been founded on rock. And everyone who hears these words of mine and does not act on them will be like a foolish man who built his house on sand. The rain fell, and the floods came, and the winds blew and beat against that house, and it fell—and great was its fall!"

- Jesus uses the everyday example of building on rock. We can think of coastal erosion, and picture a house gradually collapsing on a cliff edge. Foundations are weak. Soon the house will disappear.
- The same is true for our decisions and purposes in life. If we build on the sands of finance, reputation, control, we can collapse. Love

of God and love of neighbour are the rock of a life that is fully human, fully alive, fully Christ-like.

Friday 29th June,
Sts. Peter and Paul, Apostles   Matthew 16:13–19

Now when Jesus came into the district of Caesarea Philippi, he asked his disciples, "Who do people say that the Son of Man is?" And they said, "Some say John the Baptist, but others Elijah, and still others Jeremiah or one of the prophets." He said to them, "But who do you say that I am?" Simon Peter answered, "You are the Messiah, the Son of the living God." And Jesus answered him, "Blessed are you, Simon son of Jonah! For flesh and blood has not revealed this to you, but my Father in heaven. And I tell you, you are Peter, and on this rock I will build my church, and the gates of Hades will not prevail against it. I will give you the keys of the kingdom of heaven, and whatever you bind on earth will be bound in heaven, and whatever you loose on earth will be loosed in heaven."

- I take care to let nothing come between me and my conversation with God. No spiritual reading, no inspiration point will answer the question that God asked of me, "Who do you say that I am?"
- I express who God is to me by the way I live; it becomes evident to others by what I say and by what I do. I pray that my faith in the living God may be seen in my words and actions.

Saturday 30th June   Matthew 8:5–13

When he entered Capernaum, a centurion came to him, appealing to him and saying, "Lord, my servant is lying at home paralyzed, in terrible distress." And he said to him, "I will come and cure him." The centurion answered, "Lord, I am not worthy to have you come under my roof; but only speak the word, and my servant will be healed. For I also am a man under

authority, with soldiers under me; and I say to one, 'Go,' and he
goes, and to another, 'Come,' and he comes, and to my slave,
'Do this,' and the slave does it." When Jesus heard him, he was
amazed and said to those who followed him, "Truly I tell you,
in no one in Israel have I found such faith. I tell you, many will
come from east and west and will eat with Abraham and Isaac
and Jacob in the kingdom of heaven, while the heirs of the kingdom will be thrown into the outer darkness, where there will be
weeping and gnashing of teeth." And to the centurion Jesus said,
"Go; let it be done for you according to your faith." And the
servant was healed in that hour.

- Here we see yet another counter-cultural action of Jesus. He offers
  to go to the house of a Gentile, an action which would make him
  unclean in the eyes of the disciples and the usual crowd that followed him.
- Jesus' life and prayer showed him that the narrow definitions of
  race, gender, and holiness were false. One eye went to those who
  welcomed him, and the other eye looked to whoever might be
  called the "outsider." We may feel like an "outsider" to God sometimes. That's a particularly rich moment for prayer if we can bring
  it honestly before God in our prayer.

july 1–7

Something to think and pray about each day this week:

Sharing the Burden

"My yoke is easy and my burden light." Lord, these lovely words are sometimes linked to a picture of you in pastel shades, in a montage of roses and golden light. But it takes strength and courage to remain gentle in face of false accusations and scheming enemies. It is you who are the strong one, not the screamers and warmongers. You call it a yoke, Lord; and indeed it rests on me from the outside. Yet it fits me as though I was made for it, this love of you. Once I am joined with you, the burden becomes light and the yoke easy. I find rest in you. "Can one reach God by toil?" asked W. B. Yeats. "He gives himself to the pure in heart. He asks nothing but our attention." Do I feel your yoke as easy and well fitting, Lord? If I feel it as a burden, then it is not your yoke I am carrying.

The Presence of God

God is with me; but more,
God is within me, giving me existence.
Let me dwell for a moment on God's life-giving presence
in my body, my mind, my heart,
and in the whole of my life.

Freedom

God is not foreign to my freedom.
Instead the Spirit breathes life into my most intimate desires,
gently nudging me towards all that is good.
I ask for the grace to let myself be enfolded by the Spirit.

Consciousness

How am I really feeling? Light-hearted? Heavy-hearted?
I may be very much at peace, happy to be here.
Equally, I may be frustrated, worried, or angry.
I acknowledge how I really am. It is the real me that the Lord loves.

The Word

I read the Word of God slowly, a few times over, and I listen
to what God is saying to me. (Please turn to your scripture on
the following pages. Inspiration points are there should you need
them. When you are ready, return here to continue.)

Conversation

How has God's Word moved me? Has it left me cold?
Has it consoled me or moved me to act in a new way?
I imagine Jesus standing or sitting beside me;
I turn and share my feelings with him.

Conclusion

Glory be to the Father, and to the Son, and to the Holy Spirit,
As it was in the beginning, is now, and ever shall be,
World without end. Amen.

Sunday 1st July,
Thirteenth Sunday in Ordinary Time   Mark 5:21–24, 35b–43

When Jesus had crossed again in the boat to the other side, a great crowd gathered round him; and he was by the lake. Now there was a woman who had been suffering from hemorrhages for twelve years. She had endured much under many physicians, and had spent all that she had; and she was no better, but rather grew worse. She had heard about Jesus, and came up behind him in the crowd and touched his cloak, for she said, "If I but touch his clothes, I will be made well." Immediately her hemorrhage stopped; and she felt in her body that she was healed of her disease. Immediately aware that power had gone forth from him, Jesus turned about in the crowd and said, "Who touched my clothes?" And his disciples said to him, "You see the crowd pressing in on you; how can you say, 'Who touched me?'" He looked all round to see who had done it. But the woman, knowing what had happened to her, came in fear and trembling, fell down before him, and told him the whole truth. He said to her, "Daughter, your faith has made you well; go in peace, and be healed of your disease."

- Faith heals people as they meet Jesus.
- Prayer is one way of strengthening faith. Prayer is an entry into the world of mystery, where we cannot name everything nor know everything. There is a knowledge of the heart which is the knowledge of faith. We are open to that through the faith-life of others.

Monday 2nd July   **Matthew 8:18–22**

Now when Jesus saw great crowds around him, he gave orders to go over to the other side. A scribe then approached and said, "Teacher, I will follow you wherever you go." And Jesus said to him, "Foxes have holes, and birds of the air have nests;

but the Son of Man has nowhere to lay his head." Another of his disciples said to him, "Lord, first let me go and bury my father." But Jesus said to him, "Follow me, and let the dead bury their own dead."

- It may be that as Jesus answered the scribe he challenged him, reminding him that he might not have anywhere to lay his head.
- Even as I say I am willing to follow Jesus, I too quickly realize where it may be difficult for me. If I am to be a disciple, I need to remain in dialogue with Jesus, listening keenly for his response.

Tuesday 3rd July, St. Thomas, Apostle   John 20:24–29

Thomas (who was called the Twin), one of the twelve, was not with them when Jesus came. So the other disciples told him, "We have seen the Lord." But he said to them, "Unless I see the mark of the nails in his hands, and put my finger in the mark of the nails and my hand in his side, I will not believe." A week later his disciples were again in the house, and Thomas was with them. Although the doors were shut, Jesus came and stood among them and said, "Peace be with you." Then he said to Thomas, "Put your finger here and see my hands. Reach out your hand and put it in my side. Do not doubt but believe." Thomas answered him, "My Lord and my God!" Jesus said to him, "Have you believed because you have seen me? Blessed are those who have not seen and yet have come to believe."

- We see that Thomas lacked faith in his brothers and sisters. His independent mind refused to accept their word, wanting to reach his own conclusions for himself. If I am to be a Christian, I am called to belong to others—to grow in trust of them if I am to grow in faith in God.

- I have not seen and yet have come to believe. Jesus speaks of me in this gospel and blesses me.

Wednesday 4th July   Matthew 8:28–34

When he came to the other side, to the country of the Gadarenes, two demoniacs coming out of the tombs met him. They were so fierce that no one could pass that way. Suddenly they shouted, "What have you to do with us, Son of God? Have you come here to torment us before the time?" Now a large herd of swine was feeding at some distance from them. The demons begged him, "If you cast us out, send us into the herd of swine." And he said to them, "Go!" So they came out and entered the swine; and suddenly, the whole herd rushed down the steep bank into the lake and perished in the water. The swineherds ran off, and on going into the town, they told the whole story about what had happened to the demoniacs. Then the whole town came out to meet Jesus; and when they saw him, they begged him to leave their neighborhood.

- Jesus was a man "of the other side." He moved to Gentile and dangerous areas with little thought to his own safety, intent on the mission of his Father. There he met the forces of evil—prejudice and hatred.

- He still calls us to unity. His vision is to unite all peoples in the love of God his Father. His vision is to unite the goodness and evil in every human heart, and to reconcile us to ourselves in the love of the Father who loves us as we are.

Thursday 5th July   Matthew 9:1–8

And after getting into a boat he crossed the water and came to his own town. And just then some people were carrying a paralyzed man lying on a bed. When Jesus saw their faith, he said to the paralytic, "Take heart, son; your sins are forgiven."

Then some of the scribes said to themselves, "This man is blaspheming." But Jesus, perceiving their thoughts, said, "Why do you think evil in your hearts? For which is easier, to say, 'Your sins are forgiven,' or to say, 'Stand up and walk'? But so that you may know that the Son of Man has authority on earth to forgive sins"—he then said to the paralytic—"Stand up, take your bed and go to your home." And he stood up and went to his home. When the crowds saw it, they were filled with awe, and they glorified God, who had given such authority to human beings.

- The people of Jesus' town were quick to judge, springing to the defence of their religious principles. They had lost sight of the bigger picture that Jesus had in view; he wanted to restore health and wholeness.
- Jesus longs for me to live fully and freely. In this time of prayer, I ask for liberty from what binds me and bring before God my desire for wholeness.

Friday 6th July   **Matthew 9:9–13**

As Jesus was walking along, he saw a man called Matthew sitting at the tax booth; and he said to him, "Follow me." And he got up and followed him. And as he sat at dinner in the house, many tax collectors and sinners came and were sitting with him and his disciples. When the Pharisees saw this, they said to his disciples, "Why does your teacher eat with tax collectors and sinners?" But when he heard this, he said, "Those who are well have no need of a physician, but those who are sick. Go and learn what this means, 'I desire mercy, not sacrifice.' For I have come to call not the righteous but sinners."

- The Pharisees asked the disciples a question but it is Jesus who answers. I consider whether my answers are too ready, too quick.

Perhaps I need to turn to Jesus first rather than always saying what I think.

- Aware of my sinfulness and failure, I may feel unworthy of God's grace. It is when I am a sinner and aware of it that I am best able to be with Jesus. God looks upon me lovingly not because I judge myself ready but because I know I am in need.

Saturday 7th July   Matthew 9:14–17

Then the disciples of John came to him, saying, "Why do we and the Pharisees fast often, but your disciples do not fast?" And Jesus said to them, "The wedding guests cannot mourn as long as the bridegroom is with them, can they? The days will come when the bridegroom is taken away from them, and then they will fast. No one sews a piece of unshrunk cloth on an old cloak, for the patch pulls away from the cloak, and a worse tear is made. Neither is new wine put into old wineskins; otherwise, the skins burst, and the wine is spilled, and the skins are destroyed; but new wine is put into fresh wineskins, and so both are preserved."

- Prayer renews us, as does any activity of faith. It can be like the new wine in fresh wineskins. It's like the joy of meeting a friend after a long time, or indeed meeting the friends we meet daily. If prayer is not refreshing and renewing our spirits, maybe we pray the wrong way.
- If we find the way to pray that enlivens us and brings us the quiet joy of God, we have found the treasure of faith.

july 8–14

Something to think and pray about each day this week:

The Patience of God

How can we live with the evil in the world? Jesus answered with the parable of the wheat and the darnel, whose force hits us every day. It is about having patience with the persistence of evil in the world. We may face malicious vandalism, like the enemy who sowed weeds in his neighbour's field. In their early stages the weeds looked like wheat, and you could not root up weeds without taking some wheat as well. So too some of the evils we face are dressed up to look respectable. We have to fight evil, but we need not give ourselves ulcers if we find that society remains far from perfect. The final judgment lies with God.

Lord, you remind me of my impatience when faced with evil in the world. Let me learn to wait for the wheat and the weeds to grow. Otherwise my judgments will likely be too hasty and mistaken. You warn us against the illusions of inquisitions which tried to eliminate sin by laws and bonfires. You do not ask us to coerce people into what we think is the right path. Part of me is impatient to root out evil, like the servants offering to weed out the darnel. You tell me to wait on God's judgment and trust that the goodness of his seed will prevail over the weeds. May I learn patience. When faced with violent people, I will not let their way of treating me determine my way of treating them.

The Presence of God

To be present is to arrive as one is and open up to the other.
At this instant, as I arrive here, God is present waiting for me.
God always arrives before me, desiring to connect with me
even more than my most intimate friend.
I take a moment and greet my loving God.

Freedom

Everything has the potential to draw forth from me a fuller love
and life.
yet my desires are often fixed, caught, on illusions of fulfillment.
I ask that God, through my freedom, may orchestrate
my desires in a vibrant, loving melody rich in harmony.

Consciousness

Knowing that God loves me unconditionally,
I can afford to be honest about how I am.
How has the last day been, and how do I feel now?
I share my feelings openly with the Lord.

The Word

I take my time to read the Word of God, slowly, a few times, allowing myself to dwell on anything that strikes me. (Please turn to your scripture on the following pages. Inspiration points are there should you need them. When you are ready, return here to continue.)

Conversation

What feelings are rising in me
as I pray and reflect on God's Word?
I imagine Jesus himself sitting or standing beside me,
and open my heart to him.

Conclusion

Glory be to the Father, and to the Son, and to the Holy Spirit,
As it was in the beginning, is now, and ever shall be,
World without end. Amen.

Sunday 8th July,
Fourteenth Sunday in Ordinary Time Mark 6:1–6

Jesus left that place and came to his hometown, and his disciples followed him. On the sabbath he began to teach in the synagogue, and many who heard him were astounded. They said, "Where did this man get all this? What is this wisdom that has been given to him? What deeds of power are being done by his hands! Is not this the carpenter, the son of Mary and brother of James and Joses and Judas and Simon, and are not his sisters here with us?" And they took offense at him. Then Jesus said to them, "Prophets are not without honor, except in their hometown, and among their own kin, and in their own house." And he could do no deed of power there, except that he laid his hands on a few sick people and cured them. And he was amazed at their unbelief. Then he went about among the villages teaching.

- People couldn't accept the ordinariness of Jesus—that he grew up in a normal family which was named and well-known in Nazareth.
- Sometimes we find it hard to see the grace of God near to us, under our noses as it were. In the ordinariness of life and love, of misunderstanding and hurt, of care and compassion, the grace of God and the love of God are active and alive.

Monday 9th July Matthew 9:20–23

Suddenly a woman who had been suffering from hemorrhages for twelve years came up behind him and touched the fringe of his cloak, for she said to herself, "If I only touch his cloak, I will be made well." Jesus turned, and seeing her he said, "Take heart, daughter; your faith has made you well." And instantly the woman was made well.

- My prayer will be poorer if I think I do not deserve Jesus' attention. I draw inspiration from the example of this woman who had the faith to reach out. In my prayer I stretch out my hand, believing that I, too, will receive God's grace.

- I listen to Jesus say to me, "Take heart, your faith has made you well."

Tuesday 10th July   Matthew 9:35–38

Then Jesus went about all the cities and villages, teaching in their synagogues, and proclaiming the good news of the kingdom, and curing every disease and every sickness. When he saw the crowds, he had compassion for them, because they were harassed and helpless, like sheep without a shepherd. Then he said to his disciples, "The harvest is plentiful, but the laborers are few; therefore ask the Lord of the harvest to send out laborers into his harvest."

- Jesus cured every disease and sickness. I bring all aspects of my life to my prayer, knowing that God wants to bring healing too.
- I may recall times when I have been too busy or too stressed. I picture Jesus looking with compassion on me then, keeping alive in his heart God's desire for me that I had lost sight of. I linger in Jesus' compassionate gaze.

Wednesday 11th July   Matthew 10:1–7

Then Jesus summoned his twelve disciples and gave them authority over unclean spirits, to cast them out, and to cure every disease and every sickness. These are the names of the twelve apostles: first, Simon, also known as Peter, and his brother Andrew; James son of Zebedee, and his brother John; Philip and Bartholomew; Thomas and Matthew the tax collector; James son of Alphaeus, and Thaddaeus; Simon the Cananaean, and Judas Iscariot, the one who betrayed him. These twelve Jesus sent out with the following instructions: "Go nowhere among the Gentiles, and enter no town of the Samaritans, but go rather to the lost sheep of the house of Israel. As you go, proclaim the good news, 'The kingdom of heaven has come near.'"

- As I read this list of the apostles, I think of my name among them. I pray that I may accept the trust that Jesus has in me.
- I can proclaim that the kingdom of heaven is near by what I do, by the way I live. I can be an illustration of God's presence, a splash of colour, an inspiration among those who may think of themselves as "lost sheep."

Thursday 12th July   Hosea 11:1, 3–4

When Israel was a child, I loved him, and out of Egypt I called my son. Yet it was I who taught Ephraim to walk, I took them up in my arms; but they did not know that I healed them. I led them with cords of human kindness, with bands of love. I was to them like those who lift infants to their cheeks. I bent down to them and fed them.

- I let the tender intimacy of this passage speak to me; it tells me how God wants to treat me. It challenges my ideas about myself, inviting me to consider myself as a child, as an infant held close to God's cheek.
- I think of the parents of newborn children, how they are so engrossed and enthralled by the miracle of new life. I let myself be gazed on by God who loves me just as much—and even more!

Friday 13th July   Hosea 14:2–10

I will heal their disloyalty; I will love them freely, for my anger has turned from them. I will be like the dew to Israel; he shall blossom like the lily, he shall strike root like the forests of Lebanon. His shoots shall spread out; his beauty shall be like the olive tree, and his fragrance like that of Lebanon. They shall again live beneath my shadow, they shall flourish as a garden; they shall blossom like the vine, their fragrance shall be like the wine of Lebanon.

- As I take this time in the presence of God, I try not to be distracted by memories or regrets. I hear the Word of God that is full of promise and accept that God wants me to flourish, to grow, and to blossom.
- The images of the reading are of abundance, colour, and fragrance. I pray that I may enrich the lives of those who live with me by living generously, freely, and fully.

Saturday 14th July   Isaiah 6:5–8

And I said: "Woe is me! I am lost, for I am a man of unclean lips, and I live among a people of unclean lips; yet my eyes have seen the King, the Lord of hosts!" Then one of the seraphs flew to me, holding a live coal that had been taken from the altar with a pair of tongs. The seraph touched my mouth with it and said: "Now that this has touched your lips, your guilt has departed and your sin is blotted out." Then I heard the voice of the Lord saying, "Whom shall I send, and who will go for us?" And I said, "Here am I; send me!"

- I hear the voice of the Lord asking, "Whom shall I send?" As I want to answer, "Send me!", I pray for the grace that I will need at this time.
- God has confidence in me, trusts me, and sends me out. I pray that I may have confidence in myself even as I rely on God.

july 15–21

Something to think and pray about each day this week:

The Healer's Touch

The fifth chapter of Mark's gospel describes two healings by Jesus: the healing of a girl dying after twelve years of life and the healing of a woman sick for twelve years. In both there is physical contact with Jesus. The woman reaches out through the crowd to touch him. Jesus takes the little girl by the hand.

A point may come in our own sickness—or that of someone close to us—when we realize that medicine alone will make no difference. We turn to the Lord and find help, maybe not in a cure, but in peace.

> When other helpers fail and comforts flee,
> Help of the helpless, O abide with me.

Lord, I cannot touch you, but I reach out to you in faith. You said of the little girl, "She is not dead but sleeping." And you woke her up. I am waiting for your hand on me, to make me more fully alive. Let me hear you say to me, "Talitha cumi."

The Presence of God
What is present to me is what has a hold on my becoming.
I reflect on the presence of God always there in love,
amidst the many things that have a hold on me.
I pause and pray that I may let God
affect my becoming in this precise moment.

Freedom
There are very few people
who realize what God would make of them
if they abandoned themselves into his hands,
and let themselves be formed by his grace (St. Ignatius).
I ask for the grace to trust myself totally to God's love.

Consciousness
In the presence of my loving Creator,
I look honestly at my feelings over the last day,
the highs, the lows, and the level ground.
Can I see where the Lord has been present?

The Word
God speaks to each one of us individually. I need to listen to what
he is saying to me. (Please turn to your scripture on the following
pages. Inspiration points are there should you need them. When
you are ready, return here to continue.)

Conversation
What is stirring in me as I pray?
Am I consoled, troubled, left cold?
I imagine Jesus himself standing or sitting at my side,
and share my feelings with him.

Conclusion
Glory be to the Father, and to the Son, and to the Holy Spirit,
As it was in the beginning, is now, and ever shall be,
World without end. Amen.

Sunday 15th July,
Fifteenth Sunday in Ordinary Time Mark 6:7–13

Jesus called the twelve and began to send them out two by two, and gave them authority over the unclean spirits. He ordered them to take nothing for their journey except a staff; no bread, no bag, no money in their belts; but to wear sandals and not to put on two tunics. He said to them, "Wherever you enter a house, stay there until you leave the place. If any place will not welcome you and they refuse to hear you, as you leave, shake off the dust that is on your feet as a testimony against them." So they went out and proclaimed that all should repent. They cast out many demons, and anointed with oil many who were sick and cured them.

- Jesus sent his disciples to preach his kingdom with little other than their dependency on him and on God. They were always pilgrims, with the sandals of the wanderer.

- Following Jesus means becoming a bit of a wanderer, both interiorly and, perhaps, externally. In our relationship with him and in our knowledge of him we are never grounded and stuck but are always on the move into new love and new knowledge. This is his gift to us, not just our achievement.

Monday 16th July Isaiah 1:16–17

Wash yourselves; make yourselves clean; remove the evil of your doings from before my eyes; cease to do evil, learn to do good; seek justice, rescue the oppressed, defend the orphan, plead for the widow.

- As I wish to learn to do good, I realize that only God can teach me. I pray for enlightenment.

- My prayer is empty unless it is brought to life in my attitudes and actions. I think of how my way of living brings justice within reach of those in need.

Tuesday 17th July   **Matthew 11:20–22**

Then Jesus began to reproach the cities in which most of his deeds of power had been done, because they did not repent. "Woe to you, Chorazin! Woe to you, Bethsaida! For if the deeds of power done in you had been done in Tyre and Sidon, they would have repented long ago in sackcloth and ashes. But I tell you, on the day of judgment it will be more tolerable for Tyre and Sidon than for you."

- If my prayer is real, I will meet not only the "gentle Jesus, meek and mild" but will be challenged by Jesus' vision—one that is greater than mine.
- As Jesus reproaches those who have been indifferent, I allow myself to feel uncomfortable. I ask forgiveness and repent.

Wednesday 18th July   **Matthew 11:25–27**

At that time Jesus said, "I thank you, Father, Lord of heaven and earth, because you have hidden these things from the wise and the intelligent and have revealed them to infants; yes, Father, for such was your gracious will. All things have been handed over to me by my Father; and no one knows the Son except the Father, and no one knows the Father except the Son and anyone to whom the Son chooses to reveal him."

- Some things are important to me though I find it difficult to put them in words; I am not even sure how I learnt them. I give thanks to God for all that is revealed in simple and quiet ways.
- I may not convince people through the strength of my logic or through my eloquence. I pray that I may rely, not on my wisdom or intelligence, but on God whom I am growing to recognize and trust.

246

Thursday 19th July   **Isaiah 26:7–9, 12**

The way of the righteous is level; O Just One, you make smooth the path of the righteous. In the path of your judgments, O Lord, we wait for you; your name and your renown are the soul's desire. My soul yearns for you in the night, my spirit within me earnestly seeks you. For when your judgments are in the earth, the inhabitants of the world learn righteousness. O Lord, you will ordain peace for us, for indeed, all that we have done, you have done for us.

- Like Isaiah, I wait for the Lord. I know that in waiting I can become impatient, disheartened, or inattentive. I bring what I desire and yearn for before God, asking for blessing.
- I think of all that I have done, considering the achievements of which I am proud. I turn to God with thanks as I pray, "All that I have done, you have done for me."

Friday 20th July   **Matthew 12:1–8**

At that time Jesus went through the grainfields on the sabbath; his disciples were hungry, and they began to pluck heads of grain and to eat. When the Pharisees saw it, they said to him, "Look, your disciples are doing what is not lawful to do on the sabbath." He said to them, "Have you not read what David did when he and his companions were hungry? He entered the house of God and ate the bread of the Presence, which it was not lawful for him or his companions to eat, but only for the priests. Or have you not read in the law that on the sabbath the priests in the temple break the sabbath and yet are guiltless? I tell you, something greater than the temple is here. But if you had known what this means, 'I desire mercy and not sacrifice,' you would not have condemned the guiltless. For the Son of Man is lord of the sabbath."

- When my Church is criticised it is easy to become defensive and self-righteous. The gospel reminds me that Jesus often experienced rebuttal and told his disciples to expect it. I pray that I may act and speak more like Jesus did.
- I am circumscribed by many laws, guidelines, and regulations. I pray for the same freedom and maturity that Jesus had to never let anything come between him and God.

Saturday 21st July   Matthew 12:14–21

But the Pharisees went out and conspired against him, how to destroy him. When Jesus became aware of this, he departed. Many crowds followed him, and he cured all of them, and he ordered them not to make him known. This was to fulfill what had been spoken through the prophet Isaiah: "Here is my servant, whom I have chosen, my beloved, with whom my soul is well pleased. I will put my Spirit upon him, and he will proclaim justice to the Gentiles. He will not wrangle or cry aloud, nor will anyone hear his voice in the streets. He will not break a bruised reed or quench a smoldering wick until he brings justice to victory. And in his name the Gentiles will hope."

- Jesus the healer has drawn enemies down on himself, and he withdraws in the face of their hostility. He is not defeated; he continues his work. But as Isaiah had foretold, it is in his suffering that his true identity will be known to all nations.
- Lord, teach me to bear my suffering with humility, to put aside the temptation to protest my innocence—for your sake.

july 22–28

Something to think and pray about each day this week:

My Life in Jesus

What did Jesus mean when he urged self-denial? "Deny yourself and take up your cross daily." I used to think this meant looking for mortifications. Lord, you have taught me that my cross is myself, my ego, the pains in my body, my awkwardness, my mistakes. Gerard Manley Hopkins put it starkly:

> I am gall, I am heartburn. God's most deep decree
> Bitter would have me taste; my taste was me.

To follow you is to move beyond ego-trips. It means coping with the business of life without trampling on others or making them suffer. There is a world here to be explored: to deny myself—to reach a point where my self is no longer the most important thing in the world; to be able to take a back seat comfortably; to be happy to listen; to accept without resentment the diminishments that come to me through time or circumstances; to see your hand, Lord, in both the bright and dark places of my life.

The Presence of God
Jesus waits silent and unseen to come into my heart.
I will respond to His call.
He comes with His infinite power and love.
May I be filled with joy in His presence.

Freedom
A thick and shapeless tree-trunk would never believe
that it could become a statue, admired as a miracle of sculpture,
and would never submit itself to the chisel of the sculptor,
who sees by her genius what she can make of it (St. Ignatius).
I ask for the grace to let myself be shaped by my loving Creator.

Consciousness
Knowing that God loves me unconditionally,
I look honestly over the last day, its events, and my feelings.
Do I have something to be grateful for? Then I give thanks.
Is there something I am sorry for? Then I ask forgiveness.

The Word
I read the Word of God slowly, a few times over, and I listen
to what God is saying to me. (Please turn to your scripture on
the following pages. Inspiration points are there should you need
them. When you are ready, return here to continue.)

Conversation
Do I notice myself reacting as I pray with the Word of God?
Do I feel challenged, comforted, angry?
Imagining Jesus sitting or standing by me,
I speak out my feelings, as one trusted friend to another.

Conclusion
Glory be to the Father, and to the Son, and to the Holy Spirit,
As it was in the beginning, is now, and ever shall be,
World without end. Amen.

Sunday 22nd July,
Sixteenth Sunday in Ordinary Time   Mark 6:30–34

The apostles gathered around Jesus, and told him all that they had done and taught. He said to them, "Come away to a deserted place all by yourselves and rest a while." For many were coming and going, and they had no leisure even to eat. And they went away in the boat to a deserted place by themselves. Now many saw them going and recognized them, and they hurried there on foot from all the towns and arrived ahead of them. As he went ashore, he saw a great crowd; and he had compassion for them, because they were like sheep without a shepherd; and he began to teach them many things.

* Prayer is a time of answering the invitation in the gospel: "Come away to a deserted place." The place of our mind can be very crowded with the cares and concerns of life. We need time to give these over to God in prayer and then time just to be still.
* Stillness is of the essence of prayer. But whether we are still or busy, the essence of prayer is to share all we are with Jesus, and to go from prayer ready to work with him in our world.

Monday 23rd July   Micah 6:6–8

With what shall I come before the Lord, and bow myself before God on high? Shall I come before him with burnt-offerings, with calves a year old? Will the Lord be pleased with thousands of rams, with tens of thousands of rivers of oil? Shall I give my firstborn for my transgression, the fruit of my body for the sin of my soul? He has told you, O mortal, what is good; and what does the Lord require of you but to do justice, and to love kindness, and to walk humbly with your God?

- It might be easier if God were to ask me to do difficult things, to put great challenges before me. I am reminded, instead, that God asks me only to be just, to love, and to follow.
- I am reminded not to make my prayer another achievement, something else that I do. It is time for my heart to be shaped, for my attitudes and desires to become what God made them to be.

Tuesday 24th July   Micah 7:18–20

Who is a God like you, pardoning iniquity and passing over the transgression of the remnant of your possession? He does not retain his anger forever, because he delights in showing clemency. He will again have compassion upon us; he will tread our iniquities under foot. You will cast all our sins into the depths of the sea. You will show faithfulness to Jacob and unswerving loyalty to Abraham, as you have sworn to our ancestors from the days of old.

- Time and again God promises me goodness, yet I often wonder where it is now. I pray that my eyes may be opened to appreciate where God is working.
- God has cast my sins into the depths of the sea and does not see me now through them nor judge me because of them. I pray that I may receive the forgiveness that God offers.

Wednesday 25th July,
St. James, Apostle   Matthew 20:20–23

Then the mother of the sons of Zebedee came to him with her sons, and kneeling before him, she asked a favor of him. And he said to her, "What do you want?" She said to him, "Declare that these two sons of mine will sit, one at your right hand and one at your left, in your kingdom." But Jesus answered, "You do not know what you are asking. Are you able to drink the cup that I am about to drink?" They said to him, "We are able." He said to them, "You will indeed drink my cup, but to sit at my right hand and at my left, this is not mine to grant, but it is for those for whom it has been prepared by my Father."

- The mother of James and John was ambitious for her sons. For them she wanted the top place at every table with Jesus. Many a parent wants the same. But Jesus sidesteps again and says that the one who serves most is the one in the honoured place with God.
- As we watch Jesus in the gospels we see he is at the beck and call of many. He is the servant of all. This is love, and it is the way Jesus shows the love of God among us.

Thursday 26th July   Jeremiah 2:1–2, 12–13

The word of the Lord came to me, saying: Go and proclaim in the hearing of Jerusalem, Thus says the Lord: I remember the devotion of your youth, your love as a bride, how you followed me in the wilderness, in a land not sown. Be appalled, O heavens, at this, be shocked, be utterly desolate, says the Lord, for my people have committed two evils: they have forsaken me, the fountain of living water, and dug out cisterns for themselves, cracked cisterns that can hold no water.

- I take this time of prayer as a time to drink deeply at the cistern God offers me. I ask God to help me to let go, to relax, to be fully present.
- The energies and talents I have are to give glory to God, for the good of others and for my growth. I ask for the help I need to use them wisely. I ask forgiveness for trying to be self-sufficient.

Friday 27th July   Jeremiah 3:15–16

I will give you shepherds after my own heart, who will feed you with knowledge and understanding. And when you have multiplied and increased in the land, in those days, says the Lord, they shall no longer say, "The ark of the covenant of the Lord." It shall not come to mind, or be remembered, or missed; nor shall another one be made.

- My time of prayer is important not just because I read the Word of God but because I make myself present to God. Everything that supports my prayer, that brings me to God, is a tool, an instrument. I attune myself to how God is present to me now.
- I pray for all those who are shepherds to me, for those who guide and lead me. I pray that I may, in turn, be a shepherd after God's own heart.

Saturday 28th July   Jeremiah 7:5–7

For if you truly amend your ways and your doings, if you truly act justly one with another, if you do not oppress the alien, the orphan, and the widow, or shed innocent blood in this place, and if you do not go after other gods to your own hurt, then I will dwell with you in this place, in the land that I gave of old to your ancestors for ever and ever.

- I ask God's blessing that I may see how I need to act justly, taking responsibility for the needy and the stranger.
- God wants to dwell with me. I make space for God by recognizing distractions and false priorities and putting them aside, by caring for what God cares about.

july 29–august 4

Something to think and pray about each day this week:

Lighting the Way

The prophet Isaiah wrote, "I will give you as a light to the nations, that my salvation may reach to the ends of the earth" (Isaiah 49:3). Is it fanciful to speak of the *Sacred Space* website and books in this way? What thanks we owe to the legions of scientists, technologists, writers, editors, and computer buffs who have made it possible to reach round the world in this way! Inspired by a vision of a worldwide web, they created the means by which we can fulfil what Isaiah barely glimpsed and enable epiphanies to happen. Epiphanies, when God shows himself, come rarely. We find ourselves briefly on Holy Ground, with a sense of awe and delight. What are we doing all through life but moving from one little piece of Holy Ground to the next?

The Presence of God
As I sit here, the beating of my heart,
the ebb and flow of my breathing, the movements of my mind
are all signs of God's ongoing creation of me.
I pause for a moment, and become aware
of this presence of God within me.

Freedom
I ask for the grace
to let go of my own concerns
and be open to what God is asking of me,
to let myself be guided and formed by my loving Creator.

Consciousness
How do I find myself today?
Where am I with God? With others?
Do I have something to be grateful for? Then I give thanks.
Is there something I am sorry for? Then I ask forgiveness.

The Word
I take my time to read the Word of God, slowly, a few times, allowing myself to dwell on anything that strikes me. (Please turn
to your scripture on the following pages. Inspiration points are
there should you need them. When you are ready, return here to
continue.)

Conversation
Remembering that I am still in God's presence,
I imagine Jesus himself standing or sitting beside me,
and say whatever is on my mind, whatever is in my heart,
speaking as one friend to another.

Conclusion
Glory be to the Father, and to the Son, and to the Holy Spirit,
As it was in the beginning, is now, and ever shall be,
World without end. Amen.

Sunday 29th July,
Seventeenth Sunday in Ordinary Time　　　　John 6:1–13

After this Jesus went to the other side of the Sea of Galilee, also called the Sea of Tiberias. A large crowd kept following him, because they saw the signs that he was doing for the sick. Jesus went up the mountain and sat down there with his disciples. Now the Passover, the festival of the Jews, was near. When he looked up and saw a large crowd coming towards him, Jesus said to Philip, "Where are we to buy bread for these people to eat?" He said this to test him, for he himself knew what he was going to do. Philip answered him, "Six months' wages would not buy enough bread for each of them to get a little." One of his disciples, Andrew, Simon Peter's brother, said to him, "There is a boy here who has five barley loaves and two fish. But what are they among so many people?" Jesus said, "Make the people sit down." Now there was a great deal of grass in the place; so they sat down, about five thousand in all. Then Jesus took the loaves, and when he had given thanks, he distributed them to those who were seated; so also the fish, as much as they wanted. When they were satisfied, he told his disciples, "Gather up the fragments left over, so that nothing may be lost." So they gathered them up, and from the fragments of the five barley loaves, left by those who had eaten, they filled twelve baskets.

- The boy with the small lunch seems to have had little to offer, but what he brought fed the crowds. We often feel that we have little to offer in the service of Jesus. His work now depends on our cooperation with him. What is offered in love—though it looks small—can have large effects.

- Our prayer time is our daily offering of love and care for others in the immediate circle of our lives and a connection to the larger world of neighbourhood, country, and universe.

Monday 30th July   Matthew 13:31–32

He put before them another parable: "The kingdom of heaven is like a mustard seed that someone took and sowed in his field; it is the smallest of all the seeds, but when it has grown it is the greatest of shrubs and becomes a tree, so that the birds of the air come and make nests in its branches."

- I see that my life of faith is sometimes evident and identifiable; at other times it is hidden and quiet. At this moment I may identify with the blossoming shrub.
- The reign of God is where God's will holds sway. I ask God to bless my imagination, that I might see signs and images of the kingdom of God in my life.

Tuesday 31st July, St. Ignatius Loyola   Jeremiah 14:17–22

You shall say to them this word: Let my eyes run down with tears night and day, and let them not cease, for the virgin daughter—my people—is struck down with a crushing blow, with a very grievous wound. If I go out into the field, look—those killed by the sword! And if I enter the city, look—those sick with famine! For both prophet and priest ply their trade throughout the land, and have no knowledge. Have you completely rejected Judah? Does your heart loathe Zion? Why have you struck us down so that there is no healing for us? We look for peace, but find no good; for a time of healing, but there is terror instead. We acknowledge our wickedness, O Lord, the iniquity of our ancestors, for we have sinned against you. Do not spurn us, for your name's sake; do not dishonor your glorious throne; remember and do not break your covenant with us. Can any idols of the nations bring rain? Or can the heavens give showers?

Is it not you, O Lord our God? We set our hope on you, for it is you who do all this.

- The honesty and pleading of Jeremiah tells me something about prayer.
- I bring all my needs to my prayer, and all those who suffer injustice, poverty, disaster, and war, acknowledging that God is the One in whom our hopes are founded.

Wednesday 1st August   Jeremiah 15:19–21

Therefore, thus says the Lord: If you turn back, I will take you back, and you shall stand before me. If you utter what is precious, and not what is worthless, you shall serve as my mouth. It is they who will turn to you, not you who will turn to them. And I will make you to this people a fortified wall of bronze; they will fight against you, but they shall not prevail over you, for I am with you to save you and deliver you, says the Lord. I will deliver you out of the hand of the wicked, and redeem you from the grasp of the ruthless.

- I do not have to be concerned with influencing or persuading: God can work through my efforts and communicate through my words.
- Even if I don't experience the ruthless and the wicked, I know there are many things that can keep me in their grasp. I turn again to God, asking for help.

Thursday 2nd August   Jeremiah 18:1–6

The word that came to Jeremiah from the Lord: "Come, go down to the potter's house, and there I will let you hear my words." So I went down to the potter's house, and there he was working at his wheel. The vessel he was making of clay was spoiled in the potter's hand, and he reworked it into another vessel, as seemed good to him. Then the word of the Lord came to me: Can I not do with you, O house of Israel, just as this potter has done? says the Lord. Just like the clay in the potter's hand, so are you in my hand, O house of Israel.

- The potter is offered as an image of God at work. Where do I see images of God's working with me?
- Do I resist the shaping of God, preferring to be as I am or as I was, not accepting the new shape that God has in mind for me?

Friday 3rd August   Matthew 13:54–58

Jesus came to his home town and began to teach the people in their synagogue, so that they were astounded and said, "Where did this man get this wisdom and these deeds of power? Is not this the carpenter's son? Is not his mother called Mary? And are not his brothers James and Joseph and Simon and Judas? And are not all his sisters with us? Where then did this man get all this?" And they took offense at him. But Jesus said to them, "Prophets are not without honor except in their own country and in their own house." And he did not do many deeds of power there, because of their unbelief.

- There are always reasons not to listen—the people of Jesus' town saw him as just a local boy. Suspicion of strangers prevents messages from being heard as well.
- I ask for the courage and honesty I need to be truthful with those close to me and for the grace I need to listen to them. I pray that I may receive the message that God has for me.

Saturday 4th August   Matthew 14:1–12

At that time Herod the ruler heard reports about Jesus; and he said to his servants, "This is John the Baptist; he has been raised from the dead, and for this reason these powers are at work in him." For Herod had arrested John, bound him, and put him in prison on account of Herodias, his brother Philip's wife, because John had been telling him, "It is not lawful for you to have her." Though Herod wanted to put him to death, he feared the crowd, because they regarded him as a prophet. But when Herod's birthday came, the daughter of Herodias danced before the company, and she pleased Herod so much that he promised on oath to grant her whatever she might ask. Prompted by her mother, she said, "Give me the head of John the Baptist here on a platter." The king was grieved, yet out of regard for his oaths and for the guests, he commanded it to be given; he sent and had John beheaded in the prison. The head was brought on a platter and given to the girl, who brought it to her mother. His disciples came and took the body and buried it; then they went and told Jesus.

- Heads have rolled throughout history when good people stood their ground. The fate of John the Baptist has been repeated in wars for justice, for religion, and for faith. It still goes on, as men and women spend years in prison for their beliefs.
- In prayer we recall and remind ourselves of modern Baptists, and we do what we can to highlight their unjust treatment. We pray they be strengthened by the power of the risen Lord Jesus.

august 5–11

Something to think and pray about each day this week:

Discerning the Way

Ignatius Loyola's Spiritual Exercises were designed in the first place as a way of making good decisions. The first thing he would say about our decision-making is that we have to learn from experience, and not commit the same errors over again. Secondly, we should reflect on our experience and see what its elements are, analyse what happened, why one thing worked while another thing did not, and so on.

It may require a special effort to discern the finger of God in the places where we work. God's grace breaks through into our lives at surprising times and in surprising ways. Crises erupt at inconvenient times. On occasion, after years of strenuous efforts in some ministry, a group of apostolic workers has come together for a sustained discernment that took weeks, searching by prayer, research, and discussion for the best way forward. Each time there were stunning results, with long-lasting consequences for their engagement in new strategies and projects and for planned withdrawal from others.

The Presence of God

I pause for a moment
and reflect on God's life-giving presence
in every part of my body, in everything around me,
in the whole of my life.

Freedom

I ask for the grace to believe
in what I could be and do
if I only allowed God, my loving Creator,
to continue to create me, guide me, and shape me.

Consciousness

In God's loving presence I unwind the past day,
starting from now and looking back, moment by moment.
I gather in all the goodness and light, in gratitude.
I attend to the shadows and what they say to me,
seeking healing, courage, forgiveness.

The Word

God speaks to each one of us individually. I need to listen to what
he is saying to me. (Please turn to your scripture on the following
pages. Inspiration points are there should you need them. When
you are ready, return here to continue.)

Conversation

How has God's Word moved me? Has it left me cold?
Has it consoled me or moved me to act in a new way?
I imagine Jesus standing or sitting beside me;
I turn and share my feelings with him.

Conclusion

Glory be to the Father, and to the Son, and to the Holy Spirit,
As it was in the beginning, is now, and ever shall be,
World without end. Amen.

Sunday 5th August,
Eighteenth Sunday in Ordinary Time   John 6:26–34

Jesus said to the crowd, "Very truly, I tell you, you are looking for me, not because you saw signs, but because you ate your fill of the loaves. Do not work for the food that perishes, but for the food that endures for eternal life, which the Son of Man will give you. For it is on him that God the Father has set his seal." Then they said to him, "What must we do to perform the works of God?" Jesus answered them, "This is the work of God, that you believe in him whom he has sent." So they said to him, "What sign are you going to give us then, so that we may see it and believe you? What work are you performing? Our ancestors ate the manna in the wilderness; as it is written, 'He gave them bread from heaven to eat.'" Then Jesus said to them, "Very truly, I tell you, it was not Moses who gave you the bread from heaven, but it is my Father who gives you the true bread from heaven. For the bread of God is that which comes down from heaven and gives life to the world." They said to him, "Sir, give us this bread always."

- Jesus continually contrasts the temporary nature of the work of God in the Hebrew scriptures and the eternal nature of his own work.

- We live in the time of Jesus, when his hour of death and resurrection have come. With him we can never only hunger or thirst for the kingdom of God, as it is near to us and within us. We thirst for more of what we already have.

Monday 6th August,
Transfiguration of the Lord   Daniel 7:13–14

I saw one like a human being coming with the clouds of heaven. And he came to the Ancient One and was presented before him. To him was given dominion and glory and kingship, that all peoples, nations, and languages should serve him. His dominion is an everlasting dominion that shall not pass away, and his kingship is one that shall never be destroyed.

- The prophet Daniel describes the reign of God as one that embraces all time and space. The Feast of the Transfiguration reminds me that my true identity lies in being drawn into this glory.
- I am held in being by the everlasting love of God. I pray that I may live in a greater awareness of this and that my way of living may offer glimpses of God's love to others.

Tuesday 7th August   Jeremiah 30:18–19

Thus says the Lord: I am going to restore the fortunes of the tents of Jacob, and have compassion on his dwellings; the city shall be rebuilt upon its mound, and the citadel set on its rightful site. Out of them shall come thanksgiving, and the sound of merrymakers. I will make them many, and they shall not be few; I will make them honored, and they shall not be disdained.

- The words of Jeremiah remind me that God has a plan for me, a vision for my growth, a desire that I thrive. I take time to let God look on me, and I allow my heart to be lifted.
- I consider how the reading mentions hope, gratitude, and joy. Where do I need to make space for these attitudes to be more present in my life?

Wednesday 8th August   Jeremiah 31:1–4

At that time, says the Lord, I will be the God of all the families of Israel, and they shall be my people. Thus says the Lord: The people who survived the sword found grace in the wilderness; when Israel sought for rest, the Lord appeared to him from far away. I have loved you with an everlasting love; therefore

I have continued my faithfulness to you. Again I will build you, and you shall be built, O virgin Israel! Again you shall take your tambourines, and go forth in the dance of the merrymakers.

- Looking back on my life, I pray for the enlightenment I need to recognize how God has blessed me, even in what seemed like wilderness times.
- I pray for all who find themselves in the wildernesses at the moment, for those from whom God's hand is hidden. I soak in the words of Jeremiah, words full of promise and confidence in God's goodness.

Thursday 9th August   Jeremiah 31:31–34

The days are surely coming, says the Lord, when I will make a new Covenant with the house of Israel and the house of Judah. It will not be like the covenant that I made with their ancestors when I took them by the hand to bring them out of the land of Egypt—a covenant that they broke, though I was their husband, says the Lord. But this is the covenant that I will make with the house of Israel after those days, says the Lord: I will put my law within them, and I will write it on their hearts; and I will be their God, and they shall be my people. No longer shall they teach one another, or say to each other, "Know the Lord," for they shall all know me, from the least of them to the greatest, says the Lord; for I will forgive their iniquity, and remember their sin no more.

- God wants to draw me into relationship, into a new agreement. I pray that I may not be held back by anything in the past but may accept the confidence that God has in me.
- The covenant is not a just a legal agreement, a contract, or a law, but a drawing together of people in love. God calls me in love. I make my loving response.

Friday 10th August, St. Lawrence

John 12:24–26

Very truly, I tell you, unless a grain of wheat falls into the earth and dies, it remains just a single grain; but if it dies, it bears much fruit. Those who love their life lose it, and those who hate their life in this world will keep it for eternal life. Whoever serves me must follow me, and where I am, there will my servant be also. Whoever serves me, the Father will honor."

- The grass sheds its seeds on the soil before it withers. The salmon swims up the stream to die. It is harder for us humans to accept the law of nature, that we too must fade away and find happiness in passing on our riches to others.

Saturday 11th August

Matthew 17:14–20

When they came to the crowd, a man came to Jesus, knelt before him, and said, "Lord, have mercy on my son, for he is an epileptic and he suffers terribly; he often falls into the fire and often into the water. And I brought him to your disciples, but they could not cure him." Jesus answered, "You faithless and perverse generation, how much longer must I be with you? How much longer must I put up with you? Bring him here to me." And Jesus rebuked the demon, and it came out of him, and the boy was cured instantly. Then the disciples came to Jesus privately and said, "Why could we not cast it out?" He said to them, "Because of your little faith. For truly I tell you, if you have faith the size of a mustard seed, you will say to this mountain, 'Move from here to there,' and it will move; and nothing will be impossible for you."

- The disciples went back to Jesus with their question. I keep this image in mind as I bring the questions of my life before Jesus.
- As I ask for greater faith, I ask for a greater ability to trust those around me. I pray for a belief in myself that is founded on God's truth.

august 12–18

Something to think and pray about each day this week:

Taking the Plunge

Conversion means a turning, moving round a corner. It can be a sharp, sudden, hairpin bend, as was Paul's on the road to Damascus, or it can be a gentle, open curve, in which we change our direction only gradually. It is the Holy Spirit who does the work of sanctification, pulling us round the bend. Come, Holy Spirit, fill the hearts of your faithful, and enkindle in them the fire of your love.

Lord, you tell me, as you told Simon Peter, to "put out into the deep water." You are ready to surprise me with the depths I can find in myself, with the work you can do through me. Save me from complacency, from settling for a routine existence. Open me to recognizing your hand in my daily encounters.

The Presence of God

The world is charged with the grandeur of God (Gerard Manley Hopkins).
I dwell for a moment on the presence of God
around me, in every part of my body,
and deep within my being.

Freedom

"In these days, God taught me
as a schoolteacher teaches a pupil" (St. Ignatius).
I remind myself that there are things God has to teach me yet,
and ask for the grace to hear them and let them change me.

Consciousness

Help me, Lord, to be more conscious of your presence.
Teach me to recognize your presence in others.
Fill my heart with gratitude for the times your love
has been shown to me through the care of others.

The Word

I read the Word of God slowly, a few times over, and I listen
to what God is saying to me. (Please turn to your scripture on
the following pages. Inspiration points are there should you need
them. When you are ready, return here to continue.)

Conversation

What feelings are rising in me
as I pray and reflect on God's Word?
I imagine Jesus himself sitting or standing beside me,
and open my heart to him.

Conclusion

Glory be to the Father, and to the Son, and to the Holy Spirit,
As it was in the beginning, is now, and ever shall be,
World without end. Amen.

Sunday 12th August,
Nineteenth Sunday in Ordinary Time   John 6:47–51

Jesus said to the crowd, "Very truly, I tell you, whoever believes has eternal life. I am the bread of life. Your ancestors ate the manna in the wilderness, and they died. This is the bread that comes down from heaven, so that one may eat of it and not die. I am the living bread that came down from heaven. Whoever eats of this bread will live forever; and the bread that I will give for the life of the world is my flesh."

- Imagine living forever. We find it hard to envisage eternal life, a quality and enjoyment of life that never ends. We have ways of describing it—like joy, love, peace.
- We are promised this life after death by our sharing the life of Jesus on earth. He gives himself in time that we may live with him in eternity.

Monday 13th August   Matthew 17:24–23

When they reached Capernaum, the collectors of the temple tax came to Peter and said, "Does your teacher not pay the temple tax?" He said, "Yes, he does." And when he came home, Jesus spoke of it first, asking, "What do you think, Simon? From whom do kings of the earth take toll or tribute? From their children or from others?" When Peter said, "From others." Jesus said to him, "Then the children are free. However, so that we do not give offense to them, go to the lake and cast a hook; take the first fish that comes up; and when you open its mouth, you will find a coin; take that and give it to them for you and me."

- Not a friendly question, Lord: "Are you tax compliant?" In your answer, you claim the privilege of children in their father's house, implying that the Son of God has no tax obligations in the house of God.

- But you point beyond that exemption in a way that pulls me up sharp: "Whatever about my rights, I do not want to cause scandal, to give unnecessary offence, to be a stumbling-block to others. I pay the tax."

Tuesday 14th August   Matthew 18:1–5

At that time the disciples came to Jesus and asked, "Who is the greatest in the kingdom of heaven?" He called a child, whom he put among them, and said, "Truly I tell you, unless you change and become like children, you will never enter the kingdom of heaven. Whoever becomes humble like this child is the greatest in the kingdom of heaven. Whoever welcomes one such child in my name welcomes me."

- Jesus is teaching the adult onlookers: in the child he sees complete trust, simple acceptance, humility, and an absence of driving ambition.
- What can I learn about my faith journey from the helpless child?

Wednesday 15th August,
Assumption of the Virgin Mary   Luke 1:39–45

In those days Mary set out and went with haste to a Judean town in the hill country, where she entered the house of Zechariah and greeted Elizabeth. When Elizabeth heard Mary's greeting, the child leapt in her womb. And Elizabeth was filled with the Holy Spirit and exclaimed with a loud cry, "Blessed are you among women, and blessed is the fruit of your womb. And why has this happened to me, that the mother of my Lord comes to me? For as soon as I heard the sound of your greeting, the child in my womb leapt for joy. And blessed is she who believed that there would be a fulfillment of what was spoken to her by the Lord."

- Even at the hour of her own need, Mary went to the aid of her cousin.
- I think of the blessings that good friends bring to us. I consider how I can reach out to offer encouragement and support.

Thursday 16th August   Matthew 18:21–22

Then Peter came and said to him, "Lord, if another member of the church sins against me, how often should I forgive? As many as seven times?" Jesus said to him, "Not seven times, but, I tell you, seventy-seven times."

- I am encouraged by Peter who, in a moment when living in the way of the Gospel seemed difficult, brought his question to Jesus.
- I speak to Jesus about my life, about how it really is.

Friday 17th August   Ezekiel 16:59–60, 62–63

Yes, thus says the Lord God: I will deal with you as you have done, you who have despised the oath, breaking the covenant; yet I will remember my covenant with you in the days of your youth, and I will establish with you an everlasting covenant. I will establish my covenant with you, and you shall know that I am the Lord, in order that you may remember and be confounded, and never open your mouth again because of your shame, when I forgive you all that you have done, says the Lord God.

- Instead of looking at my life in fragments, thinking of times of faithfulness contrasted with the times when I was less careful, I accept that God sees continuity in my discipleship.
- I listen to the words, "I forgive all that you have done." I take time to let God speak them to me, allowing them to rest in my heart.

Saturday 18th August   **Ezekiel 18:30–32**

R epent and turn from all your transgressions; otherwise iniquity will be your ruin. Cast away from you all the transgressions that you have committed against me, and get yourselves a
new heart and a new spirit! Why will you die, O house of Israel?
For I have no pleasure in the death of anyone, says the Lord God.
Turn, then, and live.

- I ask God for the new heart and new spirit that I need, acknowledging my need of life and energy.
- God calls me to life, asking me to turn from whatever drags me
down or belittles me. I bring before God any regrets, habits, or
attitudes that hold me back and ask God's help to cast them away.

Something to think and pray about each day this week:

Where Do I Stand?

In the Bible, poverty is an evil to be corrected; wealth is not an evil but a necessity for the well-being of the kingdom. However, the love of riches can lead to neglect of God and of the poor. The Christian community has always tried to make the care of the poor its priority. Is it mine?

"What stress are you under?" Jesus asks of us. It stems from his mission. He is sent by the Father to purify, and to distinguish what is genuine from dross. Life according to the Beatitudes has its share of conflict. For those who hunger and thirst for justice, this world is not a comfortable place. As Simeon prophesied to Mary, Jesus was "destined to be a sign that is rejected" (Luke 2:34). What about me? Do I merge seamlessly and comfortably with the values of this world? Do I hunger and thirst for anything? If the behaviour of the Beatitudes were a criminal offence, would I be in prison?

The Presence of God
As I sit here, God is present,
breathing life into me and into everything around me.
For a few moments, I sit silently,
and become aware of God's loving presence.

Freedom
If God were trying to tell me something, would I know?
If God were reassuring me or challenging me, would I notice?
I ask for the grace to be free of my own preoccupations
and open to what God may be saying to me.

Consciousness
How am I really feeling? Light-hearted? Heavy-hearted?
I may be very much at peace, happy to be here.
Equally, I may be frustrated, worried, or angry.
I acknowledge how I really am. It is the real me that the Lord loves.

The Word
I take my time to read the Word of God, slowly, a few times, allowing myself to dwell on anything that strikes me. (Please turn to your scripture on the following pages. Inspiration points are there should you need them. When you are ready, return here to continue.)

Conversation
What is stirring in me as I pray?
Am I consoled, troubled, left cold?
I imagine Jesus himself standing or sitting at my side,
and share my feelings with him.

Conclusion
Glory be to the Father, and to the Son, and to the Holy Spirit,
As it was in the beginning, is now, and ever shall be,
World without end. Amen.

276

Sunday 19th August,
Twentieth Sunday in Ordinary Time   John 6:51–58

I am the living bread that came down from heaven. Whoever eats of this bread will live forever; and the bread that I will give for the life of the world is my flesh." The Jews then disputed among themselves, saying, "How can this man give us his flesh to eat?" So Jesus said to them, "Very truly, I tell you, unless you eat the flesh of the Son of Man and drink his blood, you have no life in you. Those who eat my flesh and drink my blood have eternal life, and I will raise them up on the last day; for my flesh is true food and my blood is true drink. Those who eat my flesh and drink my blood abide in me, and I in them. Just as the living Father sent me, and I live because of the Father, so whoever eats me will live because of me. This is the bread that came down from heaven, not like that which your ancestors ate, and they died. But the one who eats this bread will live forever."

- What we receive in the Eucharist is the gift of life from Jesus. This is a sharing in the life of God; in the fragility of the bread and wine is strong food, and joyful drink.
- In the Eucharist, God is close to his creation. In Jesus we can recognize God near at hand. As Pope Benedict writes, "We have to rediscover God, not just any God, but the God that has a human face, because when we see Jesus Christ, we see God."

Monday 20th August   Matthew 19:16–22

Then someone came to Jesus and said, "Teacher, what good deed must I do to have eternal life?" And he said to him, "Why do you ask me about what is good? There is only one who is good. If you wish to enter into life, keep the commandments." He said to him, "Which ones?" And Jesus said, "You shall not murder; You shall not commit adultery; You shall not steal; You shall not bear false witness; Honor your father and mother; also, You shall love your neighbor as yourself." The young man said to him, "I have kept all these; what do I still lack?" Jesus said to him, "If you wish to be perfect, go, sell your possessions, and give the money to the poor, and you will have treasure in heaven; then come, follow me." When the young man heard this word, he went away grieving, for he had many possessions.

- The young man who approached Jesus had many things to ask, but his questions seemed to be ways of keeping God's message at a distance. Jesus finally said aloud what he may already have known: following God means not just a change of mind but leads to a change of heart.
- As God reveals to me what I must do, I am also given the strength to do it. Bend my heart to your will, O God.

Tuesday 21st August   **Matthew 19:23–26**

Jesus said to his disciples, "Truly I tell you, it will be hard for a rich person to enter the kingdom of heaven. Again I tell you, it is easier for a camel to go through the eye of a needle than for someone who is rich to enter the kingdom of God." When the disciples heard this, they were greatly astounded and said, "Then who can be saved?" But Jesus looked at them and said, "For mortals it is impossible, but for God all things are possible."

- The things to which I am most attached can slow me down. I may sometimes tell others why they are important, and sometimes may convince myself. I allow God to speak to me about what is truly important, to draw me into the perspective of God's love.
- It is easy for me to measure myself against others and to let my admiration become envy. I pray that I may be able to let go of some of my ideas about what I want for myself.

Wednesday 22nd August Matthew 20:1–16

Jesus said to his disciples, "For the kingdom of heaven is like a
landowner who went out early in the morning to hire laborers
for his vineyard. After agreeing with the laborers for the usual
daily wage, he sent them into his vineyard. When he went out
about nine o'clock, he saw others standing idle in the marketplace; and he said to them, 'You also go into the vineyard, and I
will pay you whatever is right.' So they went. When he went out
again about noon and about three o'clock, he did the same. And
about five o'clock he went out and found others standing around;
and he said to them, 'Why are you standing here idle all day?'
They said to him, 'Because no one has hired us.' He said to them,
'You also go into the vineyard.' When evening came, the owner of
the vineyard said to his manager, 'Call the laborers and give them
their pay, beginning with the last and then going to the first.'
When those hired about five o'clock came, each of them received
the usual daily wage. Now when the first came, they thought they
would receive more; but each of them also received the usual daily
wage. And when they received it, they grumbled against the landowner, saying, 'These last worked only one hour, and you have
made them equal to us who have borne the burden of the day
and the scorching heat.' But he replied to one of them, 'Friend, I
am doing you no wrong; did you not agree with me for the usual
daily wage? Take what belongs to you and go; I choose to give to
this last the same as I give to you. Am I not allowed to do what
I choose with what belongs to me? Or are you envious because I
am generous?' So the last will be first, and the first will be last."

• The workers received the proper daily wage and were happy—
until they made comparisons with one another. Help me, Lord, to
focus on what you have given to me and not to hanker after what
you have given to others.

- I give care, attention, and respect to the people I meet with. I think of how I acknowledge those who serve me in small ways and in bigger ones.

Thursday 23rd August   Ezekiel 36:24–28

I will take you from the nations, and gather you from all the countries, and bring you into your own land. I will sprinkle clean water upon you, and you shall be clean from all your uncleannesses, and from all your idols I will cleanse you. A new heart I will give you, and a new spirit I will put within you; and I will remove from your body the heart of stone and give you a heart of flesh. I will put my spirit within you, and make you follow my statutes and be careful to observe my ordinances. Then you shall live in the land that I gave to your ancestors; and you shall be my people, and I will be your God.

- I think today not of what I want to do for God but of what God wants to do for me. God cares for me in all of my being—body, heart, and soul—wanting to refresh me, invigorate me, and call me back to life.
- I pray that I may let God be God and think of what it means for me to be a child of God.

Friday 24th August,
St. Bartholomew, Apostle   John 1:45–51

Philip found Nathanael and said to him, "We have found him about whom Moses in the law and also the prophets wrote, Jesus son of Joseph from Nazareth." Nathanael said to him, "Can anything good come out of Nazareth?" Philip said to him, "Come and see." When Jesus saw Nathanael coming towards him, he said of him, "Here is truly an Israelite in whom there is no deceit!" Nathanael asked him, "Where did you come to know me?" Jesus answered, "I saw you under the fig tree before

Philip called you." Nathanael replied, "Rabbi, you are the Son of God! You are the King of Israel!" Jesus answered, "Do you believe because I told you that I saw you under the fig tree? You will see greater things than these." And he said to him, "Very truly, I tell you, you will see heaven opened and the angels of God ascending and descending upon the Son of Man."

- Philip's announcement about meeting Jesus received a cynical response. He might have found it difficult to see the good in Nathanael that Jesus recognised. I pray for the wisdom I need to see beyond the dismissive answer and ask for patience.
- Jesus sees me "under the fig trees" of my life, recognizing what is in my heart. I relax in the knowledge that I am known and loved.

Saturday 25th August　　　　　　　　　　　**Matthew 23:1–3**

Then Jesus said to the crowds and to his disciples, "The scribes and the Pharisees sit on Moses' seat; therefore, do whatever they teach you and follow it; but do not do as they do, for they do not practice what they teach."

- Jesus acknowledges authority, but warns that actions are much more important than mere words. His charge against the scribes and Pharisees is one of hypocrisy.
- Do I struggle with this too, like the scribes and Pharisees? Am I careful of appearances? Do I present myself carefully while holding others to a standard that I don't truly meet?

august 26–september 1

Something to think and pray about each day this week:

Placing Myself with God

How do you pray? What is your body's posture in prayer? Human beings are like one another, so it is not surprising that even in widely different cultures, there is some agreement on how to set about prayer. John Callanan, S.J., summarises this wisdom, "When you settle into prayer, look first to your breathing. Slow down. Taste the air flowing through your nostrils. Fill your body deeply with it, and then empty it slowly by gently breathing out. Continue this breathing, slowly and deeply, with lips slightly open, inhaling through the nose and exhaling through the mouth. Think of your mind as a pool whose surface, when ruffled by the winds of anger or desire, is unable to reflect the sun. You are trying to find an interior reflection of God's goodness in your life."

The Presence of God
As I sit here with my book, God is here—
around me, in my sensations, in my thoughts, and deep within me.
I pause for a moment, and become aware
of God's life-giving presence.

Freedom
I need to close out the noise, to rise above the noise—
the noise that interrupts, that separates,
the noise that isolates.
I need to listen to God again.

Consciousness
Knowing that God loves me unconditionally,
I can afford to be honest about how I am.
How has the last day been, and how do I feel now?
I share my feelings openly with the Lord.

The Word
God speaks to each one of us individually. I need to listen to what
he is saying to me. (Please turn to your scripture on the following
pages. Inspiration points are there should you need them. When
you are ready, return here to continue.)

Conversation
Do I notice myself reacting as I pray with the Word of God?
Do I feel challenged, comforted, angry?
Imagining Jesus sitting or standing by me,
I speak out my feelings, as one trusted friend to another.

Conclusion
Glory be to the Father, and to the Son, and to the Holy Spirit,
As it was in the beginning, is now, and ever shall be,
World without end. Amen.

Sunday 26th August,
Twenty-first Sunday in Ordinary Time   John 6:66–69

Because of Jesus' teaching many of his disciples turned back and no longer went about with him. So Jesus asked the twelve, "Do you also wish to go away?" Simon Peter answered him, "Lord, to whom can we go? You have the words of eternal life. We have come to believe and know that you are the Holy One of God."

- Love welcomes us to the companionship of Jesus. In the enjoyment and the challenge of such love, would we want to go elsewhere? Some did, and the evidence is that their departure from Jesus did not bring happiness.
- What Jesus offers reaches deep into all our human desires, joys, tears, laughter, and love.

Monday 27th August   2 Thessalonians 1:1–5, 11–12

Paul, Silvanus, and Timothy, To the church of the Thessalonians in God our Father and the Lord Jesus Christ: Grace to you and peace from God our Father and the Lord Jesus Christ. We must always give thanks to God for you, brothers and sisters, as is right, because your faith is growing abundantly, and the love of every one of you for one another is increasing. Therefore we ourselves boast of you among the churches of God for your steadfastness and faith during all your persecutions and the afflictions that you are enduring. This is evidence of the righteous judgment of God, and is intended to make you worthy of the kingdom of God, for which you are also suffering. To this end we always pray for you, asking that our God will make you worthy of his call and will fulfil by his power every good resolve and work of faith, so that the name of our Lord Jesus may be glorified in you, and you in him, according to the grace of our God and the Lord Jesus Christ.

- Encouraged by Paul, I pray for those who matter most to me. I pray for their good; I give thanks; I rejoice in their gifts.
- I think of all who are in need, bringing to mind those who endure persecutions or afflictions. I think of what I might do to ease their burden now in my prayer or, later, in other ways.

Tuesday 28th August   Matthew 23:23–24

Jesus said, "Woe to you, scribes and Pharisees, hypocrites! For you tithe mint, dill, and cummin, and have neglected the weightier matters of the law: justice and mercy and faith. It is these you ought to have practiced without neglecting the others. You blind guides! You strain out a gnat but swallow a camel!"

- Prayer always purifies the heart. We are the better for praying, as moments of contact with God bring us into contact with the One who heals, strengthens, and forgives us.
- Real religion is the religion of the heart—bringing us in touch with the heart of God, and then caring from the heart for others.

Wednesday 29th August   2 Thessalonians 3:6–10, 16–17

Now we command you, beloved, in the name of our Lord Jesus Christ, to keep away from believers who are living in idleness and not according to the tradition that they received from us. For you yourselves know how you ought to imitate us; we were not idle when we were with you, and we did not eat anyone's bread without paying for it; but with toil and labor we worked night and day, so that we might not burden any of you. This was not because we do not have that right, but in order to give you an example to imitate. For even when we were with you, we gave you this command: Anyone unwilling to work should not eat. Now may the Lord of peace himself give you peace at all times in all ways. The Lord be with all of you.

- I pray for balance as I live in a world that exaggerates both leisure and busyness. As I pray, I keep in mind that God loves me for who I am and asks me to show this love in what I do for others.
- I have many examples to follow as I seek to live a Christian life. I take care to pay attention to them, seeking how I might imitate them.

Thursday 30th August   1 Corinthians 1:4–7

I give thanks to my God always for you because of the grace of God that has been given you in Christ Jesus, for in every way you have been enriched in him, in speech and knowledge of every kind—just as the testimony of Christ has been strengthened among you—so that you are not lacking in any spiritual gift as you wait for the revealing of our Lord Jesus Christ.

- I think of the spiritual gifts that I have been given and give thanks for them. I linger prayerfully, recalling the gifts of the Spirit— wisdom, understanding, counsel, courage, knowledge, piety, and reverence.
- I consider what gifts I need—or those that need strengthening— and express myself to God who will "strengthen me to the end."

Friday 31st August   1 Corinthians 1:17–25

For Christ did not send me to baptize but to proclaim the gospel, and not with eloquent wisdom, so that the cross of Christ might not be emptied of its power. For the message about the cross is foolishness to those who are perishing, but to us who are being saved it is the power of God. For it is written, "I will destroy the wisdom of the wise, and the discernment of the discerning I will thwart." Where is the one who is wise? Where is the scribe? Where is the debater of this age? Has not God made foolish the wisdom of the world? For since, in the wisdom of God, the world did not know God through wisdom, God decided, through the foolishness of our proclamation, to save those who believe. For Jews demand signs and Greeks desire wisdom, but we proclaim Christ crucified, a stumbling-block to Jews and foolishness to Gentiles, but to those who are the called, both Jews and Greeks, Christ the power of God and the wisdom of God. For God's foolishness is wiser than human wisdom, and God's weakness is stronger than human strength.

- The cross is emptied of its power when I forget the love it represents. Crosses are often used as mere decoration or as empty symbols.
- I might take more time to notice the crosses around me and to think of what they mean.

Saturday 1st September   **1 Corinthians 1:26–31**

Consider your own call, brothers and sisters: not many of you were wise by human standards, not many were powerful, not many were of noble birth. But God chose what is foolish in the world to shame the wise; God chose what is weak in the world to shame the strong; God chose what is low and despised in the world, things that are not, to reduce to nothing things that are, so that no one might boast in the presence of God. He is the source of your life in Christ Jesus, who became for us wisdom from God, and righteousness and sanctification and redemption, in order that, as it is written, "Let the one who boasts, boast in the Lord."

- I am reminded that I do not become like Jesus through my own efforts. In my weakness I ask God for what I really need.
- I take some reassurance from the fact that I do not have to win every argument and to have the last word. I pray for the help I need to live as well as I can, but to realize that, even in my weakness, God's grace may be evident.

september 2–8

Something to think and pray about each day this week:

The Sound of Stillness
When you meet somebody who is physically restless, with twitchy muscles and restless gaze, you do not feel present to them or they to you. Bodily calm is part of our presence to people, and also to God. You may be on your knees, standing, sitting, or prostrate. You try to stop the body moving. You focus on something physical: the breath flowing into you, or the sounds that invade your stillness, or the awareness of your enveloping skin. Then you give space to the Lord who created you, who is more central to your being than your own mind is, yet who is beyond your imagination.

The Presence of God

I pause for a moment, aware that God is here.
I think of how everything around me,
the air I breathe, my whole body,
is tingling with the presence of God.

Freedom

I will ask God's help,
to be free from my own preoccupations,
to be open to God in this time of prayer,
to come to love and serve him more.

Consciousness

In the presence of my loving Creator,
I look honestly at my feelings over the last day,
the highs, the lows, and the level ground.
Can I see where the Lord has been present?

The Word

I read the Word of God slowly, a few times over, and I listen
to what God is saying to me. (Please turn to your scripture on
the following pages. Inspiration points are there should you need
them. When you are ready, return here to continue.)

Conversation

Remembering that I am still in God's presence,
I imagine Jesus himself standing or sitting beside me,
and say whatever is on my mind, whatever is in my heart,
speaking as one friend to another.

Conclusion

Glory be to the Father, and to the Son, and to the Holy Spirit,
As it was in the beginning, is now, and ever shall be,
World without end. Amen.

Sunday 2nd September,
Twenty-second Sunday in Ordinary Time   Mark 7:1–8

Now when the Pharisees and some of the scribes who had come from Jerusalem gathered around Jesus they noticed that some of his disciples were eating with defiled hands, that is, without washing them. (For the Pharisees, and all the Jews, do not eat unless they thoroughly wash their hands, thus observing the tradition of the elders; and they do not eat anything from the market unless they wash it; and there are also many other traditions that they observe, the washing of cups, pots, and bronze kettles.) So the Pharisees and the scribes asked him, "Why do your disciples not live according to the tradition of the elders, but eat with defiled hands?" He said to them, "Isaiah prophesied rightly about you hypocrites, as it is written, 'This people honors me with their lips, but their hearts are far from me; in vain do they worship me, teaching human precepts as doctrines.' You abandon the commandment of God and hold to human tradition."

- God sees the heart and its fluctuations. He judges us on the love of our lives and our efforts to love. In the evening of life God sees not just what we did but the heart of goodness by which we lived.
- A practical way of letting the good flow is to be grateful. On any day we can always think of something to be thankful for. In thanks, the spirit of joy and blessing flow into us and through us.

Monday 3rd September   1 Corinthians 2:1–5

When I came to you, brothers and sisters, I did not come proclaiming the mystery of God to you in lofty words or wisdom. For I decided to know nothing among you except Jesus Christ, and him crucified. And I came to you in weakness and in fear and in much trembling. My speech and my proclamation were not with plausible words of wisdom, but with a demonstration of the Spirit and of power, so that your faith might rest not on human wisdom but on the power of God.

- St. Paul reminds me that I do not have to be preoccupied with what I do or say. I may need to be "weak" enough for the Spirit of God to work.
- My witness to Christ is not only through my words, but is seen in the way I am. As my relationship with Jesus deepens, I grow in trust and confidence.

Tuesday 4th September   1 Corinthians 2:12–13

Now we have received not the spirit of the world, but the Spirit that is from God, so that we may understand the gifts bestowed on us by God. And we speak of these things in words not taught by human wisdom but taught by the Spirit, interpreting spiritual things to those who are spiritual.

- I take time to notice the gifts that God has given to me, so that I may appreciate how God has answered my prayers.
- This time of prayer is a time for the Spirit to speak to me. I receive the gifts that the Spirit brings, leaving aside for now "the spirit of the world" that claims my attention too.

Wednesday 5th September   1 Corinthians 3:1–9

And so, brothers and sisters, I could not speak to you as spiritual people, but rather as people of the flesh, as infants in Christ. I fed you with milk, not solid food, for you were not ready for solid food. Even now you are still not ready, for you are still of the flesh. For as long as there is jealousy and quarrelling among you, are you not of the flesh, and behaving according to human inclinations? For when one says, "I belong to Paul," and another, "I belong to Apollos," are you not merely human? What then is Apollos? What is Paul? Servants through whom you came to believe, as the Lord assigned to each. I planted, Apollos watered, but God gave the growth. So neither the one who plants nor the one who waters is anything, but only God who gives the growth. The one who plants and the one who waters have a common purpose, and each will receive wages according to the labor of each. For we are God's servants, working together; you are God's field, God's building.

- It is natural to welcome appreciation; I sometimes look for credit for what I do.
- I think of myself as God's field, God's building. The care that others take with their homes or possessions is nothing to God's care for me. I consider the work that God is doing in me.

Thursday 6th September   **1 Corinthians 3:18–23**

Do not deceive yourselves. If you think that you are wise in this age, you should become fools so that you may become wise. For the wisdom of this world is foolishness with God. For it is written, "He catches the wise in their craftiness," and again, "The Lord knows the thoughts of the wise, that they are futile." So let no one boast about human leaders. For all things are yours, whether Paul or Apollos or Cephas or the world or life or death or the present or the future—all belong to you, and you belong to Christ, and Christ belongs to God.

- It is often difficult to be thought of as a fool, so I may seek the last word and strive to prove myself, if not wise, at least reasonable. I pray for enough humour, humility, and detachment to allow myself to be thought foolish for being a disciple.
- Human achievements bring many good things, but the Spirit of God brings blessings. I ask for the wisdom I need to discern the Spirit that I might follow.

Friday 7th September   **1 Corinthians 4:1–5**

Think of us in this way, as servants of Christ and stewards of God's mysteries. Moreover, it is required of stewards that they should be found trustworthy. But with me it is a very small thing that I should be judged by you or by any human court. I do not even judge myself. I am not aware of anything against myself, but I am not thereby acquitted. It is the Lord who judges me. Therefore do not pronounce judgment before the time, before the Lord comes, who will bring to light the things now hidden in darkness and will disclose the purposes of the heart. Then each one will receive commendation from God.

- Being a servant of Christ is not a mission reserved for the ordained. By my Baptism, I am called into service and trusted by Jesus with the tasks closest to his heart.
- If others are to think of me as Christ's servant, that is how I must think of myself. Like Ignatius of Loyola, I ask, "What have I done for Christ, what am I doing for Christ, what will I do for Christ?"

Saturday 8th September,
Birthday of the Blessed Virgin Mary   **Romans 8:28–30**

We know that all things work together for good for those who love God, who are called according to his purpose. For those whom he foreknew he also predestined to be conformed to the image of his Son, in order that he might be the firstborn within a large family. And those whom he predestined he also called; and those whom he called he also justified; and those whom he justified he also glorified.

- God calls me into cooperation. I consider the dignity and honour that I am given and ask that I may act in a way that shows my appreciation of God working with me.

- I take time to think of how God has turned things to my good in the past, giving thanks for blessings, letting go of the plans that I had for myself.

september 9–15

Something to think and pray about each day this week:

Looking to Meet God

One conviction is central to Christian prayer: that God is active in it. We turn to meditation not so much as an exercise in self-improvement as an opening of ourselves to our heavenly Father who is waiting for us. Three hundred years ago, Jean-Pierre de Caussade wrote of the Sacrament of the Present Moment. It is only in the Now that we have access to God. Looking forward or back exercises the mind and imagination, but that distracts us from the true meeting of prayer, with the Lord who is present in my inmost soul. "Be still and know that I am God" (Psalm 46). There is a stage in prayer where we go beyond words and thoughts—the hard bit is to stop thinking. A mystic is quoted as hearing from God, "I will not have thy thoughts instead of thee." As we grow older, prayer becomes less wordy, less brainy, more like the peasant whom the Curé of Ars used to see in his church—"I look at the good God and the good God looks at me."

The Presence of God
For a few moments, I think of God's veiled presence in things:
in the elements, giving them existence;
in plants, giving them life; in animals, giving them sensation;
and finally, in me, giving me all this and more,
making me a temple, a dwelling-place of the Spirit.

Freedom
God is not foreign to my freedom.
Instead the Spirit breathes life into my most intimate desires,
gently nudging me towards all that is good.
I ask for the grace to let myself be enfolded by the Spirit.

Consciousness
Knowing that God loves me unconditionally,
I look honestly over the last day, its events, and my feelings.
Do I have something to be grateful for? Then I give thanks.
Is there something I am sorry for? Then I ask forgiveness.

The Word
I take my time to read the Word of God, slowly, a few times, allowing myself to dwell on anything that strikes me. (Please turn
to your scripture on the following pages. Inspiration points are
there should you need them. When you are ready, return here to
continue.)

Conversation
How has God's Word moved me? Has it left me cold?
Has it consoled me or moved me to act in a new way?
I imagine Jesus standing or sitting beside me;
I turn and share my feelings with him.

Conclusion
Glory be to the Father, and to the Son, and to the Holy Spirit,
As it was in the beginning, is now, and ever shall be,
World without end. Amen.

298

Sunday 9th September,
Twenty-third Sunday in Ordinary Time   Mark 7:31–37

Then he returned from the region of Tyre, and went by way of Sidon towards the Sea of Galilee, in the region of the Decapolis. They brought to him a deaf man who had an impediment in his speech; and they begged him to lay his hand on him. He took him aside in private, away from the crowd, and put his fingers into his ears, and he spat and touched his tongue. Then looking up to heaven, he sighed and said to him, "Ephphatha," that is, "Be opened." And immediately his ears were opened, his tongue was released, and he spoke plainly. Then Jesus ordered them to tell no one; but the more he ordered them, the more zealously they proclaimed it. They were astounded beyond measure, saying, "He has done everything well; he even makes the deaf to hear and the mute to speak."

- The healing work of Jesus involved the body as well as the mind and soul. Our body is the "place" of the Holy Spirit, and through words, touch, and feeling, we affect the lives of others.
- In prayer we thank God for the sacredness of our bodies and ask that we care well for them. We offer this care to the Lord in the ways we eat, drink, touch, and taste. We believe that Jesus, Son of God, is present and incarnate today in our bodies.

Monday 10th September   1 Corinthians 5:6–8

Your boasting is not a good thing. Do you not know that a little yeast leavens the whole batch of dough? Clean out the old yeast so that you may be a new batch, as you really are unleavened. For our paschal lamb, Christ, has been sacrificed. Therefore, let us celebrate the festival, not with the old yeast, the yeast of malice and evil, but with the unleavened bread of sincerity and truth.

- Advertisers spend fortunes to prod my pride in myself. But how does God see and love me? I am created for good and am so much greater than the deficiencies that the world may see in me.
- The yeast of the world can have an effect of distorting the pure shape that God has in heart and in mind for me. I remind myself that success, appearance, performance, and possessions are not the true measures of who I am.

Tuesday 11th September   **Psalm 149:1–4**

Praise the Lord! Sing to the Lord a new song, his praise in the assembly of the faithful. Let Israel be glad in its Maker; let the children of Zion rejoice in their King. Let them praise his name with dancing, making melody to him with tambourine and lyre. For the Lord takes pleasure in his people; he adorns the humble with victory.

- Praise for God flows from the whole community of believers in full voice, with dancing and joyful new songs.
- Lord, teach me to put aside inhibition and open myself to the love and majesty of the God who loves me.

Wednesday 12th September   **Luke 6:20–23**

Then Jesus looked up at his disciples and said: "Blessed are you who are poor, for yours is the kingdom of God. Blessed are you who are hungry now, for you will be filled. Blessed are you who weep now, for you will laugh. Blessed are you when people hate you, and when they exclude you, revile you, and defame you on account of the Son of Man. Rejoice in that day and leap for joy, for surely your reward is great in heaven; for that is what their ancestors did to the prophets."

- How much do I really believe that there is a blessing in hardship, in poverty, hunger, sadness, hostility? Jesus discovered in his own life that blessings abound everywhere and enrich our lives and the lives of those around us.

- It may not always happen this way. We can become the constant victim of the past. Suffering can make us better people or bitter people. What have I done with my suffering? Teach me, Lord.

Thursday 13th September   1 Corinthians 8:1–6

Now concerning food sacrificed to idols: we know that "all of us possess knowledge." Knowledge puffs up, but love builds up. Anyone who claims to know something does not yet have the necessary knowledge; but anyone who loves God is known by him. Hence, as to the eating of food offered to idols, we know that "no idol in the world really exists," and that "there is no God but one." Indeed, even though there may be so-called gods in heaven or on earth—as in fact there are many gods and many lords—yet for us there is one God, the Father, from whom are all things and for whom we exist, and one Lord, Jesus Christ, through whom are all things and through whom we exist.

- My living as a Christian is not measured by what I know, by my command of "Christian doctrine." The love that I embody and show to others is the true indication that God's Spirit is alive in me.
- I pray for those who serve "gods" and "lords" that do not lead them to life. I ask for a deep compassion for them, praying that they may discover their true worth and identity as people loved by God.

Friday 14th September,
Triumph of the Holy Cross   Numbers 21:4–5

Jesus said, "And just as Moses lifted up the serpent in the wilderness, so must the Son of Man be lifted up, that whoever believes in him may have eternal life. For God so loved the world that he gave his only Son, so that everyone who believes in him may not perish but may have eternal life. Indeed, God did not send the Son into the world to condemn the world, but in order that the world might be saved through him."

- There are times when, like the people in the desert, I wonder about God's presence and providence.
- I pray for a deeper faith and for the ability to recognize God's movements in my life. I pray with compassion for all those who struggle, for any who seek light in their lives at this moment.
- I ask God now to open my eyes to help me to see how I am blessed in ways that I may have come to think of as ordinary.

Saturday 15th September   1 Corinthians 10:14–22

Therefore, my dear friends, flee from the worship of idols. I speak as to sensible people; judge for yourselves what I say. The cup of blessing that we bless, is it not a sharing in the blood of Christ? The bread that we break, is it not a sharing in the body of Christ? Because there is one bread, we who are many are one body, for we all partake of the one bread. Consider the people of Israel; are not those who eat the sacrifices partners in the altar? What do I imply then? That food sacrificed to idols is anything, or that an idol is anything? No, I imply that what pagans sacrifice, they sacrifice to demons and not to God. I do not want you to be partners with demons. You cannot drink the cup of the Lord and the cup of demons. You cannot partake of the table of the Lord and the table of demons. Or are we provoking the Lord to jealousy? Are we stronger than he?

- I acknowledge that it is easy for me to pay attention to what divides and separates. I consider all that makes me one with others, and I take strength and encouragement.
- I pray for my community, thinking of their differences and difficulties. I ask God to bless us with a deeper appreciation of how we are one.

Something to think and pray about each day this week:

The Mystery of Joy

As we grow older and have fewer tasks ahead of us, we have leisure to indulge our memories. We should choose with care the memories we indulge. Even in old age they shape our moods. If we are seduced into what you might call sore memories—resentments and grievances—then people will avoid us. The world is hard enough without doses of other people's gloom to darken it. But we can lift our own and others' moods if we linger on the joyful mysteries of our life, on the people we loved and the experiences that we felt as blessings. We don't want to bore our friends with complacency or boastfulness. Gratitude for God's gifts is different. It is one of the basic themes of any mature spirituality, and it makes us easy to live with.

The Presence of God

Jesus waits silent and unseen to come into my heart.
I will respond to His call.
He comes with His infinite power and love.
May I be filled with joy in His presence.

Freedom

Everything has the potential to draw forth from me a fuller love and life.
Yet my desires are often fixed, caught, on illusions of fulfillment.
I ask that God, through my freedom, may orchestrate
my desires in a vibrant, loving melody rich in harmony.

Consciousness

How do I find myself today?
Where am I with God? With others?
Do I have something to be grateful for? Then I give thanks.
Is there something I am sorry for? Then I ask forgiveness.

The Word

God speaks to each one of us individually. I need to listen to what he is saying to me. (Please turn to your scripture on the following pages. Inspiration points are there should you need them. When you are ready, return here to continue.)

Conversation

What feelings are rising in me
as I pray and reflect on God's Word?
I imagine Jesus himself sitting or standing beside me,
and open my heart to him.

Conclusion

Glory be to the Father, and to the Son, and to the Holy Spirit,
As it was in the beginning, is now, and ever shall be,
World without end. Amen.

304

Sunday 16th September,
Twenty-fourth Sunday in Ordinary Time   Mark 8:27–32

Jesus went on with his disciples to the villages of Caesarea
Philippi; and on the way he asked his disciples, "Who do
people say that I am?" And they answered him, "John the Baptist; and others, Elijah; and still others, one of the prophets." He
asked them, "But who do you say that I am?" Peter answered
him, "You are the Messiah." And he sternly ordered them not
to tell anyone about him. Then he began to teach them that the
Son of Man must undergo great suffering, and be rejected by the
elders, the chief priests, and the scribes, and be killed, and after
three days rise again. He said all this quite openly.

- People seemed to wonder who Jesus was. After hearing him speak
  or watching him healing the sick, they might compare him to John
  the Baptist or one of the prophets, and they wondered if these
  prophets had come back to life. They knew that there was more to
  him than met the eye, more to the meaning of his words than they
  would initially hear.

- Jesus can always surprise us; every time we read a bit of the gospel
  we can learn something new about him or about ourselves.

Monday 17th September   1 Corinthians 11:23–26

For I received from the Lord what I also handed on to you,
that the Lord Jesus on the night when he was betrayed took a
loaf of bread, and when he had given thanks, he broke it and said,
"This is my body that is for you. Do this in remembrance of me."
In the same way he took the cup also, after supper, saying, "This
cup is the new covenant in my blood. Do this, as often as you
drink it, in remembrance of me." For as often as you eat this bread
and drink the cup, you proclaim the Lord's death until he comes.

- As I recall Jesus' giving of himself at the Last Supper, I draw strength from the life he offers to me. When I am challenged, confronted, or seem overwhelmed, I return to this source of life that Jesus offers to me—his own life and very presence.
- Proclaiming the Lord's death leads me to accept the cross in my life, knowing that, as I embrace it, Jesus leads me to new life.

Tuesday 18th September — Luke 7:11–17

Soon afterwards he went to a town called Nain, and his disciples and a large crowd went with him. As he approached the gate of the town, a man who had died was being carried out. He was his mother's only son, and she was a widow; and with her was a large crowd from the town. When the Lord saw her, he had compassion for her and said to her, "Do not weep." Then he came forward and touched the bier, and the bearers stood still. And he said, "Young man, I say to you, rise!" The dead man sat up and began to speak, and Jesus gave him to his mother. Fear seized all of them; and they glorified God, saying, "A great prophet has risen among us!" and "God has looked favorably on his people!" This word about him spread throughout Judea and all the surrounding country.

- The compassion which can invade our hearts at the time of the death of a young person was also in Jesus' heart for a young widow. He wanted to reach out to her, hold her to his heart, and make her life better. This is the same with any suffering we have.
- The raising up of this young son is a symbol of how Jesus raises us when we are down. The compassion of his heart lets us know that we are understood, accepted, and welcomed in the loving heart of God.

Wednesday 19th September — 1 Corinthians 13:9–13

We know only in part, and we prophesy only in part; but when the complete comes, the partial will come to an end. When I was a child, I spoke like a child, I thought like a child,

I reasoned like a child; when I became an adult, I put an end to childish ways. For now we see in a mirror, dimly, but then we will see face to face. Now I know only in part; then I will know fully, even as I have been fully known. And now faith, hope, and love abide, these three; and the greatest of these is love.

- As I come before God in prayer, I ask for the help I need to recognize how little I know. Even my own life is, in some ways, a mystery to me; my perspective is limited. I allow myself time to accept that God sees who I really am and waits for me to be drawn into this fuller light.
- I pray for the maturity that is proper to me. I put aside anything that is not worthy of me and look at my life with love.

Thursday 20th September   1 Corinthians 15:9–11

For I am the least of the apostles, unfit to be called an apostle, because I persecuted the church of God. But by the grace of God I am what I am, and his grace towards me has not been in vain. On the contrary, I worked harder any of them—though it was not I, but the grace of God that is with me. Whether then it was I or they, so we proclaim and so you have come to believe.

- I pray for the humility that Paul displays; I recognize that I am not the greatest apostle but know that I am not less in the eyes of God because of that.
- The good that I do is done through the Spirit of God working in me. I give thanks for God's Spirit and pray that I may recognize how God acts in my actions and speaks even in my words.

Friday 21st September,
St. Matthew, Apostle and Evangelist   Ephesians 4:1–7, 11–13

I therefore, the prisoner in the Lord, beg you to lead a life worthy of the calling to which you have been called, with all humility and gentleness, with patience, bearing with one another in love, making every effort to maintain the unity of the Spirit in the bond of peace. There is one body and one Spirit, just as you were called to the one hope of your calling, one Lord, one faith, one baptism, one God and Father of all, who is above all and through all and in all. But each of us was given grace according to the measure of Christ's gift. The gifts he gave were that some would be apostles, some prophets, some evangelists, some pastors and teachers, to equip the saints for the work of ministry, for building up the body of Christ, until all of us come to the unity of the faith and of the knowledge of the Son of God, to maturity, to the measure of the full stature of Christ.

- I recognize the many gifts that are given to those around me, and I pray for the humility to be able to rely on them, trusting in God's Spirit given to them.
- I give thanks to God for the Spirit given to me and pray that I may give witness to that Spirit by what I say and do.

Saturday 22nd September   1 Corinthians 15:36, 42–44

What you sow does not come to life unless it dies. And as for what you sow, you do not sow the body that is to be, but a bare seed, perhaps of wheat or of some other grain. So it is with the resurrection of the dead. What is sown is perishable, what is raised is imperishable. It is sown in dishonor, it is raised in glory. It is sown in weakness, it is raised in power. It is sown a physical body, it is raised a spiritual body. If there is a physical body, there is also a spiritual body.

- Our modern care for comfort, appearance, and health help us to bring dignity to the body but can easily lead us to think that the journey is in physical perfection.
- I pray for a greater awareness of the spiritual work that God wants to do in me.

september 23–29

Something to think and pray about each day this week:

Coming and Going—Together

Preparing for death used to be clear-cut, getting things off one's chest, clearing one's conscience, using the help of a priest. As a priest I remember lovely encounters of this sort. An old Irish dock worker in New York, who had drifted away from his roots and from the Church, was overjoyed to see a priest as he faced the end, and found that he still knew the words of the "Hail Mary." The anonymous but familiar figure of a priest makes it easier to talk about the death you face—easier than when talking to family, who may feel it their duty to deny the approach of the end.

It should not be this way. Of the many ways to die alone, the most comfortless and solitary is when family and friends conspire to deny the approach of death. They may feel, "I couldn't take away her hope." But without acceptance of the truth, they remove the possibility of spiritual companionship at the end. Dr. Nuland, in his extraordinary book *How We Die*, remembers with regret how the family conspired to avoid the truth when his beloved Aunt Rose was dying. "We knew—she knew—we knew she knew—she knew we knew—and none of us would talk about it when we were all together. We kept up the charade to the end. Aunt Rose was deprived, and so were we, of the coming together that should have been, when we might finally tell her what her life had given us. In this sense, my Aunt Rose died alone."

The Presence of God

"I stand at the door and knock," says the Lord.
What a wonderful privilege
that the Lord of all creation desires to come to me.
I welcome His presence.

Freedom

Lord, grant me the grace to be free from the excesses of this life.
Let me not get caught up with the desire for wealth.
Keep my heart and mind free to love and serve You.

Consciousness

"There is a time and place for everything," as the saying goes.
Lord, grant that I may always desire
to spend time in your presence, to hear your call.

The Word

God speaks to each one of us individually. I need to listen to what
he is saying to me. (Please turn to your scripture on the following
pages. Inspiration points are there should you need them. When
you are ready, return here to continue.)

Conversation

The gift of speech is a wonderful gift.
May I use this gift with kindness.
May I be slow to utter harsh words,
hurtful words, and words spoken in anger.

Conclusion

Glory be to the Father, and to the Son, and to the Holy Spirit,
As it was in the beginning, is now, and ever shall be,
World without end. Amen.

Sunday 23rd September,
Twenty-fifth Sunday in Ordinary Time   Mark 9:30–35

They went on from there and passed through Galilee. He did not want anyone to know it; for he was teaching his disciples, saying to them, "The Son of Man is to be betrayed into human hands, and they will kill him, and three days after being killed, he will rise again." But they did not understand what he was saying and were afraid to ask him. Then they came to Capernaum; and when he was in the house he asked them, "What were you arguing about on the way?" But they were silent, for on the way they had argued with one another who was the greatest. He sat down, called the twelve, and said to them, "Whoever wants to be first must be last of all and servant of all."

- Ambition is part of our makeup, and it was no different for some of the apostles. For Jesus, the proper ambition is to be more like him, to serve and suffer for others as he served and suffered.
- Somebody once told St. Ignatius that Francis Xavier was a very ambitious young man. Ignatius replied, "He is not ambitious enough." His later ambitions were Gospel ambitions. Prayer renews and refreshes our desire to be like and for Jesus in the world.

Monday 24th September   Proverbs 3:27–31

Do not withhold good from those to whom it is due, when it is in your power to do it. Do not say to your neighbor, "Go, and come again; tomorrow I will give it"—when you have it with you. Do not plan harm against your neighbor who lives trustingly beside you. Do not quarrel with anyone without cause, when no harm has been done to you. Do not envy the violent and do not choose any of their ways.

- The Book of Proverbs reminds me just how simple and straightforward the Word of God can be. I consider how, even after hundreds of years, caring for our neighbour is a first test of discipleship.

- I pray for those who live around me, bringing them before God and asking God to bless them. I give thanks for relationships that bring me life and pray for healing for those which do not.

Tuesday 25th September   Luke 8:19–21

Then his mother and his brothers came to him, but they could not reach him because of the crowd. And he was told, "Your mother and your brothers are standing outside, wanting to see you." But he said to them, "My mother and my brothers are those who hear the Word of God and do it."

- Our prime relationship in life is our relationship with God. This explains Jesus' words about his mother and brothers: we belong to God before we belong to anyone else. Our relationship to each other is deepest in our common belonging to God.
- Our relationship with God grows by listening to his Word, praying over his Word, and translating his Word into Christian life and service.

Wednesday 26th September   Proverbs 30:5–9

Every word of God proves true; he is a shield to those who take refuge in him. Do not add to his words, or else he will rebuke you, and you will be found a liar. Two things I ask of you; do not deny them to me before I die: Remove far from me falsehood and lying; give me neither poverty nor riches; feed me with the food that I need, or I shall be full, and deny you, and say, "Who is the Lord?" or I shall be poor, and steal, and profane the name of my God.

- My prayer is my time for hearing the Word of God, not only in the scripture, but listening for the Word that God speaks to me in my heart. I take the time I need, putting aside text and recitation, to be present to the voice of God who loves me.

- It is easy to be full—filled and satisfied—with the wrong food. I review my "diet" with the Lord, and ask myself if where I draw consolation and nourishment is the place God has in mind for me.

Thursday 27th September   Ecclesiastes 1:2–7

Vanity of vanities, says the Teacher, vanity of vanities! All is vanity. What do people gain from all the toil at which they toil under the sun? A generation goes, and a generation comes, but the earth remains for ever. The sun rises and the sun goes down, and hurries to the place where it rises. The wind blows to the south, and goes round to the north; round and round goes the wind, and on its circuits the wind returns. All streams run to the sea, but the sea is not full; to the place where the streams flow, there they continue to flow.

- Jesus points us to the world of nature so that we might realize what we might do. Consider how Jesus would have read this text.
- Effectiveness, rewards, and results are commonly sought in daily life. I realize that my prayer is not open to the same measures but is a conversation in love between God and me.

Friday 28th September   Ecclesiastes 3:1–10

For everything there is a season, and a time for every matter under heaven: a time to be born, and a time to die; a time to plant, and a time to pluck up what is planted; a time to kill, and a time to heal; a time to break down, and a time to build up; a time to weep, and a time to laugh; a time to mourn, and a time to dance; a time to throw away stones, and a time to gather stones together; a time to embrace, and a time to refrain from embracing; a time to seek, and a time to lose; a time to keep, and a time to throw away; a time to tear, and a time to sew; a time to keep silence, and a time to speak; a time to love, and a time to hate; a time for war, and a time for peace.

- I bring my life before God. I allow my desires, regrets, and hopes to be reviewed in the presence of God who loves me. I let go of the expectations I have of myself and listen to where God is calling me—both to rest and to growth.
- I pray for presence of mind when I act, asking that whatever I do may be done with God. I ask for the courage I may need to refrain from action or from speaking as I remind myself that I do not always need to have the final say.

Saturday 29th September,
Sts. Michael, Gabriel, and Raphael   Revelation 12:10–12

Then I heard a loud voice in heaven, proclaiming, "Now have come the salvation and the power and the kingdom of our God and the authority of his Messiah, for the accuser of our comrades has been thrown down, who accuses them day and night before our God. But they have conquered him by the blood of the Lamb and by the word of their testimony, for they did not cling to life even in the face of death. Rejoice then, you heavens and those who dwell in them! But woe to the earth and the sea, for the devil has come down to you with great wrath, because he knows that his time is short!"

- The Book of Revelation describes John's vision of the world to come. He wrote, not to distract people from their real lives, but to help them understand their lives in the light of God's promises and action. I pray that I may be without fear and enjoy the freedom to which God calls me. God's love for me is stronger than any voice that accuses me.
- The voice of the accuser does not speak for my good. On this feast of God's messengers, I pray for the strength I need to resist any message that is not God's word for me.

september 30–october 6

Something to think and pray about each day this week:

Opening Up

The catechism definition of prayer is useful: the raising of the heart and mind to God. Not that we need a definition. Prayer is something we do in our own way. We breathe, smile, and metabolize food without defining the operations—so too with prayer. But we can consciously put ourselves in the way of prayer, quieting the body. One traditional method is to sit with the backbone straight, from your bottom to the top of your head, the eyes half-closed, the breathing slow and easy, the hands on your lap with the palms facing upwards in openness to God's gifts. Then we aim to become present to God as he is always present to us. He has ears to listen to what our heart is saying.

The Presence of God
I remind myself that, as I sit here now,
God is gazing on me with love and holding me in being.
I pause for a moment and think of this.

Freedom
Lord, grant me the grace to be free from the excesses of this life.
Let me not get caught up with the desire for wealth.
Keep my heart and mind free to love and serve You.

Consciousness
How am I really feeling? Light-hearted? Heavy-hearted?
I may be very much at peace, happy to be here.
Equally, I may be frustrated, worried, or angry.
I acknowledge how I really am. It is the real me that the Lord loves.

The Word
I take my time to read the Word of God, slowly, a few times, allowing myself to dwell on anything that strikes me. (Please turn to your scripture on the following pages. Inspiration points are there should you need them. When you are ready, return here to continue.)

Conversation
Do I notice myself reacting as I pray with the Word of God?
Do I feel challenged, comforted, angry?
Imagining Jesus sitting or standing by me,
I speak out my feelings, as one trusted friend to another.

Conclusion
Glory be to the Father, and to the Son, and to the Holy Spirit,
As it was in the beginning, is now, and ever shall be,
World without end. Amen.

Sunday 30th September,
Twenty-sixth Sunday in Ordinary Time   Mark 9:38–41

John said to Jesus, "Teacher, we saw someone casting out demons in your name, and we tried to stop him, because he was not following us." But Jesus said, "Do not stop him; for no one who does a deed of power in my name will be able soon afterwards to speak evil of me. Whoever is not against us is for us. For truly I tell you, whoever gives you a cup of water to drink because you bear the name of Christ will by no means lose the reward."

- We never know the effects of kindness and goodness. Even something good done for a person years ago can still be well remembered. Somewhat like water having its effect wherever it flows, our goodness always gives life, even in the future. These are the unremembered acts of kindness and of love.
- In the small things we show our love, which may be the strongest part of any love.

Monday 1st October   Job 1:21–22

Then Job arose, tore his robe, shaved his head, and fell on the ground and worshiped. He said, "Naked I came from my mother's womb, and naked shall I return there; the Lord gave, and the Lord has taken away; blessed be the name of the Lord." In all this Job did not sin or charge God with wrongdoing.

- Job enjoyed the good things of the earth but receives the news of great calamity with acceptance of God's will.
- I bless the name of the Lord for all of the good things I enjoy, recognizing them and recognizing their source in God who loves me.

Tuesday 2nd October   Job 3:1–3, 11–12

After this Job opened his mouth and cursed the day of his birth. Job said: "Let the day perish on which I was born, and the night that said, 'A man-child is conceived.' Why did I not die at birth, come forth from the womb and expire? Why were there knees to receive me, or breasts for me to suck?"

- If we are shocked to read Job's despairing words, it may be because our prayer is quieter and more polite. Job speaks frankly to God about the anger and pain that he experiences.
- I bring my life before God who knows and loves me, praying that I not be afraid to speak honestly and openly.

Wednesday 3rd October   Luke 9:57–62

As they were going along the road, someone said to him, "I will follow you wherever you go." And Jesus said to him, "Foxes have holes, and birds of the air have nests; but the Son of Man has nowhere to lay his head." To another he said, "Follow me." But he said, "Lord, first let me go and bury my father." But Jesus said to him, "Let the dead bury their own dead; but as for you, go and proclaim the kingdom of God." Another said, "I will follow you, Lord; but let me first say farewell to those at my home." Jesus said to him, "No one who puts a hand to the plow and looks back is fit for the kingdom of God."

- Jesus is not suggesting we neglect our parents or those close to us. In his strong way, he prods us to remain alive to the challenges of the present moment, and to take our futures in hand.
- There always seem to be excuses about following him, and he breaks through these with the call to depth in our following of him, to live our lives with the depth worthy of our humanity and of this calling by him.
- Let me take some time today to look closely at my "excuses."

318

Thursday 4th October,
St. Francis of Assisi   Job 19:22–27

Job said, "O that my words were written down! O that they
were inscribed in a book! O that with an iron pen and with
lead they were engraved on a rock forever! For I know that my
Redeemer lives, and that at the last he will stand upon the earth;
and after my skin has been thus destroyed, then in my flesh I
shall see God, whom I shall see on my side, and my eyes shall
behold, and not another. My heart faints within me!"

- The Book of Job tells of his confidence, trust, and faith as well
  as his doubt, struggle, and debate with God. Job asks that he be
  remembered only for his profession of faith.
- Job imagines a book being written or a monument being inscribed.
  Is there an insight that I might record—for my good or for the
  good of others?

Friday 5th October   Job 38:1, 12–21; 40:3–5

Then the Lord answered Job out of the whirlwind: "Have you
commanded the morning since your days began, and caused
the dawn to know its place, so that it might take hold of the skirts
of the earth, and the wicked be shaken out of it? It is changed like
clay under the seal, and it is dyed like a garment. Light is with-
held from the wicked, and their uplifted arm is broken. Have you
entered into the springs of the sea, or walked in the recesses of the
deep? Have the gates of death been revealed to you, or have you
seen the gates of deep darkness? Have you comprehended the
expanse of the earth? Declare, if you know all this. Where is the
way to the dwelling of light, and where is the place of darkness,
that you may take it to its territory and that you may discern the
paths to its home? Surely you know, for you were born then, and
the number of your days is great!" Then Job answered the Lord:
"See, I am of small account; what shall I answer you? I lay my

hand on my mouth. I have spoken once, and I will not answer; twice, but will proceed no further."

- The Lord invites Job to consider the marvels of creation. As I take some time in prayer to give thanks to God for the wonders around me, I may have to pray for a deeper appreciation of God's presence in the people, places, and things that are all about.
- I know that when my prayer consists only of asking I can lose sight of how God has already answered me. I take time to consider how God already blesses me, and I give thanks.

Saturday 6th October   **Job 42:1–3, 5–6**

Then Job answered the Lord: "I know that you can do all things, and that no purpose of yours can be thwarted. 'Who is this that hides counsel without knowledge?' Therefore I have uttered what I did not understand, things too wonderful for me, which I did not know. I had heard of you by the hearing of the ear, but now my eye sees you; therefore I despise myself, and repent in dust and ashes."

- As I become aware of the greatness of God, I may react by feeling smaller and thinking less of myself. I pray that I may appreciate the dignity I am given by being called to live as a child of God.
- Jesus affirms that God does not receive the humble reluctantly or dutifully, but awaits us with love and joy. I take care not to let false humility come between me and the love God offers me.

Something to think and pray about each day this week:

Moving Towards God

We are never stationary on the path to God. Our prayer changes. Many, many good people move from using well-rehearsed vocal prayers and pious reflections, to a more silent, wordless sort of presence. Be still and know that I am God. I will not have thy thoughts instead of thee. The old peasant, whom the Curé of Ars found spending hours in the church, explained it, "I look at the good God and the good God looks at me." With our oldest friends we do not need to talk.

The Presence of God

In the silence of my innermost being,
in the fragments of my yearned-for wholeness,
can I hear the whispers of God's presence?
Can I remember when I felt God's nearness?—
when we walked together and I let myself be embraced by God's love.

Freedom

I ask for the grace
to let go of my own concerns
and be open to what God is asking of me,
to let myself be guided and formed by my loving Creator.

Consciousness

I exist in a web of relationships—links to nature, people, God.
I trace out these links, giving thanks
for the life that flows through them.
Some links are twisted or broken:
I may feel regret, anger, disappointment.
I pray for the gift of acceptance and forgiveness.

The Word

The Word of God comes down to us through the scriptures.
May the Holy Spirit enlighten my mind and my heart to respond
to the gospel teachings. (Please turn to your scripture on the following pages. Inspiration points are there should you need them.
When you are ready, return here to continue.)

Conversation

Remembering that I am still in God's presence,
I imagine Jesus himself standing or sitting beside me,
and say whatever is on my mind, whatever is in my heart,
speaking as one friend to another.

Conclusion

Glory be to the Father, and to the Son, and to the Holy Spirit,
As it was in the beginning, is now, and ever shall be,
World without end. Amen.

Sunday 7th October,
Twenty-seventh Sunday in Ordinary Time   Mark 10:2–16

Some Pharisees came, and to test Jesus they asked, "Is it lawful for a man to divorce his wife?" He answered them, "What did Moses command you?" They said, "Moses allowed a man to write a certificate of dismissal and to divorce her." But Jesus said to them, "Because of your hardness of heart he wrote this commandment for you. But from the beginning of creation, 'God made them male and female.' 'For this reason a man shall leave his father and mother and be joined to his wife, and the two shall become one flesh.' So they are no longer two, but one flesh. Therefore what God has joined together, let no one separate." Then in the house the disciples asked him again about this matter. He said to them, "Whoever divorces his wife and marries another commits adultery against her; and if she divorces her husband and marries another, she commits adultery." People were bringing little children to him in order that he might touch them; and the disciples spoke sternly to them. But when Jesus saw this, he was indignant and said to them, "Let the little children come to me; do not stop them; for it is to such as these that the kingdom of God belongs. Truly I tell you, whoever does not receive the kingdom of God as a little child will never enter it." And he took them up in his arms, laid his hands on them, and blessed them.

- Two "cares" feature in the gospel today: care for marriage and care for children.
- Perhaps in our prayer today we can bring to mind people who are close to us and who have marriage or family cares, and pray for them. Help us, Lord, to truly care for the earth, for marriage, and for children in our society.

Monday 8th October   Galatians 1:6–12

I am astonished that you are so quickly deserting the one who called you in the grace of Christ and are turning to a different gospel—not that there is another gospel, but there are some who are confusing you and want to pervert the gospel of Christ. But even if we or an angel from heaven should proclaim to you a gospel contrary to what we proclaimed to you, let that one be accursed! As we have said before, so now I repeat, if anyone proclaims to you a gospel contrary to what you received, let that one be accursed! Am I now seeking human approval, or God's approval? Or am I trying to please people? If I were still pleasing people, I would not be a servant of Christ. For I want you to know, brothers and sisters, that the gospel that was proclaimed by me is not of human origin; for I did not receive it from a human source, nor was I taught it, but I received it through a revelation of Jesus Christ.

- I pray with compassion for all people who are distracted by other gospels, by messages which are not for their good or for their growth.
- I think of how God's working has been revealed in my life. I savour these revelations and give thanks.

Tuesday 9th October   Galatians 1:13–24

You have heard, no doubt, of my earlier life in Judaism. I was violently persecuting the church of God and was trying to destroy it. I advanced in Judaism beyond many among my people of the same age, for I was far more zealous for the traditions of my ancestors. But when God, who had set me apart before I was born and called me through his grace, was pleased to reveal his Son to me, so that I might proclaim him among the Gentiles, I did not confer with any human being, nor did I go up to Jerusalem to those who were already apostles before me, but I went away at once into Arabia, and afterwards I returned to Damascus. Then after three years I did go up to Jerusalem to visit Cephas and stayed with him for fifteen days; but I did not see any other apostle except James the Lord's brother. In what I am writing to you, before God, I do not lie! Then I went into the regions of Syria and Cilicia, and I was still unknown by sight to the churches of Judea that are in Christ; they only heard it said, "The one who formerly was persecuting us is now proclaiming the faith he once tried to destroy." And they glorified God because of me.

- Paul's writings have inspired the Church for centuries. I think of my own "missionary history," remembering how I have brought good news to people in different ways.
- I think of how Paul was able to change his life from being a persecutor of Christians to being a proclaimer of the Gospel. I pray for the courage and the humility I need to change my habits for the better.

Wednesday 10th October · Galatians 2:1–2

Then after fourteen years I went up again to Jerusalem with Barnabas, taking Titus along with me. I went up in response to a revelation. Then I laid before them (though only in a private meeting with the acknowledged leaders) the gospel that I proclaim among the Gentiles, in order to make sure that I was not running, or had not run, in vain.

- I lay before God "the gospel that I proclaim," asking God to help me to recognize more clearly where I might speak or stay silent, act or be still.
- Paul took care about where he spoke and to whom. I ask forgiveness for times when my words have been inappropriate or unhelpful, and pray for God's Spirit to be with me into the future.

Thursday 11th October   Galatians 3:1–5

You foolish Galatians! Who has bewitched you? It was before your eyes that Jesus Christ was publicly exhibited as crucified! The only thing I want to learn from you is this: Did you receive the Spirit by doing the works of the law or by believing what you heard? Are you so foolish? Having started with the Spirit, are you now ending with the flesh? Did you experience so much for nothing?—if it really was for nothing. Well then, does God supply you with the Spirit and work miracles among you by your doing the works of the law, or by your believing what you heard?

- Paul calls the Galatians to account as he questions them closely on their faithfulness to the Gospel. It is easy to become indignant or defensive when questions arise.
- I pray for the humility I need to be able to examine my life and bring it before God who knows me well and loves me dearly.

Friday 12th October   Galatians 3:13–14

Christ redeemed us from the curse of the law by becoming a curse for us—for it is written, "Cursed is everyone who hangs on a tree"—in order that in Christ Jesus the blessing of Abraham might come to the Gentiles, so that we might receive the promise of the Spirit through faith.

- Jesus was prepared to take the lowest place, even to risk losing his reputation, his good name—as Paul says, "he became a curse." He did this for me. I give thanks to God, and I renew my commitment to give what I can in Jesus' name.
- I think of the situations and relationships in my life that need to be more open to the presence of the Holy Spirit. I bring them before God aware of the promise of blessings that God gives to me.

Saturday 13th October   **Galatians 3:23–29**

Now before faith came, we were imprisoned and guarded under the law until faith would be revealed. Therefore the law was our disciplinarian until Christ came, so that we might be justified by faith. But now that faith has come, we are no longer subject to a disciplinarian, for in Christ Jesus you are all children of God through faith. As many of you as were baptized into Christ have clothed yourselves with Christ. There is no longer Jew or Greek, there is no longer slave or free, there is no longer male and female; for all of you are one in Christ Jesus. And if you belong to Christ, then you are Abraham's offspring, heirs according to the promise.

• Analysts and commentators always divide people into different categories and groups. It is easy—and sometimes attractive—to think of oneself as part of a particular sector. Paul reminds me that such divisions may limit my view of God's action. I consider what it is like to let go of distinctions, remembering what it means to be "one in Christ."

• Sometimes I can become my own disciplinarian, living by rules and limits that I have set down. I pray that I may receive and live in the freedom that Jesus wishes for me.

october 14–20

Something to think and pray about each day this week:

Imagining Jesus

One way into prayer is through the imagination. Take a gospel scene such as the question put to Jesus (Matthew 22:17): is it lawful to pay tribute to Caesar? Read the text slowly; then read it again. Place yourself in the scene, standing beside Jesus, watching him as the Pharisees lay a trap with their question. If you can, see the place, the people, the coin of tribute. Imagine the tension provoked by their words. Be present with Jesus as he asks for the denarius. Hear his voice as he exposes the hypocrisy of their flattery, but takes their question seriously and gives an answer that has echoed down the centuries: give therefore to the emperor the things that are the emperor's and to God the things that are God's. Savor its implications.

The Presence of God

God is with me; but more,
God is within me, giving me existence.
Let me dwell for a moment on God's life-giving presence
in my body, my mind, my heart,
and in the whole of my life.

Freedom

I ask for the grace to believe
in what I could be and do
if I only allowed God, my loving Creator,
to continue to create me, guide me, and shape me.

Consciousness

Knowing that God loves me unconditionally,
I can afford to be honest about how I am.
How has the last day been, and how do I feel now?
I share my feelings openly with the Lord.

The Word

I read the Word of God slowly, a few times over, and I listen
to what God is saying to me. (Please turn to your scripture on
the following pages. Inspiration points are there should you need
them. When you are ready, return here to continue.)

Conversation

How has God's Word moved me? Has it left me cold?
Has it consoled me or moved me to act in a new way?
I imagine Jesus standing or sitting beside me;
I turn and share my feelings with him.

Conclusion

Glory be to the Father, and to the Son, and to the Holy Spirit,
As it was in the beginning, is now, and ever shall be,
World without end. Amen.

Sunday 14th October,
Twenty-eighth Sunday in Ordinary Time Mark 10:17–27

As Jesus was setting out on a journey, a man ran up and knelt before him, and asked him, "Good Teacher, what must I do to inherit eternal life?" Jesus said to him, "Why do you call me good? No one is good but God alone. You know the commandments: 'You shall not murder; You shall not commit adultery; You shall not steal; You shall not bear false witness; You shall not defraud; Honor your father and mother.'" He said to him, "Teacher, I have kept all these since my youth." Jesus, looking at him, loved him and said, "You lack one thing; go, sell what you own, and give the money to the poor, and you will have treasure in heaven; then come, follow me." When he heard this, he was shocked and went away grieving, for he had many possessions. Then Jesus looked around and said to his disciples, "How hard it will be for those who have wealth to enter the kingdom of God!" And the disciples were perplexed at these words. But Jesus said to them again, "Children, how hard it is to enter the kingdom of God! It is easier for a camel to go through the eye of a needle than for someone who is rich to enter the kingdom of God." They were greatly astounded and said to one another, "Then who can be saved?" Jesus looked at them and said, "For mortals it is impossible, but not for God; for God all things are possible."

- The man who had great wealth found sadness in his wealth. Somehow the Lord's invitation to give away and to share threatened him badly. Jesus knows the way possessions and wealth and comforts can tie us down. He knows that his compassion makes up for much human weakness.

- We offer to the Lord in prayer all we are and all we have, asking for help in using wisely what we possess and living easily without what we might like to possess but cannot.

Monday 15th October,
St. Teresa of Avila   Galatians 5:1

For freedom Christ has set us free. Stand firm, therefore, and do not submit again to a yoke of slavery.

- I take time to consider the freedom that God has in mind for me. I name and speak to God about my deepest desires, recognizing what holds me back.

- I can surrender my freedom easily by letting habits and patterns develop, by thinking of things I "must" do. I think of how I might turn away from what does not bring me life and allow time for God to surprise me. I ask God to help me to be free.

Tuesday 16th October   Galatians 5:1, 4–5

For freedom Christ has set us free. Stand firm, therefore, and do not submit again to a yoke of slavery. You who want to be justified by the law have cut yourselves off from Christ; you have fallen away from grace. For through the Spirit, by faith, we eagerly wait for the hope of righteousness.

- Seeking to be justified by the law is sometimes attractive; observation of the law brings a human satisfaction. Living in the freedom to which Jesus calls us means taking risks.

- The freedom that Jesus has in mind for me does not leave me lost or directionless. I am pointed in hope, waiting on the word of the Lord. I ask for God's grace to help me to live freely.

Wednesday 17th October   Galatians 5:22–25

The fruit of the Spirit is love, joy, peace, patience, kindness, generosity, faithfulness, gentleness, and self-control. There is no law against such things. And those who belong to Christ Jesus have crucified the flesh with its passions and desires. If we live by the Spirit, let us also be guided by the Spirit.

- Paul lists the fruits of the Spirit. I consider them now, imagining God "stocktaking," rejoicing at the discovery of each of these gifts in my life, cherishing what is there while offering me more.
- For Paul, the attractions of the flesh represent everything that distracts us from what God offers. As I come to pray, I recognize whatever it is that may come between me and the freedom God has in mind for me.

Thursday 18th October, St. Luke, Evangelist — 2 Timothy 4:9–13

Do your best to come to me soon, for Demas, in love with this present world, has deserted me and gone to Thessalonica; Crescens has gone to Galatia, Titus to Dalmatia. Only Luke is with me. Get Mark and bring him with you, for he is useful in my ministry. I have sent Tychicus to Ephesus. When you come, bring the cloak that I left with Carpus at Troas, also the books, and above all the parchments.

- In Paul's reliance on Timothy, Luke, and Mark, and his request for some possessions he values, we are reminded of how the gospel is proclaimed in everyday, real-life circumstances.
- I think of the people who surround me and give thanks for those upon whom I rely, and I pray for the other people who come to mind. I give thanks to God for the possessions that help me.

Friday 19th October — Ephesians 1:11–14

In Christ we have also obtained an inheritance, having been destined according to the purpose of him who accomplishes all things according to his counsel and will, so that we, who were the first to set our hope on Christ, might live for the praise of his glory. In him you also, when you had heard the word of truth, the gospel of your salvation, and had believed in him, were marked with the seal of the promised Holy Spirit; this is the pledge of our inheritance towards redemption as God's own people, to the praise of his glory.

- The inheritance that we have in Christ was a great consolation to Teresa of Avila, whose feast we celebrated this week. She wrote, "Whoever has God lacks nothing: God alone is enough."
- The gifts that we are given by God bring us joy and fulfil our lives. We pray that we may see in them an assurance that God's Spirit is with us and that we may always be moved to give praise to God.

Saturday 20th October   **Ephesians 1:17–20**

I pray that the God of our Lord Jesus Christ, the Father of glory, may give you a spirit of wisdom and revelation as you come to know him, so that, with the eyes of your heart enlightened, you may know what is the hope to which he has called you, what are the riches of his glorious inheritance among the saints, and what is the immeasurable greatness of his power for us who believe, according to the working of his great power.

- As I see Paul pray generously for his friends, I think of my own friends. I call a friend to mind and read this passage again, praying for them from my heart.
- I ask for a spirit of wisdom and revelation that I may look at my life wisely and recognize God's gifts. I allow God to expand my hope to realize that what God desires for me is far beyond anything I might ask for myself.

Something to think and pray about each day this week:

The Depth of Prayer

Our faith is a mixture of light and darkness. We look to the holy people of history to give us some light on the quest for God. St. John of the Cross, who reformed the Carmelites and was imprisoned for his pains, "distrusted whatever removed the soul from the obscure faith where the understanding must be left behind in order to go to God by love." One of his greatest Carmelite followers, Thérèse of Lisieux, lived her religious life in darkness. Her biographer described her state in these words, "The whole area of religion seemed remote and unreal to her, not arousing the least response, either friendly or antagonistic, in her mind and heart. It was as though religion had become simply something remembered, grey, cold and unimportant."

St. Paul wrote about our inability to pray, "The Spirit helps us in our weakness; when we do not know how to pray as we ought, that very Spirit intercedes with sighs too deep for words. And God, who searches the heart, knows what is the mind of the Spirit, because the Spirit intercedes for the saints according to the will of God" (Romans 8:26). The dialogue with God continues even when our mind and heart are weary.

The Presence of God

To be present is to arrive as one is and open up to the other.
At this instant, as I arrive here, God is present waiting for me.
God always arrives before me, desiring to connect with me
even more than my most intimate friend.
I take a moment and greet my loving God.

Freedom

"In these days, God taught me
as a schoolteacher teaches a pupil" (St. Ignatius).
I remind myself that there are things God has to teach me yet,
and ask for the grace to hear them and let them change me.

Consciousness

In the presence of my loving Creator,
I look honestly at my feelings over the last day,
the highs, the lows, and the level ground.
Can I see where the Lord has been present?

The Word

I take my time to read the Word of God, slowly, a few times, allowing myself to dwell on anything that strikes me. (Please turn to your scripture on the following pages. Inspiration points are there should you need them. When you are ready, return here to continue.)

Conversation

What feelings are rising in me
as I pray and reflect on God's Word?
I imagine Jesus himself sitting or standing beside me,
and open my heart to him.

Conclusion

Glory be to the Father, and to the Son, and to the Holy Spirit,
As it was in the beginning, is now, and ever shall be,
World without end. Amen.

Sunday 21st October,
Twenty-ninth Sunday in Ordinary Time   Mark 10:42–45

J esus called them and said to them, "You know that among the Gentiles those whom they recognize as their rulers lord it over them, and their great ones are tyrants over them. But it is not so among you; but whoever wishes to become great among you must be your servant, and whoever wishes to be first among you must be slave of all. For the Son of Man came not to be served but to serve, and to give his life a ransom for many."

- Many titles of the Lord include the word "servant": servant king, servant Messiah, servant Lord. This is one of Jesus' deepest identities—he is among us as one who serves. Watch him in the gospel teaching his disciples to be like him, one who serves others in love.
- Jesus teaches this to each of us in prayer.

Monday 22nd October   Ephesians 2:4–10

B ut God, who is rich in mercy, out of the great love with which he loved us even when we were dead through our trespasses, made us alive together with Christ—by grace you have been saved—and raised us up with him and seated us with him in the heavenly places in Christ Jesus, so that in the ages to come he might show the immeasurable riches of his grace in kindness towards us in Christ Jesus. For by grace you have been saved through faith, and this is not your own doing; it is the gift of God—not the result of works, so that no one may boast. For we are what he has made us, created in Christ Jesus for good works, which God prepared beforehand to be our way of life.

- God freely gifts each one of us with salvation, through the Christ, his son Jesus. This generosity brings wealth beyond compare.
- In what I do today, let me give thanks. Lord, build my faith.

Tuesday 23rd October **Ephesians 2:19–22**

You are no longer strangers and aliens, but you are citizens with the saints and also members of the household of God, built upon the foundation of the apostles and prophets, with Christ Jesus himself as the cornerstone. In him the whole structure is joined together and grows into a holy temple in the Lord; in whom you also are built together spiritually into a dwelling-place for God.

- The dignity that I am given in being a member of God's household is not something that I have deserved or earned—it is God's gracious gift, given in love. I place myself in prayer before God, who attends to me as a family member.
- I think of all who are estranged, left out, or feel marginalized. I think of how my words and attitudes to them can remind them of their true dignity, can help them to realize that we are called into one family in God.

Wednesday 24th October **Ephesians 3:7–12**

Of this gospel I have become a servant according to the gift of God's grace that was given to me by the working of his power. Although I am the very least of all the saints, this grace was given to me to bring to the Gentiles the news of the boundless riches of Christ, and to make everyone see what is the plan of the mystery hidden for ages in God who created all things; so that through the church the wisdom of God in its rich variety might now be made known to the rulers and authorities in the heavenly places. This was in accordance with the eternal purpose that he has carried out in Christ Jesus our Lord, in whom we have access to God in boldness and confidence through faith in him.

- Paul was able to consider that he was "a servant" and "the least" while he valued the dignity he was given by being a member of God's household.
- In prayer, I consider how I am linked with the generations of people who handed on the message that St. Paul proclaimed, the Good News that Jesus left us.

Thursday 25th October   Ephesians 3:14–21

For this reason I bow my knees before the Father, from whom every family in heaven and on earth takes its name. I pray that, according to the riches of his glory, he may grant that you may be strengthened in your inner being with power through his Spirit, and that Christ may dwell in your hearts through faith, as you are being rooted and grounded in love. I pray that you may have the power to comprehend, with all the saints, what is the breadth and length and height and depth, and to know the love of Christ that surpasses knowledge, so that you may be filled with all the fullness of God. Now to him who by the power at work within us is able to accomplish abundantly far more than all we can ask or imagine, to him be glory in the church and in Christ Jesus to all generations, for ever and ever. Amen.

- This time I spend in prayer is time for my inner being to grow stronger. I take care to note and to cherish any intuition, revelation, or sign of God's presence in me.
- I allow myself to take some moments in the presence of God who is so much greater than my imagining or comprehension. Believing that God can accomplish more than I can ask or imagine, I take care not to let God's work be limited by any narrow boundaries that I set.

Friday 26th October   Ephesians 4:1–6

I therefore, the prisoner in the Lord, beg you to lead a life worthy of the calling to which you have been called, with all humility and gentleness, with patience, bearing with one another in love, making every effort to maintain the unity of the Spirit in the bond of peace. There is one body and one Spirit, just as you were called to the one hope of your calling, one Lord, one faith, one baptism, one God and Father of all, who is above all and through all and in all.

- Christian living calls me into care for other people. I belong to others in the Body of Christ; they can depend on me.
- St. Paul lists humility, patience, gentleness, and love as characteristics of the Spirit. I ask God to strengthen these graces in me, thinking of how I need them at this time.

Saturday 27th October   Ephesians 4:14–16

We must no longer be children, tossed to and fro and blown about by every wind of doctrine, by people's trickery, by their craftiness in deceitful scheming. But speaking the truth in love, we must grow up in every way into him who is the head, into Christ, from whom the whole body, joined and knitted together by every ligament with which it is equipped, as each part is working properly, promotes the body's growth in building itself up in love.

- Building up the Body of Christ in a visible or tangible way may seem attractive. I trust that my prayer knits together the ligaments of Christ's body, and offer this as my invisible work to be measured only by God.
- I will be tossed about by every wind of doctrine if I forget my growth into Christ. I pray now with all others who create their *Sacred Space* in prayer today; I pray for all who are in need.

Something to think and pray about each day this week:

Remembering

This is the month when we relish what is called the Communion of Saints, the oneness of all who have lived and died. Customs vary across the world, but we may pray for them, remember them at Masses, visit and pray at graves, and tell stories. This is not in memory of saints with haloes and floating bodies, but rather those who suffered and survived, who tried and sometimes failed, as Paddy Kavanagh wrote:

> To be a poet and not know the trade,
> To be a lover and repel all women;
> Twin ironies by which great saints are made,
> The agonising pincer-jaws of Heaven.

Presence of God

What is present to me is what has a hold on my becoming.
I reflect on the presence of God always there in love,
amidst the many things that have a hold on me.
I pause and pray that I may let God
affect my becoming in this precise moment.

Freedom

If God were trying to tell me something, would I know?
If God were reassuring me or challenging me, would I notice?
I ask for the grace to be free of my own preoccupations
and open to what God may be saying to me.

Consciousness

Knowing that God loves me unconditionally,
I look honestly over the last day, its events, and my feelings.
Do I have something to be grateful for? Then I give thanks.
Is there something I am sorry for? Then I ask forgiveness.

The Word

God speaks to each one of us individually. I need to listen to what
he is saying to me. (Please turn to your scripture on the following
pages. Inspiration points are there should you need them. When
you are ready, return here to continue.)

Conversation

What is stirring in me as I pray?
Am I consoled, troubled, left cold?
I imagine Jesus himself standing or sitting at my side,
and share my feelings with him.

Conclusion

Glory be to the Father, and to the Son, and to the Holy Spirit,
As it was in the beginning, is now, and ever shall be,
World without end. Amen.

Sunday 28th October,
Thirtieth Sunday in Ordinary Time   Mark 10:46–52

They came to Jericho. As he and his disciples and a large crowd were leaving Jericho, Bartimaeus son of Timaeus, a blind beggar, was sitting by the roadside. When he heard that it was Jesus of Nazareth, he began to shout out and say, "Jesus, Son of David, have mercy on me!" Many sternly ordered him to be quiet, but he cried out even more loudly, "Son of David, have mercy on me!" Jesus stood still and said, "Call him here." And they called the blind man, saying to him, "Take heart; get up, he is calling you." So throwing off his cloak, he sprang up and came to Jesus. Then Jesus said to him, "What do you want me to do for you?" The blind man said to him, "My teacher, let me see again." Jesus said to him, "Go; your faith has made you well." Immediately he regained his sight and followed him on the way.

- Without his cloak the blind man could be even more lost—he would lose protection from the elements. It was one of his most essential possessions. In going to Jesus, he let it go.
- Letting go is an integral part of prayer. We hand over hurts, grief, and disappointments as best we can. We hand them over to the One who loves us and gives much more in return.

Monday 29th October   Ephesians 4:32–5:2, 8

Be kind to one another, tender-hearted, forgiving one another, as God in Christ has forgiven you. Therefore be imitators of God, as beloved children, and live in love, as Christ loved us and gave himself up for us, a fragrant offering and sacrifice to God. For once you were darkness, but now in the Lord you are light. Live as children of light—for the fruit of the light is found in all that is good and right and true.

- The first tasks I am given are not dramatic, demanding, or far away. I am asked to be kind and forgiving to those around me. Before I think of what I might do, I take time to consider that Christ has forgiven me.
- I imagine myself as a light, a source of illumination and comfort, bringing clarity and hope. I ask God to help me to live as a child of the light in my ordinary circumstances.

Tuesday 30th October **Ephesians 5:21, 29–33**

Be subject to one another out of reverence for Christ. For no one ever hates his own body, but he nourishes and tenderly cares for it, just as Christ does for the church, because we are members of his body. "For this reason a man will leave his father and mother and be joined to his wife, and the two will become one flesh." This is a great mystery, and I am applying it to Christ and the church. Each of you, however, should love his wife as himself, and a wife should respect her husband.

- I think about how the Word of God speaks to me in prayer. I pray for all who live in committed relationships, that they may give witness to Christ by living in mutual reverence, love, and respect.
- I am reminded that Christ cares for the Church; I take time to allow myself to be blessed by God, aware that I am a member of Christ's body.

Wednesday 31st October **Ephesians 6:1–9**

Children, obey your parents in the Lord, for this is right. "Honor your father and mother"—this is the first commandment with a promise: "so that it may be well with you and you may live long on the earth." And, fathers, do not provoke your children to anger, but bring them up in the discipline and instruction of the Lord. Slaves, obey your earthly masters with fear and trembling, in singleness of heart, as you obey Christ;

344

not only while being watched, and in order to please them, but as slaves of Christ, doing the will of God from the heart. Render service with enthusiasm, as to the Lord and not to men and women, knowing that whatever good we do, we will receive the same again from the Lord, whether we are slaves or free. And, masters, do the same to them. Stop threatening them, for you know that both of you have the same Master in heaven, and with him there is no partiality.

- Paul saw the roles he was familiar with—parent, child, slave—as models of how the Christian relates to God. I think of those who take different roles around me and pray that I may learn from them how better to be a disciple.
- I consider the different roles that I might occupy in the course of the day and ask God to give me the presence of mind to be gracious in each.

Thursday 1st November, Feast of All Saints   Matthew 5:2–9

He began to speak, and taught them, saying: "Blessed are the poor in spirit, for theirs is the kingdom of heaven. Blessed are those who mourn, for they will be comforted. Blessed are the meek, for they will inherit the earth. Blessed are those who hunger and thirst for righteousness, for they will be filled. Blessed are the merciful, for they will receive mercy. Blessed are the pure in heart, for they will see God. Blessed are the peacemakers, for they will be called children of God."

- It is hard for us today to grasp just how radical Jesus' teaching is; perhaps familiarity and misunderstanding dull our responses. Here we can glimpse the kingdom. It is our future promise; this is our invitation to accept God as the core of daily life.
- Lord, teach me to live your way, not mine.

345

Friday 2nd November, Feast of All Souls   Romans 5:5

Hope does not disappoint us, because God's love has been poured into our hearts through the Holy Spirit that has been given to us.

- It is our custom this day to pray for the dead, for those who go before us. We join with them in our prayer.
- When I pray, I am not alone: I join with all those who are alive to God, whether in this world or in God's presence.

Saturday 3rd November   Philippians 1:22–26

If I am to live in the flesh, that means fruitful labor for me; and I do not know which I prefer. I am hard pressed between the two: my desire is to depart and be with Christ, for that is far better; but to remain in the flesh is more necessary for you. Since I am convinced of this, I know that I will remain and continue with all of you for your progress and joy in faith, so that I may share abundantly in your boasting in Christ Jesus when I come to you again.

- The most important thing for St. Paul is to give glory to Christ; he is able to say that it does not matter whether he lives or dies. Most people will immediately conclude that life must be better.
- Before God, I am reminded of what my life is for, praying that I may be strengthened to give glory to God, to be of service to others, and to continue to grow in love.

november 4–10

Something to think and pray about each day this week:

Welcome to Prayer

The spiritual writer Anthony de Mello contrasted the Judgment God with what he called the God of Welcomes. He described God getting excited like a child because you are coming to pray, "God has all these angels with golden trumpets. They are to get ready to welcome you. God has this infinite, red carpet: roll it out, he says to another group of angels." And de Mello ended by challenging his audience, "you think my pictures are silly and childish. I tell you, they are much more true than the images you may have, especially if you have some picture in the back of your head of a distant and bored and sulky God."

Perhaps even after years of study and prayer, false pictures of God can still lurk in our imaginations, so that we too become false. We put on prayer masks. We do our religious duty. We try to bargain with this boss or placate this judge. We have forgotten that the Lord takes delight in people. In more ordinary language, God is "thrilled to see us."

So get yourselves ready patiently. But remember the true God of love to whom you come. Then, some days at least, those ten minutes of yours can flow naturally and easily, and most importantly of all, leave you strengthened for a life of love.

The Presence of God

God is with me; but more, God is within me.
Let me dwell for a moment on God's life-giving presence
in my body, in my mind, in my heart,
as I sit here, right now.

Freedom

I need to close out the noise, to rise above the noise—
the noise that interrupts, that separates,
the noise that isolates.
I need to listen to God again.

Consciousness

I remind myself that I am in the presence of the Lord.
I will take refuge in His loving heart.
He is my strength in times of weakness.
He is my comforter in times of sorrow.

The Word

I read the Word of God slowly, a few times over, and I listen
to what God is saying to me. (Please turn to your scripture on
the following pages. Inspiration points are there should you need
them. When you are ready, return here to continue.)

Conversation

Do I notice myself reacting as I pray with the Word of God?
Do I feel challenged, comforted, angry?
Imagining Jesus sitting or standing by me,
I speak out my feelings, as one trusted friend to another.

Conclusion

Glory be to the Father, and to the Son, and to the Holy Spirit,
As it was in the beginning, is now, and ever shall be,
World without end. Amen.

348

Sunday 4th November,
Thirty-first Sunday in Ordinary Time   Mark 12:28–34

One of the scribes came near and heard them disputing with one another, and seeing that Jesus answered them well, he asked him, "Which commandment is the first of all?" Jesus answered, "The first is, 'Hear, O Israel: the Lord our God, the Lord is one; you shall love the Lord your God with all your heart, and with all your soul, and with all your mind, and with all your strength.' The second is this, 'You shall love your neighbor as yourself.' There is no other commandment greater than these." Then the scribe said to him, "You are right, Teacher; you have truly said that 'he is one, and besides him there is no other'; and 'to love him with all the heart, and with all the understanding, and with all the strength,' and 'to love one's neighbor as oneself,' —this is much more important than all whole burnt offerings and sacrifices." When Jesus saw that he answered wisely, he said to him, "You are not far from the kingdom of God." After that no one dared to ask him any question.

- The Jewish lawyers were blamed for multiplying regulations, but they also liked to seek out the essentials of the law, to give the whole of their religion in one sound-bite. The rabbi Hillel was once asked to instruct someone in the whole law while he stood on one leg.
- Jesus takes the lawyer's question seriously and points us to an interior religion, one of the heart, not of rule keeping or ritual.

Monday 5th November   Luke 14:12–14

Jesus said also to the one who had invited him, "When you give a luncheon or a dinner, do not invite your friends or your brothers or your relatives or rich neighbors, in case they may invite you in return, and you would be repaid. But when you give a banquet, invite the poor, the crippled, the lame, and the blind. And you will be blessed, because they cannot repay you, for you will be repaid at the resurrection of the righteous."

- Although he promises reward, Jesus wants us to do good simply because it is good. I ask that I may recognize what is best and act with confidence.
- Giving without hope of reward means letting go even my rational satisfaction. Sometimes I may not be sure about the best thing to do, but I ask God to strengthen my faith as I do what I can.

Tuesday 6th November   **Luke 14:15–24**

One of the dinner guests said to Jesus, "Blessed is anyone who will eat bread in the kingdom of God!" Then Jesus said to him, "Someone gave a great dinner and invited many. At the time for the dinner he sent his slave to say to those who had been invited, 'Come; for everything is ready now.' But they all alike began to make excuses. The first said to him, 'I have bought a piece of land, and I must go out and see it; please accept my apologies.' Another said, 'I have bought five yoke of oxen, and I am going to try them out; please accept my apologies.' Another said, 'I have just been married, and therefore I cannot come.' So the slave returned and reported this to his master. Then the owner of the house became angry and said to his slave, 'Go out at once into the streets and lanes of the town and bring in the poor, the crippled, the blind, and the lame.' And the slave said, 'Sir, what you ordered has been done, and there is still room.' Then the master said to the slave, 'Go out into the roads and lanes, and compel people to come in, so that my house may be filled. For I tell you, none of those who were invited will taste my dinner.'"

- God's invitation is from the heart. God's love, like a generous banquet, is for all. The story presents God as being disappointed and even angry that we do not respond. Whatever anger God has does not last; the empty chairs at the banquet are to be filled by people who might not expect an invitation. All are invited to pray, to love, and to worship.

- Like the people invited to feast, I often resist God's invitation; I take time now just to be present with God who loves my company.

Wednesday 7th November   Luke 14:25–27

Now large crowds were travelling with him; and he turned and said to them, "Whoever comes to me and does not hate father and mother, wife and children, brothers and sisters, yes, and even life itself, cannot be my disciple. Whoever does not carry the cross and follow me cannot be my disciple."

- How much am I able to let go? I ask God to help me to grow in freedom, to be ready to follow and to serve in new ways.
- As I consider the freedom to which Jesus calls me, patterns and habits that limit me may come to mind. I bring them before God for the healing that I need.

Thursday 8th November   Luke 15:1–10

Now all the tax-collectors and sinners were coming near to listen to him. And the Pharisees and the scribes were grumbling and saying, "This fellow welcomes sinners and eats with them." So he told them this parable: "Which one of you, having a hundred sheep and losing one of them, does not leave the ninety-nine in the wilderness and go after the one that is lost until he finds it? When he has found it, he lays it on his shoulders and rejoices. And when he comes home, he calls together his friends and neighbors, saying to them, 'Rejoice with me, for I have found my sheep that was lost.' Just so, I tell you, there will be more joy in heaven over one sinner who repents than over ninety-nine righteous people who need no repentance. Or what woman having ten silver coins, if she loses one of them, does not light a lamp, sweep the house, and search carefully until she finds it? When she has found it, she calls together her friends and neighbors, saying, 'Rejoice with me, for I have found the coin that I had lost.' Just so, I tell you, there is joy in the presence of the angels of God over one sinner who repents."

- The finding of the coin seems such a simple joy. I realize that possessions and property may blind me to simple blessings. As I think of what is really of value, I may realize that I have to seek it again, perhaps sweeping and searching.
- Those around me may know what is really important to me. Thinking of the woman in Jesus' story, I may need to remind them of what I really value.

Friday 9th November,
Dedication of the Lateran Basilica   John 2:13–22

The Passover of the Jews was near, and Jesus went up to Jerusalem. In the temple he found people selling cattle, sheep, and doves, and the money changers seated at their tables. Making a whip of cords, he drove all of them out of the temple, both the sheep and the cattle. He also poured out the coins of the money changers and overturned their tables. He told those who were selling the doves, "Take these things out of here! Stop making my Father's house a marketplace!" His disciples remembered that it was written, "Zeal for your house will consume me." The Jews then said to him, "What sign can you show us for doing this?" Jesus answered them, "Destroy this temple, and in three days I will raise it up." The Jews then said, "This temple has been under construction for forty-six years, and will you raise it up in three days?" But he was speaking of the temple of his body. After he was raised from the dead, his disciples remembered that he had said this; and they believed the scripture and the word that Jesus had spoken.

- With anger and passion, Jesus pushes us to look beyond the externals—temple, church, structure, commerce—to focus on the essential: the presence of God among us.
- Lord, teach me to fix my gaze on you, and not be diverted.

Saturday 10th November   Luke 16:9–13

Jesus said to the disciples, "And I tell you, make friends for yourselves by means of dishonest wealth so that when it is gone, they may welcome you into the eternal homes. Whoever is faithful in a very little is faithful also in much; and whoever is dishonest in a very little is dishonest also in much. If then you have not been faithful with the dishonest wealth, who will entrust to you the true riches? And if you have not been faithful with what belongs to another, who will give you what is your own? No slave can serve two masters; for a slave will either hate the one and love the other, or be devoted to the one and despise the other. You cannot serve God and wealth."

- I might look again at the advertising that is all around. I think of what these messages say to me about the values of the world and consider how my way of living might be a "billboard" for the message of Jesus.
- It is easy to be preoccupied by concerns and priorities. I take time now to be in the presence of God who loves me, laying aside other distractions or bringing them before God.

Something to think and pray about each day this week:

Glimpsing Love

George Herbert, an Anglican minister who was also a great poet, once wrote a sonnet on prayer. It's famous in the world of literature for having no sentences, just phrases that describe prayer in many different ways. Some of them evoke prayer as petition, as a battering ram against the Almighty. Some of them compare prayer to hearing heavenly music. I think that Herbert is deliberately giving eloquent descriptions in order to surprise us with his simple conclusion. The last words of the poem are "something understood." I like that. It suggests that when we pray the heart learns something in its own strange way. Even if the going is tough. Even if I don't feel much. Perhaps only at the end is "something understood." I don't think Herbert means that I have worked something out with the mind. Instead I have understood something more deeply and on another level—about God, or about love, or about myself, or about others. A glimpse of love that gives food for living.

Do I get something out of prayer? Yes, my horizon expands and attitudes get healed by being in the presence of God. So an important fruit of prayer is genuine peace and the courage to love. And this can happen even without strong feelings.

The Presence of God
As I sit here, the beating of my heart,
the ebb and flow of my breathing, the movements of my mind
are all signs of God's ongoing creation of me.
I pause for a moment, and become aware
of this presence of God within me.

Freedom
Lord, grant me the grace to be free from the excesses of this life.
Let me not get caught up with the desire for wealth.
Keep my heart and mind free to love and serve You.

Consciousness
In God's loving presence I unwind the past day,
starting from now and looking back, moment by moment.
I gather in all the goodness and light, in gratitude.
I attend to the shadows and what they say to me,
seeking healing, courage, forgiveness.

The Word
I take my time to read the Word of God, slowly, a few times, allowing myself to dwell on anything that strikes me. (Please turn to your scripture on the following pages. Inspiration points are there should you need them. When you are ready, return here to continue.)

Conversation
Remembering that I am still in God's presence,
I imagine Jesus himself standing or sitting beside me,
and say whatever is on my mind, whatever is in my heart,
speaking as one friend to another.

Conclusion
Glory be to the Father, and to the Son, and to the Holy Spirit,
As it was in the beginning, is now, and ever shall be,
World without end. Amen.

Sunday 11th November,
Thirty-second Sunday in Ordinary Time   Mark 12:41–44

Jesus sat down opposite the treasury, and watched the crowd putting money into the treasury. Many rich people put in large sums. A poor widow came and put in two small copper coins, which are worth a penny. Then he called his disciples and said to them, "Truly I tell you, this poor widow has put in more than all those who are contributing to the treasury. For all of them have contributed out of their abundance; but she out of her poverty has put in everything she had, all she had to live on."

- Jesus did not seem to believe in appearances. Shows of piety and religiousness did not of themselves impress him. He saw behind the tiny amount of money to the huge generosity of the heart in the case of the poor widow.

- Jesus often pointed out that religious appearances can be empty and hypocritical. Let me reflect on that this week.

Monday 12th November   Luke 17:1–6

Jesus said to his disciples, "Occasions for stumbling are bound to come, but woe to anyone by whom they come! It would be better for you if a millstone were hung around your neck and you were thrown into the sea than for you to cause one of these little ones to stumble. Be on your guard! If another disciple sins, you must rebuke the offender, and if there is repentance, you must forgive. And if the same person sins against you seven times a day, and turns back to you seven times and says, 'I repent,' you must forgive." The apostles said to the Lord, "Increase our faith!" The Lord replied, "If you had faith the size of a mustard seed, you could say to this mulberry tree, 'Be uprooted and planted in the sea,' and it would obey you."

- I am challenged. I ask God to help me when I need to give witness by my words or actions. I ask that I may know when to speak and when simply to give example through my way of living.
- As I ask forgiveness for any bad example I have given, I realize that God receives me with joy.

Tuesday 13th November   Luke 17:7–10

Jesus said to his disciples, "Who among you would say to your slave who has just come in from plowing or tending sheep in the field, 'Come here at once and take your place at the table'? Would you not rather say to him, 'Prepare supper for me, put on your apron and serve me while I eat and drink; later you may eat and drink'? Do you thank the slave for doing what was commanded? So you also, when you have done all that you were ordered to do, say, 'We are worthless slaves; we have done only what we ought to have done!'"

- Jesus reminds us that we are children of God through grace and generosity. In worship we are responding to God's generosity; our own human powers are quite inadequate without the gifts of grace.
- Lord, teach me to be the humble servant. Give me the grace to glorify you in whatever I do.

Wednesday 14th November   Luke 17:11–19

On the way to Jerusalem Jesus was going through the region between Samaria and Galilee. As he entered a village, ten lepers approached him. Keeping their distance, they called out, saying, "Jesus, Master, have mercy on us!" When he saw them, he said to them, "Go and show yourselves to the priests." And as they went, they were made clean. Then one of them, when he saw that he was healed, turned back, praising God with a loud voice. He prostrated himself at Jesus' feet and thanked him. And he was a Samaritan. Then Jesus asked, "Were not ten made clean?

358

But the other nine, where are they? Was none of them found to return and give praise to God except this foreigner?" Then he said to him, "Get up and go on your way; your faith has made you well."

- The lepers were able to recognize their need and call on Jesus to help them. One among them, the Samaritan "outsider," wanted to express his appreciation for the gift that he had received.
- Jesus recognized the faith of the man who saw the source of the healing he had enjoyed. I see that sometimes my faith is demonstrated in how ready I am to see God at work and to attribute blessings to their source.

Thursday 15th November   Luke 17:20–25

Once Jesus was asked by the Pharisees when the kingdom of God was coming, and he answered, "The kingdom of God is not coming with things that can be observed; nor will they say, 'Look, here it is!' or 'There it is!' For, in fact, the kingdom of God is among you." Then he said to the disciples, "The days are coming when you will long to see one of the days of the Son of Man, and you will not see it. They will say to you, 'Look there!' or 'Look here!' Do not go, do not set off in pursuit. For as the lightning flashes and lights up the sky from one side to the other, so will the Son of Man be in his day. But first he must endure much suffering and be rejected by this generation."

- The reign of God is in our midst; it is within my reach. I ask God to help me to live this day in awareness that God is present.
- There are many voices calling for my attention, saying, "Look here!" or "Look there!" I prepare myself not to be distracted by the messages that do not build up the reign of God.

Page 359

Friday 16th November — Luke 17:26–37

Just as it was in the days of Noah, so too it will be in the days of the Son of Man. They were eating and drinking, and marrying and being given in marriage, until the day Noah entered the ark, and the flood came and destroyed all of them. Likewise, just as it was in the days of Lot: they were eating and drinking, buying and selling, planting and building, but on the day that Lot left Sodom, it rained fire and sulfur from heaven and destroyed all of them—it will be like that on the day that the Son of Man is revealed. On that day, anyone on the housetop who has belongings in the house must not come down to take them away; and likewise anyone in the field must not turn back. Remember Lot's wife. Those who try to make their life secure will lose it, but those who lose their life will keep it. I tell you, on that night there will be two in one bed; one will be taken and the other left. There will be two women grinding meal together; one will be taken and the other left.

- The readings speak of the "end times" as the liturgical year comes to a close. I use them as an opportunity to recognize who I am and where I am going: I am created by God and am being drawn to live fully with God.
- I consider that everything I enjoy—even life itself—is a gift. I humbly give thanks.

Saturday 17th November,
St. Elizabeth of Hungary — Luke 18:1–8

Then Jesus told them a parable about their need to pray always and not to lose heart. He said, "In a certain city there was a judge who neither feared God nor had respect for people. In that city there was a widow who kept coming to him and saying, 'Grant me justice against my opponent.' For a while he refused;

but later he said to himself, 'Though I have no fear of God and no respect for anyone, yet because this widow keeps bothering me, I will grant her justice, so that she may not wear me out by continually coming.'" And the Lord said, "Listen to what the unjust judge says. And will not God grant justice to his chosen ones who cry to him day and night? Will he delay long in helping them? I tell you, he will quickly grant justice to them. And yet, when the Son of Man comes, will he find faith on earth?"

- Jesus saw that people in his time needed encouragement in their prayer, so he encouraged them. I think of him wanting to encourage me now, realizing that he knows how I feel.
- I look at my life and situations, wondering how I might help others not to lose heart. My words, deeds, and attitudes can do for others what Jesus wanted for the people he met.

november 18–24

Something to think and pray about each day this week:

The World Renewed

Familiarity tends to dull the senses. Places lose their magic. People are taken for granted, and at times we even take God for granted. So let us look again at the familiar: the tree-lined streets of our cities, the rivers, streams and canals, the creatures of the woodland and field, the birds of the air, the people with whom we live or meet daily in work or play, and see something of beauty and goodness. If I lost my sight, how I would long to see the texture and colour and movement in the world around me! Open my eyes and my heart to your love in the world, O Lord.

The Presence of God
As I sit here, the beating of my heart,
the ebb and flow of my breathing, the movements of my mind
are all signs of God's ongoing creation of me.
I pause for a moment, and become aware
of this presence of God within me.

Freedom
I will ask God's help,
to be free from my own preoccupations,
to be open to God in this time of prayer,
to come to love and serve him more.

Consciousness
Help me, Lord, to be more conscious of your presence.
Teach me to recognize your presence in others.
Fill my heart with gratitude for the times your love
has been shown to me through the care of others.

The Word
I take my time to read the Word of God, slowly, a few times, allowing myself to dwell on anything that strikes me. (Please turn to your scripture on the following pages. Inspiration points are there should you need them. When you are ready, return here to continue.)

Conversation
Remembering that I am still in God's presence,
I imagine Jesus himself standing or sitting beside me,
and say whatever is on my mind, whatever is in my heart,
speaking as one friend to another.

Conclusion
Glory be to the Father, and to the Son, and to the Holy Spirit,
As it was in the beginning, is now, and ever shall be,
World without end. Amen.

Sunday 18th November,
Thirty-third Sunday in Ordinary Time   Mark 13:28–32

Jesus said to Peter, James, John, and Andrew, "From the fig tree learn its lesson: as soon as its branch becomes tender and puts forth its leaves, you know that summer is near. So also, when you see these things taking place, you know that he is near, at the very gates. Truly I tell you, this generation will not pass away until all these things have taken place. Heaven and earth will pass away, but my words will not pass away. But about that day or hour no one knows, neither the angels in heaven, nor the Son, but only the Father."

- It is good to find something in life that cannot pass away. We want that: we want it in love, in our friendships, and in our trusting in the future.
- The Word of God spoken in love, always a light in life, will never pass away. Prayer is our inserting of ourselves into the reality of that Word and that love.

Monday 19th November   Luke 18:35–43

As he approached Jericho, a blind man was sitting by the roadside begging. When he heard a crowd going by, he asked what was happening. They told him, "Jesus of Nazareth is passing by." Then he shouted, "Jesus, Son of David, have mercy on me!" Those who were in front sternly ordered him to be quiet; but he shouted even more loudly, "Son of David, have mercy on me!" Jesus stood still and ordered the man to be brought to him; and when he came near, he asked him, "What do you want me to do for you?" He said, "Lord, let me see again." Jesus said to him, "Receive your sight; your faith has saved you." Immediately he regained his sight and followed him, glorifying God; and all the people, when they saw it, praised God.

- I take time to picture the blind man who asks what is happening, addresses Jesus, approaches him, and is healed. As I state my needs, Jesus asks me to draw close and offers me healing. Jesus values my faith.

- The blind man was used to begging, used to raising his voice despite those who wanted him to be silent. I take time to consider my ability to ask for help and to receive it graciously.

Tuesday 20th November   Luke 19:1–10

Jesus entered Jericho and was passing through it. A man was there named Zacchaeus; he was a chief tax-collector and was rich. He was trying to see who Jesus was, but on account of the crowd he could not, because he was short in stature. So he ran ahead and climbed a sycamore tree to see him, because he was going to pass that way. When Jesus came to the place, he looked up and said to him, "Zacchaeus, hurry and come down; for I must stay at your house today." So he hurried down and was happy to welcome him. All who saw it began to grumble and said, "He has gone to be the guest of one who is a sinner." Zacchaeus stood there and said to the Lord, "Look, half of my possessions, Lord, I will give to the poor; and if I have defrauded anyone of anything, I will pay back four times as much." Then Jesus said to him, "Today salvation has come to this house, because he too is a son of Abraham. For the Son of Man came to seek out and to save the lost."

- Zacchaeus used his imagination to see above the heads of those who came between him and Jesus.
- Do I allow someone to stop me from seeing Jesus?
- Jesus saw what was holding Zacchaeus back from living fully and freely.
- I ask Jesus to speak to me about my life, to help and to heal me.

Wednesday 21st November,
Presentation of the Blessed Virgin Mary   Luke 19:11–28

As they were listening to this, he went on to tell a parable, because he was near Jerusalem, and because they supposed that the kingdom of God was to appear immediately. So he said, "A nobleman went to a distant country to get royal power for himself and then return. He summoned ten of his slaves, and gave them ten pounds, and said to them, 'Do business with these until I come back.' But the citizens of his country hated him and sent a delegation after him, saying, 'We do not want this man to rule over us.' When he returned, having received royal power, he ordered these slaves, to whom he had given the money, to be summoned so that he might find out what they had gained by trading. The first came forward and said, 'Lord, your pound has made ten more pounds.' He said to him, 'Well done, good slave! Because you have been trustworthy in a very small thing, take charge of ten cities.' Then the second came, saying, 'Lord, your pound has made five pounds.' He said to him, 'And you, rule over five cities.' Then the other came, saying, 'Lord, here is your pound. I wrapped it up in a piece of cloth, for I was afraid of you, because you are a harsh man; you take what you did not deposit, and reap what you did not sow.' He said to him, 'I will judge you by your own words, you wicked slave! You knew, did you, that I was a harsh man, taking what I did not deposit and reaping what I did not sow? Why then did you not put my money into the bank? Then when I returned, I could have collected it with interest.' He said to the bystanders, 'Take the pound from him and give it to the one who has ten pounds.' (And they said to him, 'Lord, he has ten pounds!') 'I tell you, to all those who have, more will be given; but from those who have nothing, even what they have will be taken away. But as for these enemies of mine who did not want me to be king over them—bring them here and slaughter them in my presence.'" After he had said this, he went on ahead, going up to Jerusalem.

- I am sometimes like the people to whom Jesus spoke: I want to see some proof, something immediate. Jesus reminds me that faith is real when it endures and acts.
- I may allow my faith to be strengthened by recognizing where God has answered my prayers.

Thursday 22nd November   **Luke 19:41–42**

As he came near and saw the city, he wept over it, saying, "If you, even you, had only recognized on this day the things that make for peace! But now they are hidden from your eyes."

- I know what it is like when friends can't see what is good for them. As I listen to Jesus yearning for Jerusalem, I allow his gaze to fall lovingly on me. What does he long for me to wake up to?
- My prayer is my practice of seeking God's perspective, a way of listening out for the voice I might otherwise miss. Perhaps I can see how I have grown, how less is hidden from my eyes.

Friday 23rd November   **Luke 19:45–48**

Then Jesus entered the temple and began to drive out those who were selling things there; and he said, "It is written, 'My house shall be a house of prayer'; but you have made it a den of robbers." Every day he was teaching in the temple. The chief priests, the scribes, and the leaders of the people kept looking for a way to kill him; but they did not find anything they could do, for all the people were spellbound by what they heard.

- The minds of the people are opening as the minds of the officials are closing. They both reacted to the same words and actions.

- Jesus calls me to the clarity with which he saw the world. I am made to give glory to God and to shed any way of living that is not worthy of the "temple" that I am.

Saturday 24th November   Luke 20:27–40

Some Sadducees, those who say there is no resurrection, came to him and asked him a question, "Teacher, Moses wrote for us that if a man's brother dies, leaving a wife but no children, the man shall marry the widow and raise up children for his brother. Now there were seven brothers; the first married, and died child-less; then the second and the third married her, and so in the same way all seven died childless. Finally the woman also died. In the resurrection, therefore, whose wife will the woman be? For the seven had married her." Jesus said to them, "Those who belong to this age marry and are given in marriage; but those who are considered worthy of a place in that age and in the resurrection from the dead neither marry nor are given in marriage. Indeed they cannot die any more, because they are like angels and are children of God, being children of the resurrection. And the fact that the dead are raised Moses himself showed, in the story about the bush, where he speaks of the Lord as the God of Abraham, the God of Isaac, and the God of Jacob. Now he is God not of the dead, but of the living; for to him all of them are alive." Then some of the scribes answered, "Teacher, you have spoken well." For they no longer dared to ask him another question.

- Jesus invites the Sadducees to see beyond the logical cleverness of their categories and ideas. I take time to allow Jesus to speak to my presumptions, asking him to soften my heart, to loosen my grip on what I have become used to.
- If God is not beyond our imagination, we will never be surprised. The tidy arguments of the Sadducees helped them to keep their

worlds in order, but kept them earthbound. I allow God to draw me beyond any narrowing view.

november 25–december 1

Something to think and pray about each day this week:

Embracing God

"What stress are you under?" Jesus asks of us. It stems from his mission. He is sent by the Father to purify and to distinguish what is genuine from dross. Life according to the Beatitudes has its share of conflict. For those who hunger and thirst for justice, this world is not a comfortable place. As Simeon prophesied to Mary, Jesus was "destined to be a sign that is rejected" (Luke 2:34). What about me? Do I merge seamlessly and comfortably with the values of this world? Do I hunger and thirst for anything? If the behaviour of the Beatitudes were a criminal offence, would I be in prison?

With scripture the conversation starts from God. It's like a friend greeting you from across the street. The friend starts the contact —you didn't even notice them.

Return to that marvellous image of how God looks after us, "as a mother comforting her child." If you want to deepen your personal prayer, here is one almost infallible way. Have the courage to linger over a phrase like this. Repeat it to yourself quietly. We can read the words so quickly. But if it is to reach more deeply, we need to take time. Then gradually the wonder of it can sink in: the image of the mother caring for a child in need of consolation is one of the simplest and yet most powerful in human experience. But here it is about God. . . .

The Presence of God
I pause for a moment
and reflect on God's life-giving presence
in every part of my body, in everything around me,
in the whole of my life.

Freedom
God is not foreign to my freedom.
Instead the Spirit breathes life into my most intimate desires,
gently nudging me towards all that is good.
I ask for the grace to let myself be enfolded by the Spirit.

Consciousness
I exist in a web of relationships—links to nature, people, God.
I trace out these links, giving thanks
for the life that flows through them.
Some links are twisted or broken:
I may feel regret, anger, disappointment.
I pray for the gift of acceptance and forgiveness.

The Word
God speaks to each one of us individually. I need to listen to what
he is saying to me. (Please turn to your scripture on the following
pages. Inspiration points are there should you need them. When
you are ready, return here to continue.)

Conversation
How has God's Word moved me? Has it left me cold?
Has it consoled me or moved me to act in a new way?
I imagine Jesus standing or sitting beside me;
I turn and share my feelings with him.

Conclusion
Glory be to the Father, and to the Son, and to the Holy Spirit,
As it was in the beginning, is now, and ever shall be,
World without end. Amen.

Sunday 25th November,
Feast of Christ the King   John 18:33–37

Then Pilate entered the headquarters again, summoned Jesus, and asked him, "Are you the King of the Jews?" Jesus answered, "Do you ask this on your own, or did others tell you about me?" Pilate replied, "I am not a Jew, am I? Your own nation and the chief priests have handed you over to me. What have you done?" Jesus answered, "My kingdom is not from this world. If my kingdom were from this world, my followers would be fighting to keep me from being handed over to the Jews. But as it is, my kingdom is not from here." Pilate asked him, "So you are a king?" Jesus answered, "You say that I am a king. For this I was born, and for this I came into the world, to testify to the truth. Everyone who belongs to the truth listens to my voice."

- For Jesus the red carpet is the tattered flooring in a poor house, and the crown is the headache he got from the sufferings of his people. In Jesus, the king, we are all brothers and sisters in the image of God. God is so big that we're all like him.
- What does that mean now? This is the big act of faith that we will soak ourselves in during Advent—that God became one like us, one of us, was born, lived, suffered, and died like the rest of us. The real God is found in real people.

Monday 26th November   Luke 21:1–4

Jesus looked up and saw rich people putting their gifts into the treasury; he also saw a poor widow put in two small copper coins. He said, "Truly I tell you, this poor widow has put in more than all of them; for all of them have contributed out of their abundance, but she out of her poverty has put in all she had to live on."

- Jesus saw the trust of the poor widow. I ask for God's help to see the best in the small and impoverished everyday gestures that I might notice. I bring these moments before God for blessing.

Tuesday 27th November   Luke 21:5–11

When some were speaking about the temple, how it was adorned with beautiful stones and gifts dedicated to God, Jesus said, "As for these things that you see, the days will come when not one stone will be left upon another; all will be thrown down." They asked him, "Teacher, when will this be, and what will be the sign that this is about to take place?" And he said, "Beware that you are not led astray; for many will come in my name and say, 'I am he!' and, 'The time is near!' Do not go after them. When you hear of wars and insurrections, do not be terrified; for these things must take place first, but the end will not follow immediately." Then he said to them, "Nation will rise against nation, and kingdom against kingdom; there will be great earthquakes, and in various places famines and plagues; and there will be dreadful portents and great signs from heaven."

- Jesus tells us to be prepared, to remain firm in faith. He calls us to be rooted and stable while also being ready to shed everything. He reminds us that without him as the centre of our lives, we will be lost.
- The telling of the daily news makes it easy to believe that our times are worse than others. While technology is used to spread gloomy and disheartening news, I give thanks that it also leads me to Jesus' truth.

Wednesday 28th November   Luke 21:12–19

Jesus said to his disciples, "But before all this occurs, they will arrest you and persecute you; they will hand you over to synagogues and prisons, and you will be brought before kings and governors because of my name. This will give you an opportunity to testify. So make up your minds not to prepare your defense in advance; for I will give you words and a wisdom that none of your opponents will be able to withstand or contradict. You will be betrayed even by parents and brothers, by relatives and friends; and they will put some of you to death. You will be hated by all because of my name. But not a hair of your head will perish. By your endurance you will gain your souls."

- Even when all seems to be ranged against us, Jesus assures us of his help. I pray that I may remain steadfast in faith, confident in the promises of Jesus.
- I bring before God all who suffer for their faith. I pray for those who find opposition from state, friends, or family.

Thursday 29th November   Psalm 99 (100):2–5

Worship the Lord with gladness; come into his presence with singing. Know that the Lord is God. It is he that made us, and we are his; we are his people, and the sheep of his pasture. Enter his gates with thanksgiving, and his courts with praise. Give thanks to him, bless his name. For the Lord is good; his steadfast love endures for ever, and his faithfulness to all generations.

- The words of the psalms were familiar to Jesus who called those who listened to him back to trust in God. I listen to the psalm as Jesus did.
- I think of myself as made by God, a sheep in God's pasture. I allow these images to shape my attitude as I reflect on my life with God.

Friday 30th November,
St. Andrew, Apostle   Psalm 18 (19):2–5

The heavens are telling the glory of God; and the firmament proclaims his handiwork. Day to day pours forth speech, and night to night declares knowledge. There is no speech, nor are there words; their voice is not heard; yet their voice goes out through all the earth, and their words to the end of the world.

- God's glory is reflected in the cosmos, and it is there for us to see day and night.
- As each day starts and finishes, let me make sure I give thanks for the gifts of my day, and the wonder of this universe in which we live.

Saturday 1st December   **Psalm 94 (95):1–2, 3–5, 6–7**

O come, let us sing to the Lord; let us make a joyful noise to the rock of our salvation! Let us come into his presence with thanksgiving; let us make a joyful noise to him with songs of praise! For the Lord is a great God, and a great King above all gods. In his hand are the depths of the earth; the heights of the mountains are his also. The sea is his, for he made it, and the dry land, which his hands have formed.

- God, who created all and holds all things in being, has time for me, waiting for me and loving me. I take a little time in thanks.
- Think of a beautiful part of creation, with its contours, colours, and textures. The joy of such a recollection is nothing to the joy God has in regarding me.